MADEIRA & PORTO SANTO

‘On the far side of the bay workmen saw,
chop and carve, making boats to a plan that
has changed little in 500 years; the air is tangy
with the smells of tar and freshly cut wood.’

CADOGANguides

Contents

About the author

Rodney Bolt grew up in Africa, was educated at Cambridge University where he read English, and now lives in Amsterdam. He has written the Cadogan Guides to Amsterdam and Bavaria, and in 1994 won the German National Tourist Office's 'Travel Writer of the Year' award. In the same year he stumbled across Madeira by chance, and immediately fell in love with the island.

Acknowledgements

My firm and continuing gratitude goes to Rachel Fielding for her original inspiration and guidance. Special thanks also to Linda McQueen for getting this new edition on to the shelves; Kicca Tommasi for her inspirational photographs; and Map Creation for their painstakingly drawn maps, which make a great contribution to the book.

Many thanks to all the people on Madeira who make my visits so pleasurable and easy – especially to Arlindo and Anna Brás, and to Dona Vitorina Côrte.

For Gerard

Cadogan Guides
Highlands House, 165 The Broadway,
London SW19 1NE
info.cadogan@virgin.net
www.cadoganguides.com

The Globe Pequot Press
246 Goose Lane, PO Box 480, Guilford,
Connecticut 06437–0480

Cover and photo essay design by Kicca Tommasi
Book design by Andrew Barker
Cover photographs © Kicca Tommasi
Maps © Cadogan Guides,
drawn by Map Creation Ltd
Managing Editor: Christine Stroyan
Editor: Linda McQueen
Art direction: Sarah Rianhard-Gardner
Proofreading: Dominique Shead
Indexing: Isobel McLean
Production: Navigator Guides Ltd

Printed in Italy by Legoprint
A catalogue record for this book is available from the British Library
ISBN 1-86011-104-1

Please help us to keep this guide up to date. We have done our best to ensure that the information in this guide is correct at the time of going to press, but places and facilities are constantly changing, and standards and prices in hotels and restaurants fluctuate. We would be delighted to receive any comments concerning existing entries or omissions. Authors of the best letters will receive a copy of the Cadogan Guide of their choice.

Madeira & Porto Santo a photo essay

by Kicca Tommasi

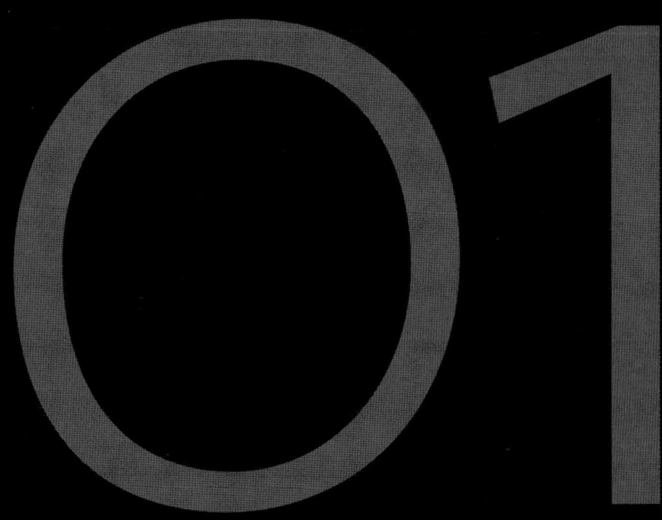

176

MARIA JOVITA
FN213L

FN 304 C
RAINHA DO
MUNDO

Pico Ruivo

Sé, Funchal

Capelo do Corpo Santo, Funchal

eucalyptus forest, Eira do Serrado

The North, inland from São Vicente

festival, Ponta Delgada

toboggan-drivers, Monte

mountain view

tropical ferns

levada walk

Reid's Hotel, Funchal

Monte Palace Tropical Garden

A-shaped thatched house, Santana

Jardim dos Loiros

Ribeiro Frio Botanical Garden

Jardim Orquídea

Bird of Paradise flower

Porto Moniz

Cabo Girão

fishing boats

market, Funchal

fishing boats, Câmara de Lobos

Old Town, Funchal

azulejos, Monte Palace Tropical Garden

About the photographer

Kicca Tommasi left sunny Rome for London to pursue photography and design. She spends much of her time travelling, trying to forget the long English winters. Her pictures are regularly published in travel guides and magazines.

Introduction

An ancient woman is carrying a pile of bracken on her head. The gigantic mound of foliage hides everything but her legs as she steps uphill with the nimbleness of a mountain goat. Two walkers balance along a narrow path, halfway up a cliff-face – bright dots in a vast volcanic landscape. A farmer parks his battered van and uncovers the baskets of fruit he has for sale: papayas, avocados, peaches and strawberries, plus a bucket or two of pink lilies. Just a mile or two away, a gentleman of the old school slides a decanter across a polished mahogany table. The wine has an aroma of toasted chestnuts. Languidly a sunbather turns over, and orders another cocktail from the beachside bar. 'Madeira,' as one 19th-century traveller put it, 'ensures almost every European comfort with every tropical luxury.'

Portugal has owned Madeira for five centuries, and the British have been residents here for three. Between them they have created a heritage of beautiful gardens, wines fit for the gods, churches filled with fine carving and rare tiles, and museums nonchalantly scattered with Flemish Old Masters and priceless *objets d'art*. The island itself, this 'semi-tropical speck in the Atlantic' some 700km off the west coast of Africa, does the rest. The mild climate and gentle pace may lull you into a dreamy indolence – but if you can rouse yourself for a walk along the water channels that criss-cross the island you will be rewarded by quite another Madeira.

What we see of Madeira are the highest points of a massive underwater mountain range, towering well over 5,000m above the sea bed. Violent submarine volcanic eruptions pushed the island up through the surface of the Atlantic during the Miocene period, around 20 million years ago (the Azores and Canary Islands made their appearance at about the same time). Lashed by wind and thrashed by waves,

Fact File

Madeira is 58km long and just 23km wide. Porto Santo, 40km to the northeast, is about 15km long and 5km wide. Two other clusters of islands complete the archipelago. Some 30km to the southeast of Madeira, the three Desertas – Ilhéu Chão, Ilhéu de Bugio and Deserta Grande – are, geologically speaking, just an extension of the main island. The channel between Madeira and these rocky outcrops is comparatively shallow. The Selvagens (the 'Savage Isles'), five barren islets 250km to the south, are closer to the Canary Islands than to Madeira. Only Madeira and Porto Santo are inhabited.

A jagged chain of mountains runs like a backbone through Madeira for some 48km, flattening out at the western end into a high plateau, the Paúl da Serra, several kilometres across and 1,000m above sea-level. Long ridges (*lomba*) separated by deep valleys run on all sides of this central spine. The highest peaks on the island are Pico Ruivo (1,861m), Pico das Torres (1,851m) and Pico Arieiro (1,810m), all in the eastern part of the island. Cabo Girão, to the west of Funchal, is the second highest sea cliff in the world, with a plunge of 589m to the breakers. The highest peak on Porto Santo is Pico do Facho (517m) in the northeast corner, but most of the island is low and flat.

Most of the population of 253,045 people live on the south side of Madeira, about 90,000 of them in Funchal. Under 5,000 people live permanently on Porto Santo.

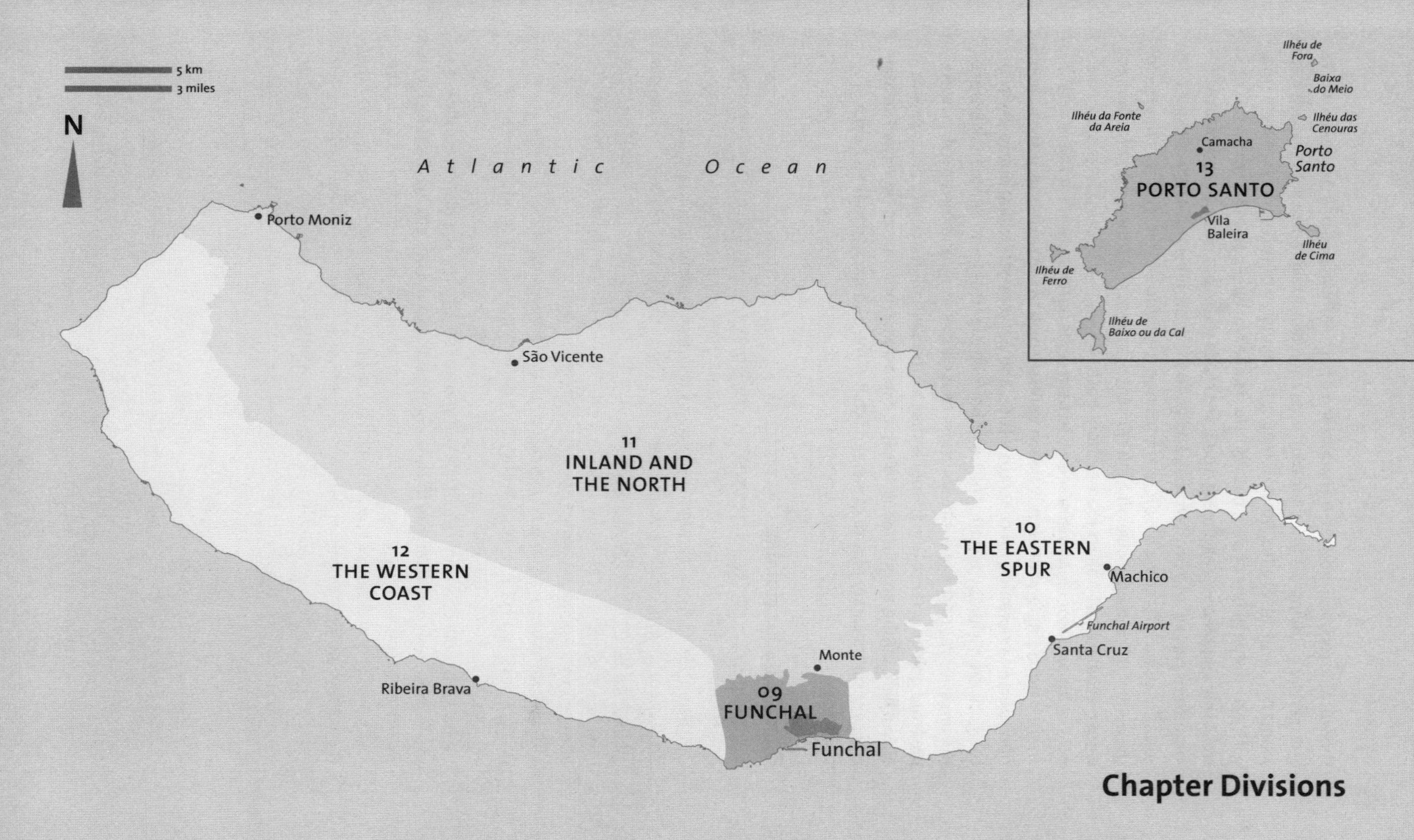

Chapter Divisions

the volcanic rock was gouged into an island of high mountains and precipitous cliffs. Strong rivers flowing off the mountain tops carved out ravine-like valleys, such as the dramatic Curral das Freiras. Most of Madeira is made up of soft, reddish-brown tufa, with occasional pillars of dark basalt. Tufa, as one traveller pointed out, can be cut as smoothly and precisely as cheese. You'll see roads sliced out of vertical cliff-faces, mountains carved into tiny terraces, and goat-sheds scooped out of the hillsides. The vertiginous rock-faces visible on land continue to plummet steeply underwater – to the delight of boys who dive off high cliffs into the sea, and fishermen, who manage a deep-sea haul just a short journey from port.

Unfortunately for us, Madeira seems to reserve its hardest rocks for the shores. There is not a single white sandy beach to be seen on the main island; instead, you'll find yourself swimming off concrete jetties, and gingerly stretching out to dry with the geckos on a lumpy terrain. The neighbouring island of Porto Santo makes up for the omission: almost the entire southern coast is one long, uninterrupted, picture-postcard golden strand. One theory is that all the sand off Madeira's beaches was blown here during an enormous volcanic explosion. From time to time the Funchal city councillors darkly plot to come and fetch some of it back to make a beach of their own.

Choosing your Holiday

Most package-holiday hotels are in the Tourist Town in Funchal, but you can have a quieter, more individualized stay in the capital by choosing accommodation in the centre or the Old Town. Though Funchal has the best museums and restaurants, a holiday entirely spent there will reveal only a fragment of what Madeira has to offer. There are a few easy walks along *levadas* around the outskirts of town, but far more interesting walks inland, and along the eastern spur. The most dramatic trek of all is between Mts Arieiro and Ruivo, the island's highest peaks.

The western coast is the least developed part of the island, offering lovely drives and gentle walks, too. For a taste of authentic, unaffected Madeira, head for the little village of San Roque do Faial.

If it's lying on a beach you're after, then you've come to the wrong place, unless you're prepared to head across to the neighbouring island of Porto Santo, which offers five miles of soft sand. The best swimming in Madeira is at the lidos of Funchal, the rock pools of Porto Moniz (teeming with tourists and Madeirense alike), and at other rocky spots along the north coast.

History

One of the beauties of Madeira is that, comparatively, it has no past... It was a virgin island. There were no aboriginal inhabitants to exterminate.

Sacheverell Sitwell

Misty Beginnings

Recorded history tells us that humans first set foot on Madeira in the early 15th century. Legends tell another story.

Ptolemy wrote of an island in the Atlantic called Erythria, the 'Red Island', because of the dye that was extracted there. (Many centuries later, Madeira would still be famous for its 'Dragon's Blood', a resin used to colour varnishes: *see* p.156). **Pliny** spoke of the 'Purple Islands', also named for their dye, that were discovered by sailors blown off course during a voyage to the Fortunate Isles (his name for the Canaries).

If the Romans were there, it is likely that the **Phoenicians** had been there before them. Certainly the **Moors** knew about the archipelago by the time they invaded the Iberian peninsula in the 8th century. They called the group 'El Ghanam', meaning 'cattle' (possibly a reference to thegoats or sheep that they found breeding freely on the islands).

Early **Christians** believed in a holy island off the coast of Africa, which was inhabited by **St Brendan** and a colony of saints, and it would mysteriously – or miraculously – disappear into swirling mist whenever sinners approached. Sailors in the 15th century saw the clouds that continually enveloped Madeira's mountains, and were sure they were looking at the Mouth of Hell. Later, they believed that the island was part of the lost continent of **Atlantis**, or the Hesperides – the islands which, according to the scholar Dr Lemprière, were 'once residence of the Amazons, a celebrated place or garden abounding with fruits of the most delicious kinds'. It was assigned as the Twelfth Labour of Hercules to fetch golden apples from this island at the world's end, wresting them from the dragon and the 'daughters of the evening' (hesperides) that guarded the tree.

Legend begins to overlap history with the tale of **Robert Machin** (or Machim) and **Anne d'Arfet**. Robert Machin was a minor English nobleman during the reign of Edward III (1327–77). He traded with Genoa, Pisa and Venice in his ship *La Welyfare*, but was banished from the kingdom. This much is fact: his banishment is registered in the Rolls of Parliament. The rest of the story has almost as many versions as it does chroniclers. Possibly the most reliable is the one that comes to us through the 15th-century writer and explorer Francisco Alcaforado, who probably had it on hearsay from sailors. Robert fell in love with Anne d'Arfet (though, as Noël Cossart points out, she could have been Anne of Dorset, Darbey or even Hertford, allowing for the mangling of the English name as the tale was told in foreign tongues). She was from a higher rung of the aristocracy than Robert, and, when her family found out about the affair with such an unsuitable candidate for their daughter's hand, they not only forbade her from seeing him, but immediately arranged a marriage for her with someone of equal status.

Anne's parents must have had some idea of Machin's daring, as they obtained a warrant from King Edward to have him imprisoned until the wedding ceremony was over. As soon as he was free of the dungeon, Machin had a message smuggled to Anne, and the two eloped on his boat. They set off from Bristol, heading for the continent, but a storm blew them out to sea. After a fortnight spent bobbing, lost, on the ocean, they came to a heavily wooded island and weighed anchor in a small bay – where the town of Machico is today. Machin went ashore to explore the island, but when he got back he found that his crew had absconded with the ship, leaving just Anne and a page on the shore. The trauma proved too much for the unfortunate Anne, who died three days later. The crew reached the Barbary Coast, where, for their sins, they were captured by Moors and sold into slavery. Robert Machin buried his lover beneath a large cedar tree, putting a simple wooden cross above her grave, together with a letter telling the tale and asking anyone who discovered the grave to build a chapel in her memory.

The Rediscovery of Madeira

Some chroniclers leave Machin to die on the island too. Others transport him to the mainland of Africa where he is captured and thrown into a dungeon. He doesn't survive long, but manages to tell his story to a cellmate who not only gets back to Europe, but relates the tale to the Portuguese adventurer João Gonçalves, known as 'Zarco' (which means 'the Squinter', or 'One-eyed').

João Gonçalves Zarco (he later took his nickname as a surname) was a fierce fighter and a gallant knight. He had lost an eye in battle against the Moors at Ceuta, fighting for Portugal under the **Infante Dom Henrique** – who is better known to English-speakers as **Prince Henry the Navigator**. Prince Henry had an English mother – **Philippa of Lancaster**, the daughter of John of Gaunt (and granddaughter of King Edward III). She had married King John (Dom João) of Portugal in 1386, a few months after the signing of the Treaty of Windsor. This agreement reaffirmed the alliance established between England and Portugal in 1376 – a pact that has remained pretty much intact ever since, making it the longest-lasting alliance in history.

Philippa, it seems, was a dynamic and intelligent woman who personally educated her children, and fired up her youngest son's imagination and sense of enquiry. In fact, apart from campaigns in Ceuta and Tangiers, Prince Henry hardly travelled at all. But he applied himself exhaustively to the study of mathematics and navigation, and always cornered any passing sea captains to glean all he could about their travels. His principal talent lay in his ability to assimilate this information, organize expeditions and inspire men to adventure.

It is quite likely that the Infante had some idea of the existence of Madeira. In the Laurentian Library in Florence is a map, known as the ***Medici Map*** and dated 1351, that clearly marks three islands off the African coast, naming them as Porto Santo, Deserta and Isola de Lolegname (Italian for Island of Woods; Noël Cossart believes that this is a corruption of the Moorish El Ghanam). The Prince, who had Genoese navigators in his employ and who had spoken to hundreds of seamen, must have had some inkling that the islands were there.

Then in 1418 Zarco and a fellow navigator, **Tristão Vaz**, were blown off the coast of Guinea, which Prince Henry had sent them to explore. They ended up on Porto Santo.

Beyond Porto Santo they found that 'there hung over the sea a thick impenetrable darkness, which was guarded by a strange noise'. After a few days' rest they made a beeline for Portugal to tell the Infante of their discovery.

The sailors were sure that the immobile mass of cloud they had seen was smoke from the Mouth of Hell. Maybe Zarco had once spoken to Machin's cellmate and knew better. More likely, it was Prince Henry who put two and two together. He lost little time in dispatching a ship under **Bartolomeu Perestrelo** to colonize Porto Santo (*see* p.201) and two more, commanded by the intrepid Zarco and Vaz, to explore further. The flotilla arrived at Porto Santo late in the summer of 1419, and early the following year Zarco and Vaz set off to investigate the distant smoke. Within it they found a mountainous island so thickly covered in trees that it was perpetually shrouded in cloud and mist. Zarco named it Madeira (Portuguese for 'wood'), either in response to these forests, or as a translation of the Italian name that Prince Henry had already made known to him.

The First Settlement

Zarco was made 'captain' of the southwestern part of the island, and Vaz (who later adopted his wife's surname, Teixeira) had jurisdiction over the northeastern part; the dividing line ran from Ponta do Tristão in the north to Ponta da Oliveira near Caniço. Vaz's capital was at Machico, where the settlers had found the grave of Anne d'Arfet and built a chapel (*see* pp.35 and 158). Zarco was the senior governor. He set up house in Câmara de Lobos, but very soon moved to the more favourable location of Funchal. His descendants were to rule in an unbroken line until the Spanish occupation in 1580; the old squinter himself lived to the impressive age of eighty. The story goes that just a year or two before his death three French pirate ships sailed into Funchal Bay. Zarco mounted his grey horse, took up his famous two-handed sword and (discreetly propped up by lieutenants on either side) took up position on the beach in front of his men. Such was the old warrior's reputation that the corsairs took one look, turned and fled.

In 1425 Dom João officially made Madeira a full province of Portugal, handing it as a gift to the Infante Dom Henrique. Colonization from the mother country began in earnest. Three strapping young nobles were sent to marry Zarco's daughters, and members of some of Portugal's grandest families came along to help swell the population. Madeiran family names such as Bettencourt, Freitas, Almeida and Ornelas date back to these first aristocratic settlers. The first children born on the island were twins, the offspring of one Gonçalo Ayres Ferreira. They were appropriately named Adam and Eve.

Fame and Fortune

One of Zarco's first acts had been to begin clearing the island for cultivation. The enormous prehistoric trees proved too much for the handful of early inhabitants, who started fires to speed things up a bit. This is supposed to have unleashed an inferno, which drove the settlers into the sea for two days, and was still smouldering in parts of the island seven years later. Tragically, the giant forests were destroyed, but the ash they left behind combined with the island's volcanic crust to make a lusciously rich soil. Prince Henry had ordered vines from Crete and sugar cane from Sicily to be grown on the island, hoping to cut in on a market monopolized by the Venetians and the Genoese. He was successful. Both crops flourished enormously, and, despite the fact that the influx of Madeiran sugar caused the market price to drop by 50 per cent by the year 1500, many people made their fortunes. Funchal became a prosperous capital – Portugal's third city after Lisbon and Porto. The wealthier landowners and merchants built grand houses in the centre of town, leaving the hard work to the peasants and slaves.

The good life was threatened only by **pirate raids**. Shipfuls of bandits would swoop in with alarming regularity and make off with rich spoils. Porto Santo, the more exposed island, had the worst of it. This, added to the fact that rabbits introduced by Perestrelo and his colonists had nibbled the island bare, caused many settlers to leave Porto Santo for Madeira.

In 1566 the French pirate **Bertrand de Montluc** fell on Funchal with a thousand men. They plundered and massacred for 15 days, then made off with 1,500,000 gold pieces before help could be fetched from the mainland. But Montluc's glee didn't last long – within days he was dead as the result of a wound he had received during the raid (*see* p.120).

The Spanish Occupation

In 1580 **Philip II of Spain** laid claim to the Portuguese crown. Portugal's coffers were empty after a disastrous campaign against Morocco. The king, Dom Sebastian, had been killed, and the line of succession wasn't clear. Philip's claim was backed by the Jesuits and wealthy Portuguese, but it was the promise of Spanish silver that tipped the scales in his favour.

In 1582 a new Spanish governor arrived on Madeira and for the first time united the two halves of the island into a single administrative entity. The Spanish modernized Madeira's fortifications, but saw the local wine industry as a threat to its own. They restricted vine-growing and wine-making severely, and exports dropped to almost nothing. The sugar and timber trades, which weren't in competition with Spanish interests, continued to boom; the Spanish Armada that famously threatened to upset Sir Francis Drake's game of bowls was made largely of Madeiran wood.

Independence and Monopolies

Spanish rule lasted until 1640, when a Catalan rebellion distracted the Castilian kings and gave the **Duke of Bragança**, a member of the old Portuguese ruling house of Avis, a chance to seize back the throne. He was crowned **King João IV**, but fighting went on until 1665 when, after the battle of Vila Viçosa, the Spanish were finally defeated and Portugal became fully independent.

By this time **Dom Afonso VI** (1656–67) had succeeded his father as king, but he was quite mad and so Portugal was ruled by his mother **Dona Luisa de Bragança**. She was keen to strengthen ties with England, as France and Spain were showing disturbing signs of making peace with each other. Dona Luisa offered her daughter **Catherine of Bragança** as a wife to the newly restored **King Charles II**. Louis XIV of France had already turned her down, and so Dona Luisa upped the stakes a bit. Catherine came with double the usual royal dowry: solid weights in silver and gold, a concession for trade with Brazil, two million *cruzados*, Bombay, Tangier and – it is said – the island of Madeira. But the scribe who was writing all this down was, reputedly, a Madeirense who couldn't bring himself to include his home island on the list. He persuaded Dona Luisa to keep Madeira back as an ultimate lure, should King Charles fail to bite. Catherine travelled to England with a secret document which added Madeira to her dowry, but she didn't need it. The Merry Monarch jumped at the opportunity of a source of funds for his lavish lifestyle. In return he agreed to defend Portugal 'as if it were England itself'.

Madeiran trade went from strength to strength. João IV had ordered Portuguese ships to call in on the island and take on wine for the colonists in Brazil, thus laying the foundations for the modern Madeiran wine trade (*see* p.52). Eventually the island became the chief stopover for all ships wanting to stock up on supplies before beginning the long haul across the Atlantic. When, in 1665, King Charles issued his ordinance forbidding exports to 'English Plantations overseas', save for goods leaving English ports in 'English bottoms', he excluded Madeira from the ban. This meant that local wine merchants had what amounted to a monopoly over trade with America and the West Indies. Madeiran wine became one of the most popular drinks in the New World, and a strong community of British merchants grew up on Madeira. They cornered the wine market, expanded into sugar and other trades and were soon leading players in the island's economy.

The British

From the end of the 17th century onwards, the British played such an integral role in island affairs that many of them seemed to regard Madeira as a colony rather than foreign territory. Though the authorities were often concerned that the British owned too much property on the island, and had their fingers (if not their fists) in too many local pies, the relationship between the two communities has, on the whole, been cordial. Feelings only became a little strained when British troops were garrisoned on the island (*see* opposite), and when an over-zealous pastor tried to convert local Portuguese to Protestantism (*see* pp.117–18) – and there was very nearly a nasty moment when **Captain Cook** visited the island in 1768.

The famous explorer, then on his first voyage in the *Endeavour*, 'battered the fort of the Loo Rock...by way of resenting an affront that had been offered to the British flag'. Exactly what the nature of the insult is we do not know, as the account was suppressed from official reports. Later, though, Cook made up for his petulance by going ashore and planting a Tulip Tree. Dr Hawksworth, the chronicler of the voyage, notes that the British consul received them 'with the kindness of a brother and the liberality of a prince'. (The tree survived until 1963, when it blew down in a storm.)

Napoleon and the British Occupations

British forces twice occupied Madeira during the **Napoleonic Wars** – from July 1801 to January 1802, and again from December 1807 to October 1814. They were friendly occupations, aimed at protecting the islands from the French, but the first one caused a diplomatic rumpus as no one had informed the Portuguese governor that he was about to be superseded. The second occupation was commanded by **General William Carr Beresford**, who was already quite a hero after campaigns in Egypt, South Africa and the Argentine.

Napoleon had tried to persuade the Portuguese to co-operate with the naval blockade of Britain. Portugal refused, and in 1807 French troops marched on Lisbon. The British whisked the Portuguese royal family away to safety in Brazil. Generals Beresford and Wellesley stayed on to deal with the French. On Christmas Eve Beresford arrived in Funchal Bay with a fleet of 24 ships, but soon realized that the island wasn't in need of quite so much protection. He left with half his garrison in 1808, though the rest of the troops stayed on until peace was finally made with France – and contributed noticeably to the island's gene pool; even today you will see the odd blond or ginger mop bobbing along in an otherwise dark school crocodile.

Napoleon himself called in on Madeira in 1815, on his way to exile in St Helena. He found an unexpected admirer in the then British consul, **Henry Veitch**. Veitch sold Boney some pipes of excellent wine (the famous Napoleon Madeira, *see* p.53) and got into hot water by addressing the ex-Emperor as 'Your Majesty' (*see* pp.191–2). He kept the gold *louis* he had received in payment, and buried them behind the foundation stone of the new English Church.

The British Factory

During the course of the 18th century British merchants came to control the wine trade almost entirely. When the dreaded diseases oidium and then phylloxera struck in the second half of the 19th century, destroying nearly all the vines (*see* p.54), many merchants moved over to sugar-refining – and soon the Brits had the grip on that too. Some time during the 18th century (no one is sure when, because all records were destroyed in a massive flood in 1806), the merchants established the **British Factory**. This was the equivalent of a Chamber of Commerce made up of the senior partners of the island's leading British firms, and based on the *feitorias* that the Portuguese had set up in the 15th and 16th centuries to guard and administer their trading posts abroad.

For decades the Factory held sway over the Madeiran British, acting almost like a small colonial government. The factors levied a tax on wine exports and built and financed a church, hospital and cemetery. They were a force not to be crossed (as young upstart traders soon learned), and adjudicated in (though sometimes propelled) the feuds that local families waged against one another. The Factory also acted as an agent for British merchants, enabling them to buy collectively, and so had enormous economic clout on the island. It was finally wound up in 1838, during a depression in the wine trade. The remaining factors started the **English Rooms**, an exclusive club on the seafront in Funchal. Later, as membership thinned out, they had to lower their standards and accept partners from less powerful firms – and even managers – into the fold, and eventually the club closed down altogether.

Miguelites and Liberals

Even after the defeat of the French in 1814, the Portuguese king **Dom João VI** (1792–1826) remained in Brazil with his family and Beresford stayed on in Lisbon as marshal of the Portuguese army. But the army staged a coup, set up a *Cortes* (parliament) elected by universal male suffrage, and devised a new constitution. Dom João returned from Brazil in 1821, content to accept the restricted powers that this constitution imposed – but his younger son, **Dom Miguel**, had other ideas. When Dom João died in 1826, his elder son and heir **Dom Pedro IV** was still living in Brazil, having been made emperor of what was by then a recently independent territory. Dom Miguel grabbed the opportunity to declare himself absolute monarch of Portugal and began a crackdown on supporters of the new constitution he had always disapproved of. Dom Pedro returned to Portugal and bloody battles ensued, in which the British actively took the side of Dom Pedro and the Liberals.

In 1828 a new Miguelite governor was sent to Madeira together with 1,000 troops. A small British force had landed a few days before to help the Madeirense, but all resistance was quashed. Over 150 people were arrested, though many leading liberal figures were able to escape to Britain on the frigate *Alligator*. Dom Miguel was eventually beaten in 1834, and exiled to Austria. The monarchy weathered badly the political turbulence and economic desiccation that followed the Miguelite rebellion. Finally, in 1910 **Dom Manuel II** (1908–10) fled to Britain and Portugal was proclaimed a republic.

The Twentieth Century

On 23 July 1905, the Paris edition of the *New York Herald* carried a report headed: 'German Company Plans to Make Madeira an Up-to-Date Resort' (a headline that, distressingly, wouldn't look out of place today). In return for a promise to build a sanatorium and hospitals and treat 40 TB patients a year free, the **Madeira Actien Gesellschaft**, headed by Prince Frederick Karl Hohenlohe, was – by arrangement with the Portuguese government – to take over all business concerns on the island. The British were in a fury. When plans for some of the hospitals were exposed as being designs for hotels and holiday camps, the Portuguese realized that they were being colonized through the back door and promptly withdrew the concession. In 1914 all German property on Madeira was confiscated. Germany declared war on Portugal in 1916 after German ships had been impounded in Lisbon harbour. Madeira got off fairly lightly during the war, though Funchal was twice shelled by German U-boats, once in 1916 and again a year later.

The decline in trade during the First World War, the Prohibition in America and the disappearance of the madeira-drinking classes after the Bolshevik Revolution in Russia knocked a large hole in the Madeiran economy. The mainland wasn't faring all that well either. The new Portuguese republic began to founder – there were 45 different governments between 1910 and 1926. Shortly after a military coup in 1926, **Dr António de Oliveira Salazar** became minister of finance. By 1932 he was prime minister, and he remained a virtual dictator until leaving office after a stroke in 1968. Although he balanced the books, his regime became increasingly cruel and repressive. In 1974, after a bloodless coup, his successor **Dr Marcello Caetano** was overthrown and the basis of the modern state of Portugal was established.

Madeira began the Salazar years on a bad footing. In 1931 a dispensation which became known as the **Hunger Law** gave a monopoly to a small group of local mill-owners. This not only caused a rise in the price of bread, but had a domino effect on investors and companies throughout the Madeiran economy which eventually led to the collapse of the island's two main banks. Thousands lost their savings. The mills were attacked and a **general strike** broke out. Lisbon sent troops, but some of the soldiers defected, joining the local garrison and a group of 300 political prisoners (who had been deported from the mainland a few months previously) to stage a coup.

General Sousa Dias, one of the deportees, was declared dictator. Many British residents hopped aboard the passing *Edinburgh Castle* and left the island. Others holed up in the luxury hotels around Reid's, protected by a small group of fusiliers and marines that had hurried over from Gibraltar. A punitive force arrived from Lisbon at the end of April, and the rebels were soon defeated. Some of the ringleaders sought asylum with the British, but most of those who had been involved in the fighting, including Dias himself, were imprisoned and taken back to Portugal.

From then on Madeira kept her grumbles to herself. Portugal remained neutral during the **Second World War** – though once again the decline in trade and tourism was bad for the island economy.

The 1974 Revolution was greeted with rejoicing, even though it too meant a momentary blow to tourism. Local supporters of Salazar made a quick break for Brazil and new political parties sprang up. But within a year civil war loomed. On Madeira, as on the mainland, there was concern about growing communist influences. A right-wing separatist movement, *Frente de Libertação Madeirense* (FLAMA, the Madeiran Liberation Front), demanded complete independence from Lisbon and is believed to have been responsible for acts of sabotage around the island. On the mainland a counter-coup was defeated in 1975, and in 1976 a new constitution was drawn up. Under this constitution Madeira was given special status within Portugal as an Autonomous Political Region. The Social Democratic Party (PSD) on the island, under **Dr Alberto João Jardim**, polled 65 per cent of the votes, while the Communists (PCP) scraped a mere 0.6 per cent. These proportions remain pretty much the same today, with a handful of other parties filling the gap and Dr Jardim still very much at the helm.

President Jardim has proved a dab hand at landing EU subsidies for Madeira. Hundreds of billions of *escudos* (and now euros) have gone into building new roads, giving a boost to the tourist industry and establishing a **Free Trade Zone**. All this is changing the face of an economy that once relied heavily on farming and fishing. Over the past few years there has been a tangible increase in Madeira's prosperity. Beggars have all but disappeared from the streets, building is going on everywhere, and the tourist industry has spread from its Funchal epicentre to benefit people all over the island. Yet, island income is way below the EU norm, with an average monthly salary of €650, and a minimum wage of around €350, and you will still find pockets of startling poverty. Madeira is certainly enjoying a boom, but locals are keeping a slightly worried eye on a not-too-distant, subsidy-less horizon.

Architecture, Arts and Crafts

04

William Wordsworth wrote a poem about 'the flowers/That in Madeira bloom and fade' – although he had never seen them. The German poet Rainer Maria Rilke composed a line or two while sitting on his balcony at Reid's. George Bernard Shaw took lessons from the hotel's dancing master, and left a signed photograph with the inscription: 'To the only man who ever taught me anything.' No doubt Albert Schweizer ran his fingers over the keys of the cathedral organ during his stay, and Camille Saint-Saëns hummed along to local folk songs while he was here. Ralph Richardson, Gregory Peck, Roger Moore and Terry-Thomas have all passed through, and Madeira has inspired Sacheverell Sitwell, AJ Cronin and countless other writers.

But Madeira's own contribution to world culture is modest – it gave Hawaii (and so the rest of us) the ukelele. Having no indigenous population, the island assumed the cultural trappings of its discoverers. Perhaps because Madeira is close to Portugal and not as exotic as the farther-flung colonies, the Portuguese made no great efforts here towards any sort of architectural or artistic display. Rich merchants built grand houses, but in styles derivative of continental trends. In the 15th and 16th centuries they bought and sometimes commissioned paintings – but by Flemish Masters. Local styles in architecture have emerged, and foreign crafts such as embroidery have been adapted and given a particularly Madeiran stamp, but Madeira's culture remains essentially Portuguese and its concerns predominantly mercantile and agrarian. The traditional dress and folk dancing, nowadays mainly dished up for tourists, are largely a product of a past peasant (and earlier slave) culture, and had all but died out until the Tourist Authority caught on to their money-earning potential.

This is not to say that Madeira is a cultural desert. During your stay you can see some exceptional painting; there are some fine museums and, here and there, an architectural gem.

Architecture

Two styles dominate island architecture: Gothic and Baroque. The former is to be seen in many of the island's early churches, the latter in public buildings, villas and refurbished church interiors. Gothic churches are often livened up by touches of decoration in the uniquely Portuguese Manueline style, or by Arab-influenced Mudéjar carving. Nineteenth-century architecture was a mish-mash of styles. Simple, regular neo-Baroque won out over most, though there are one or two examples of neoclassicism (the English church in Funchal being the finest). Modern buildings that are not eyesores are as rare as Madeirense who don't eat *espada*. The Mercado dos Lavradores (*see* p.136) and the Hotel do Navio (built in the 1970s to resemble an ocean liner), both in Funchal, are notable exceptions.

Gothic

Madeiran Gothic is very different from the delicate tracery and soaring spires of 13th-century northern European buildings such as Notre Dame or Cologne Cathedral. Writing in the 1950s about the Sé in Funchal (built 1485–1514), Robin Bryans sums up the differences with: 'Too late to be true Gothic, and too southern to be non-classical, the wide bays and slender piers suggest a static heaven rather than the soaring heaven of northern architecture.' Madeiran Gothic is solid and earthbound, closer in style to 14th-century buildings in Florence or Siena than to the flighty fantasies in Germany or France. Windows are small, and interiors cool and gloomy – though you will notice familiar vaulting and pointed arches. The main attraction of the buildings is often the carved ceiling or decorative stonework done in exuberant Manueline or geometric Mudéjar style.

Manueline and Mudéjar

Manueline – named after King Manuel I 'the Fortunate' (1495–1521) – is a style of decoration that bursts with the confidence, the excitement and the spoils of the Age of Discovery. It is, explains one commentator, 'the transposition into stone, not only of the *conquistadores*' dreams, but also of their trophies'. Shell and fish motifs, exotic fruit and strange leaves adorn altars. Monstrous swirls, ship's sails and endless cables snake around arches, burgeon above doors and windows, and dress up austere Gothic surfaces. These bare Gothic planes 'were the superb backgrounds for the upsurging desire to decorate exuberantly, to froth the stone, to twist it into cables, to knot, to loop, to hang, to carve it into vines and mottoes, to treat it as lace...'

On Madeira, Manueline outbursts are fairly restrained, confined to the odd decorative doorway or window-frame, carved ceilings (such as in the chapel at Loreto, *see* p.195) and sudden excrescences from otherwise sober buildings (the southeast corner of the Sé, *see* p.114). But a few minutes spent poking around an old island church is almost sure to reward you with a glimpse of some stonemason's expression of the pride and vision characteristic of the intrepid 15th-century navigators.

Manueline went hand in hand with a revival of an earlier Moorish style, called **Mudéjar**. Influenced by the abstract, geometric patterns of Arabic design, Mudéjar decoration tends to be simpler and more repetitive than Manueline, but intricate nonetheless. Madeira has some stunning examples of Mudéjar work in the ceilings of the Sé (*see* p.114) and the church at Calheta (*see* p.196).

Baroque

Madeiran Baroque is of the imposing, four-square, regular-featured variety. The cream walls, green shutters and regularly spaced windows of Funchal's Baroque buildings struck such a chord with the locals that the style was maintained well into the 20th century, and it is probably this image of the city that you will carry away with you. From time to time these elegant, though somewhat sober façades are dotted with little clover-leaf windows; or delicate waves break up the straight lines (such as in the House of the Consuls, *see* p.123).

If your taste is for more flamboyant, extravagant Baroque you will need to look inside the churches. Pulpits, picture frames, pillars and altars have all been subject to enthusiastic carving – not only in churches built in the 17th and 18th centuries, but also in earlier ones that have been given a facelift. Festoons ribbon out and volutes swirl, cherubs burst forth from tangles of vines, and carved drapes and tassels

Azulejos and Where to Find Them

Portugal's blue and white tiles don't, as you might expect, get their name from *azul*, the Portuguese word for 'blue'. Their origin is Moorish and their name comes from the Arabic word *zulayche* or *zulaija*, which means 'small burnt stone'. Later, when much blue (*azraq*) was being used in their manufacture, the words were combined and corrupted into *azulejos*. On Madeira you'll find them lining patios and churches, brightening up corridors and decorating the façades of buildings.

The Arabs borrowed the idea from the Persians, and by the 12th century were using tiles to embellish their mosques and palaces on the Iberian peninsula. The Persians decorated their tiles with birds, monkeys and tangles of flowers, but the Koran forbids the depiction of animals and humans in art and so the Moors developed the beautiful, intricate patterns we now call arabesques. The tiles were richly coloured in deep greens, blues, turquoise and red. At first, monochrome tiles were cut up and pieced together in a mosaic. Later a mould stamped a pattern into the wet clay. The lines of the pattern were filled with linseed oil, and the colours painted on to the surface. The oil kept the colours separate and turned black when baked, making an outline. Some tilemakers would stamp the motif in relief; the raised edges would keep the colours from intermingling. On very old tiles (such as those in the Quinta das Cruzes Museum or the Santa Clara nunnery) you can see this uneven surface. Early *azulejo* designs are very much in the abstract, geometrical Mudéjar style.

In the 16th century an Italian craftsman, Niculoso Pisano, developed the majolica technique of first covering tiles with white enamel, then painting the dyes directly on to it before glazing. This caught on in Spain, Italy and the Netherlands, and spread to Portugal during the Spanish Occupation of 1580–1640. These smoother tiles were easier to make, and led to much larger surfaces being covered with *azulejos de tapete* ('carpet tiles'), which often did resemble Moorish textiles in their design. Sometimes the entire nave of a church would be tiled (the church of São Pedro in Funchal is a

abound – everything covered in a layer of Brazilian gold leaf. It can all be a bit much, especially when combined (as Isabella de França lamented) with 'the most disgraceful daubs imaginable'. Heavy-handed restoration of many of these churches in the 19th and early 20th centuries has not helped. But there are some truly splendid examples of the style – the Colégio Church in Funchal (which also has witty *trompe l'œil* and precious *azulejos*; *see* p.120) puts all the others in the shade.

Local Touches

Beautifully worked **stucco ceilings** were a feature of many 18th- and 19th-century buildings. Designs ranged from abundant displays of flowers and fruit to copies of Wedgwood china and delicate rococo tendrils. Many of these were commissioned for private homes and company offices, and can still be seen in *quinta* hotels and houses that are now museums. A quick peek up the stair-well or from the first-floor landing in some of the old clubs or business institutes around town will also often reveal a ceiling encrusted with plaster figures or blossom. Another particularly Madeiran good example). At about this time both the Portuguese and the Dutch, influenced by the Chinese porcelain their trading ships brought back from the East, began to make tiles exclusively in blue and white – though the Portuguese sometimes added sunny yellow to the colour scheme. The Dutch were quick to spot a market for their tiles in Portugal, and it is probably under their influence, towards the end of the 17th century, that the *azulejos* depicting flowers and fruit, and later scenes from the lives of the saints, began to appear.

In the 18th century the art of the *azulejo* reached its zenith. Vast panels showing religious events, animals, ships or pictures of everyday life, and framed with Baroque cartouches, scrolls or acanthus leaves, set a style that is still imitated today. The Madeirans ignored the mainlanders' 19th-century penchant for covering the outside of their houses with mass-produced tiles (though recently emigrants returning with their pockets full of foreign currency have taken to the idea with gaudy glee). Rather, they succumbed to nostalgia. Many of the *azulejos* put up in the late 19th and early 20th centuries hark back to earlier designs. (The tiles in the Câmara Municipal in Funchal, for example, are a 1940s imitation of a Baroque design.)

The Pick of Madeira's *Azulejos*

16th century: On the spire of the Sé (cathedral) in Funchal.

Mudéjar and 17th century: Santa Clara, Funchal; Ponta do Sol parish church; Quinta das Cruzes museum and Colégio church, Funchal.

'Carpet'-style: Colégio church, Funchal; São Pedro church, Funchal.

18th century: Quinta Vigia chapel, Funchal; Sé (rear entrance), Funchal; Capela de São Roque, Machico; Colégio church, Funchal.

19th and 20th centuries: Chamber of Commerce, Avenida Arriaga, Funchal; sea wall, Avenida do Mar, Funchal (scenes of various island villages, but in bad condition); fountain opposite the Madeira Carlton hotel, Funchal.

feature of houses built in these centuries is the ***casa de prazer***, a garden teahouse, often done up in chintzy fabrics and embroidery (*see* p.123).

Madeira's only really indigenous buildings are the **A-shaped thatched houses** from the Santana region. Surprisingly spacious inside (see a full-scale model of one at the Casa do Turista in Funchal), they served as family homes to farmers for centuries – though now many have been demoted to serving as cattle sheds.

Painting and Sculpture

Painting is not a local forte. After one look at the official **portraits** of Funchal's governors, Isabella de França remarked in her diary that they were 'all painted in a style that would disgrace a signpost'. The beautiful pictures that once graced local chapels were usually Flemish, and now hang in the Museum of Sacred Art in Funchal (*see* pp.121–2). With rare exceptions, the paintings that remain in churches are crude and often brash. The most accomplished Madeiran **landscapes** are usually those done by foreign visitors; the Quinta das Cruzes Museum and the Frederico de Freitas Museum in Funchal are the best places to find these. The de Freitas Museum has an especially good collection of early engravings, prints and water-colours of the island.

Madeira's one claim to wider fame in the world of the arts is **Francisco Franco** (1885–1955). He was born near Ponta do Pargo, on the western tip of the island, but studied art in Lisbon and later spent four heady years in Paris at the time, just before the First World War, when it was the centre of innovation in art. His monumental statues, usually commemorating local notables, are much influenced by the work of Rodin and can be seen all over Portugal (*see also* p.123).

Music

Fado – gravel-voiced singers and poker-faced guitarists rendering fatalistic ballads – belongs to the mainland, though you can hear it in Madeira (*see* p.110). The local musical offering, ***xaramba*** (or *charamba*) is a jollier affair that involves a number of singers and a whole band of musicians. Songs may be wistful, though they usually bounce along at a jigging rate. Often, in a form called the ***despique***, they provide a useful vent for the pressures of island life, with improvised verses and snatches of gossip about the musicians and their friends that can get rather spiteful.

A number of uniquely Madeiran instruments feature in a *xaramba* band. The ***braguinha*** is a minuscule four-stringed guitar-like instrument, based on one that came to the island from the north Portuguese city of Braga with one of the early settlers. That was not the end of its journey. In the 19th century one Manuel Nunes left the island for Hawaii. When he got there, he and two other Madeiran craftsmen set up shop making *braguinhas*, though the Hawaiians called them ukeleles (which means 'jumping flea'). The ***rajão*** is a larger, five-stringed version of the *braguinha*. There are usually a few more bowed or plucked string instruments in the line-up – such as the richly toned, eight-string ***viola de arme***. A piano accordion or two join in to jostle things along. Percussion is amply supplied by drums, tambourines, castanets, triangles, *raspadeiras* (a rachet-like instrument known on the mainland as a *reque-reque*) and a ***brinquinho***, which consists of circles of dolls rising in tiers up a stick, which dance and jangle their metal clappers in response to rhythmic tugging.

Folk-dancing is also a communal affair. A revival of interest in the 1930s and 1940s rescued many regional dances from disappearing altogether. Villagers formed groups to study and perform their local dances. Many perform mainly as a display for tourists, but some – such as the *Grupo Folclórico da Camacha* – take their work seriously and keep up a high standard; the best place to catch these is at local village fiestas, rather than the 'folkloric evenings' arranged by hotels. Most of the dances have their origins in mainland Portugal, but have become mingled with rhythms and styles brought to the island by African slaves, and steps that reflect the movements of farm work. There is a foot-stomping grape-crushing dance, a load-carrying dance, and the *baile*, where dancers shuffle in a circle, heads bowed, in a dance that comes down from Moorish slaves who were shackled at the ankles and forbidden to look their masters in the eye.

Crafts

Embroidery

The flower and leaf motifs of Madeiran embroidery, stitched on to cotton and linen and worked into the cloth with so much filigree in between that the end-product is sometimes called lace, are known the world over. In the 19th century Madeiran cloths graced all the best tables in Britain, on the Continent and in the USA.

The craft arrived on the island with the first settlers. Rich 16th- and 17th-century vestments stitched by the nuns of Santa Clara can still be seen at the Museum of Sacred Art in Funchal. But it was **Elizabeth Phelps**, daughter of a local wine merchant, who put the industry on its feet. She did charity work in an orphanage run by the nuns, and helped teach some of the children to embroider. When she visited England in the late 1840s, she took a few samples of Madeiran lace with her; the ladies of Queen Victoria's court snapped them up, and soon Madeiran embroidery was an essential feature in the trousseau of any young bride. By 1851 Madeiran embroidery was winning prizes at trade fairs and had had a special display at the Great Exhibition in London. At one time it was estimated that there were around 70,000 women stitching away on the island for what was largely an export market.

Towards the end of the 19th century, though, the fashion was beginning to wane. A German, **Otto von Streit**, speeded up manufacture by introducing a method of printing (rather than pre-stitching) designs on to the fabric. He gave the industry another boost by targeting German and American markets, and for the early part of the 20th century the embroidery factories on the island were mostly German.

'Embroidery factory' is a bit of a misnomer. The work is still done by women (mainly) at home all over the island. It is then handed over to an agent (who takes a cut of the payment) or delivered to the 'factory' itself, where it is paid for by the stitch. Apart from cleaning and ironing, the only work that goes on at the factory is merchandising. Some work is sold (usually at shop prices) at the factory, but most is packed up for export, or sold on to shops around town. Profit percentages rise geometrically with every step along this journey. Madeiran embroidery ends up being very expensive, but only a small proportion of the price finds its way back to the person who did all that careful stitching in the first place. *See* **Funchal**, pp.98 and 123.

Tapestry was a later introduction to the island, promoted mainly by German companies, and has never caught on quite as strongly as embroidery. Nowadays the *Instituto do Bordado, Tapeçarias e Artesanato da Madeira* (Institute of Embroidery, Tapestry and Handicrafts, *see* p.123) keeps an eye on quality and gives authentic work a lead seal.

Wicker

British and German tastes were also behind the growth of wicker as a cottage industry. The story goes that a Madeiran prisoner serving time in Lisbon in the 1850s picked up the craft and taught his fellow villagers when he got home. Other versions have curious servants picking at cane furniture in *quintas* belonging to British families, then copying the work. Certainly cane furniture was all the rage in the mid-19th century, and it was a Briton, **William Hinton**, who was behind putting the craft on a more commercial footing – first to supply local hotels and later for export. But *barreleiros*, the distinctive cone-shaped baskets used to transport fruit and sometimes to hump rocks and soil about the terraces, were around long before people started making basket chairs to contain plump British tourists. Today the wicker industry is still very much a cottage industry and is centred on **Camacha**, in the south-eastern part of the island. Most of the reeds are grown in the damper climes along the north coast on the other side of the island, but William Hinton lived in Camacha, and it is here that he encouraged farmers to take to weaving. Things change slowly on Madeira. (*See* also p.161).

Carving

On an island of such forests it is surprising that you don't come across woodcarvers on every corner, whittling away at animals and figurines in an age-old tradition. Very little carving goes on in Madeira at all, though out-of-work whalers in Caniçal have taken to fashioning delicate boats and other scrimshaw out of whalebone (*see* pp.153 and 159).

The island was once renowned for its **furniture-makers**. Many of the 'Regency' and 'Victorian' pieces you see in smart hotels and antique shops were locally made. Even simpler guesthouses may be full of solidly constructed old Madeiran furniture, often covered in heavy carving. Keep an eye open for *caixas de açúcar*, hefty trunks made in the 16th and 17th centuries out of the packing cases once used to transport sugar. Another island speciality are *caixas-presépio* – carved nativity scenes within boxes and enclosed in an ornate frame. They don't only come out at Christmas, but can be seen all the year round in some churches and museums.

Traditional Dress

The richness and variety of Madeira's regional dress have all but disappeared under the wave of mass-produced costume encouraged by the Tourist Authority. Flower-sellers, toboggan drivers and 'folkloric' dancers dress up in variations on a basic theme: baggy trousers that reach to the knee and white shirts for men, sometimes with a waistcoat; brightly coloured skirts, white shirts and red waistcoats for women. The various folk-dancing societies do try a bit harder to give their outfits a traditional regional style, but it is rare to see someone in genuine, old, traditional dress.

Two items of clothing have survived the onslaught – the tough leather **ankle boots** (trimmed with red for women) and the ***carapuça***, a blue skull-cap with an odd flexible spike sticking out of the top – long ago, the height of this spike indicated your social status.

Wine, Walks and Wildflowers

05

Madeira Wine

Why, this same Madeira-wine has made me as light as a grasshopper...
William Congreve, *The Old Bachelor*, 1693

A glass of Madeiran wine sealed the signing of the American Declaration of Independence, and madeira is still used to toast anyone offered the Freedom of the City of London. George Washington got through a pint a night with his dinner. Shakespeare's 'arrant-malmsey-nose knave' Falstaff got his glowing conk from madeira, and was accused of selling his soul to the devil for 'a Cup of Madera and a cold Capon's legge'. In *Richard III*, the Bard has the poor old Duke of Clarence despatched in a Malmsey butt. ('Malmsey', 'malvasia', 'sack' and 'bastard' were all names for wines from Madeira and the Canaries.) As recently as the 1970s, revue entertainers Flanders and Swann sang of an old lecher who has his wicked way after befuddling his prey with 'madeira, m'dear'.

What is all the fuss about? The 16th-century explorer Diego Lopes had a go at describing what he thought of madeira with 'Malvasia wine is the best in the universe'. Others exhaust words like 'nutty', 'rich' and 'oaky' in attempting to put the taste into words. Some don't even try: 'Wine is inimical to description,' wrote Robin Bryans (*see* p.214), having knocked back a few glasses of 150-year-old Malmsey. But most wine buffs seem agreed that madeira has few rivals.

The History of Madeira Wine

Today's Madeira wine is fortified, like port or sherry, and comes in a range of flavours from dry to lusciously sweet. This was not always the case. Falstaff could 'score a pint of bastard in the Half Moon' with considerably less ill effect than you could nowadays. The wine that he quaffed would have been sweet but unfortified, and so much weaker than madeira today. (Though had Falstaff really existed he wouldn't have drunk madeira at all, as the play is set before Madeira was discovered – a mistake on Shakespeare's part.)

The first vines came to Madeira with Zarco's original group of settlers. The plants were from Crete, but the Portuguese called the sweet grapes *malvasia*, a corruption of Monemvasia, the Peloponnese port through which much Greek produce was exported in those days. Soon the first barrels of malvasia wine were on the market. As wine is rich in vitamins that prevent scurvy, the ships that called in at Madeira on their way to America, the West Indies and India began loading up with this nutritious sweet Malmsey.

During the 16th century, as Brazil began to dominate the sugar market, Madeiran farmers uprooted their cane and planted more profitable grape vines instead. The fame of their wines spread. One Christopher Jefferson of St Kitts declared, 'there is no commoditie better in these parts than Madeira Wines. They are soe generally and soe plentifully drunk, being the only strong drink that is naturale here, except brandy and rum, which are too hott.'

Then in 1665 the English king, Charles II, issued an ordinance that gave Madeira a virtual monopoly over the wine trade with the New World (*see* p.38). Soon Madeira swarmed with British merchants who encouraged more and more farmers to grow vines, made wine and traded either directly with passing ships, or through a network of agents across India, the Americas and Britain. Families such as the Blandys, the Leacocks, the Cossarts and the Gordons established dynasties that became the bedrock of the new industry. Their names still appear on classier wines.

But along the way something odd happened to Madeira wine. At some time around 1700 (or so the story goes), dock-hands unloading a ship in an eastern port overlooked a barrel of wine in a dark corner of the hold. When the ship called again at Funchal the captain discovered that the barrel was still there. Certain that the wine must have spoiled after jolting about on a round trip which had lasted many months, the captain was about to throw it out. But a sodden sailor who was happy that his jaded palate could cope with free wine, however nasty, cracked open the barrel – and found the contents to be delicious beyond all imagining. Those months of gradual warming in the hold as the ship crossed the equator, and perhaps even the rolling movement on the high seas, had done something that infinitely improved the taste of the wine.

Napoleon Madeira

When the ship carrying Napoleon to exile in St Helena called in at Funchal in 1815, the British consul on Madeira persuaded the famous prisoner to take on board a pipe (418 litres) of 1792 vintage madeira. On arrival in St Helena, Napoleon found that Longwood, the house he was supposed to occupy, was not yet ready, so he put up with a local English family at a cottage called The Briars. The household got through 24 bottles of madeira a month – but the ex-emperor's barrels were judged to be too young, and so remained unopened.

Napoleon suffered from a gastric complaint that put madeira off limits, so the barrels were still untapped at his death. Consul Henry Veitch maintained that, although he had paid the merchant for the wine out of his own pocket, he had received no renumeration from Napoleon, nor any reimbursment from the British government (he chose to ignore a 'gift' of gold *louis* that Bonaparte had made him). Claiming that the madeira was, therefore, his property, Veitch applied for its return. This 'Napoleon madeira' arrived back on the island in 1822, and was sold to the Blandys, who demijohned it in 1840.

Madeira wine is renowned for its longevity, and Napoleon madeira is regarded as one of the finest of the breed. You may still come across bottles at auctions – though it must be said that the contents of Boney's barrel would appear to have miraculously expanded. The entire 1792 harvest seems to have ended up as 'Napoleon madeira'. One of the authentic 1840 demijohns was opened for Sir Winston Churchill when he visited Madeira in the 1950s. The ageing premier was so touched by the gesture that he personally poured a glass for all the guests at the table, pointing out that the wine was vintaged when Marie-Antoinette was still alive.

For the next few decades merchants persuaded passing captains to use barrels of Madeiran wine as ballast, taking them on a journey across the equator and back. This ***vinho da roda*** (wine of the round voyage) was often named after the ship that it travelled in, as each batch took on a unique taste. Meanwhile, on the island, wine-makers experimented with more convenient methods of re-creating the effect of this long, warming journey. It wasn't until later in the 18th century that an abbot tumbled to the ***estufa*** process (*see* below). Around the same time merchants began to fortify Madeiran wine with French brandy or local spirits, producing the sort of madeira we know today.

This new-tasting wine was even more popular than the old one had been. Americans continued to consume vast quantities, madeira became popular at the Czar's court, and in Britain the Prince Regent declared it his favourite tipple, starting a fashion for the wine that was to last well into the 19th century.

But in 1851 disaster struck, in the form of *Oidium tuckeri*, a mildew disease which attacks the vine leaves, then the stem and eventually kills the plant. The disease arrived on Madeira in some specimens belonging to a French botanist. By 1852 it had spread over the entire island. By 1854 an annual wine production of 20 million hectolitres had plummeted to just 600. Only 15 of the 70 British wine-trading companies survived. A guide book of the time states that 'The wine of Madeira...will soon be no more than a thing of history'. It was a local farmer, João Vicente da Silva, who saved the day. He discovered that dusting the vines with sulphur put a stop to the mildew, and gradually the disease was defeated.

Then in 1872 another fiend appeared – *Phylloxera vastatrix*, the dreaded vine louse. Ironically, the phylloxera arrived on vines that had been imported from America because they were immune to oidium. The louse comes in two forms, one that attacks the root, and one that devours the leaves. When they are not eating, the insects are frantically breeding, each louse producing 25 to 30 million offspring a season. In Madeira's warm climate the phylloxera didn't even take time off for their customary winter hibernation, and the crops were devastated. Again it was a local grower, Thomas Slapp Leacock, who pioneered a remedy that was to be used all over the world – tar on the roots and copper sulphate on the leaves.

By 1883 the pests were beginning to come under control, and in the same year the government lifted a ban on importing American vines. Fresh stocks were grafted on to the old plants, and very slowly the industry began to rebuild itself. It was not until the turn of the last century that wine production was back on its feet – but by this time madeira had lost its market to sherry and port. It has never really recovered its popularity. Production is dropping, sometimes by as much as 14 per cent per year, as vineyards are gobbled up by land developers. This is especially true in the important Câmara de Lobos area, which is gradually becoming part of Funchal, as the town's boundaries sprawl outwards.

Making Madeira Wine

Madeira has the longest vintage in the world. Grapes are harvested from mid-August until the end of October, or even early November. Generally, grapes in low-lying areas ripen first and high-growing varieties, such as **Sercial** (which grows 700m above sea level) are harvested last.

As late as the 1960s most pressing was done by foot. Four men at a time would stand in a *lagar* – a metre-high wooden trough – and stamp away to the accompaniment of singers playing *machetes* (*see* 'Music', p.48). The slow, rather stately treading song strung together improvised verses about the vineyard owner and fellow workers with a refrain calling for *aguardente* and *ponche*. When they had squeezed out as much *mosto* (must) as they could, the treaders climbed out of the trough, the music hotted up, lyrics became spicier, and workers and spectators join in a spirited dance. The remaining grape pulp was coiled up in a thick rope and squeezed in a wooden press to make *vinho da corda* (wine of the rope), a must of inferior quality. The skins and mush that were left after this pressing were soaked in water, then strained to make *agua pé* (foot water), which only the thirsty grape-treaders would touch.

Workers poured the *mosto* into 12-gallon (55-litre) containers, each made from a single goatskin tied at the legs. These were carried down to the wine lodges (which were usually in Funchal) by men called ***borracheiros***. The *borracheiros* jogged along in single file, singing their own song to help them along the way. (They were also not averse to a sip of the *mosto* – hence their name, which means 'drunkard'.)

Today foot-pressing and *borracheiro* processions take place mainly for the benefit of tourists. Most grapes are taken whole to the lodges (which makes it easier for the wine-makers to check that only one variety goes into the must). Here they are pressed mechanically. Purists lament that foot-pressing, which is gentle and doesn't crush stalks and bitter pips, gave a more flavoursome wine.

In the wine lodges the must ferments for two to four weeks. These days this usually happens in a concrete tank, though top-quality must gets the wooden-vat treatment. The addition of spirit alcohol and more unfermented grape juice stops the fermentation process and determines the degree of sweetness. Later, more alcohol is added to 'fortify' the wine. Fortified madeira is called ***vinho generoso*** and usually has an alcohol content of around 17 per cent.

After fermentation comes a process that is uniquely Madeiran. The wine is slowly warmed in imitation of those long voyages across the equator. The abbot who first had the idea of doing this heated his wine in a greenhouse, or ***estufa*** – and the name has stuck. In the traditional *estufa* the wine is put into oak barrels and kept in tiered, heated attics (hence wine lodges rather than wine cellars). Today only the best wines get this treatment. Others are warmed in enormous vats (also called *estufas*). Wines are gradually taken up to temperatures of between 40°C and 50°C over a minimum period of three months. (Good wines get to stay in the *estufa* for around six months.)

The *estufa* process gives madeira a delicious burnt taste, and has a number of other curious results. Madeiran wine is extraordinarily long-lived, and doesn't spoil once opened. Even the best ports begin to decline after 40 years or so, yet madeira can be nectar well over a century after it has been made. Once the bottle has been opened, normal wines turn sour overnight. Even sherries and ports will only last a month or

Grape Types and Madeira Labels

Malmsey: The queen of madeiras. Rich, dark and full. Malmsey is an ideal after-dinner wine or nightcap.

Bual (in Portuguese: *Boal*): Also rich, fruity and sweet, though lighter than Malmsey. Once a great favourite of Indian Army officers, and taken 'for medicinal purposes' with a little fruit cake by lonely colonial wives.

Verdelho: Golden-coloured medium-dry wine that makes an excellent accompaniment to soup.

Sercial: Nutty, mellow and dry. Drunk too young, a Sercial may taste harsh, but with age it becomes soft and rich. As an aperitif it puts dry sherry and white port in the shade. Like Verdelho, Sercial is often served lightly chilled.

Bastardo: A heavy sweet wine.

Terrantez: Fresh and dry.

Tinta Negra Mole: These days the bulk of Madeiran wine is made from this juicy black grape. Tinta Negra Mole is a jack-of-all-trades that can take on the qualities of anything from a Malmsey to a Sercial, depending on where it is grown and how it is treated. Most madeiras that do not specify a grape type on the bottle are made from Tinta Negra Mole or a blend largely based on the grape. These madeiras will be given labels such as 'Fine Rich' or 'Pale Dry' and may have romantic, historical-sounding brand names such as 'Duke of Clarence'. They must be at least three years old. The better-quality blended wines will have the additional tag of **Extra Reserve** (over 15 years old), **Special Reserve** (over 10 years old), or **Reserve** (over 5 years old).

Rainwater Madeira: This is a pale, medium-dry wine made from a blend of Verdelho and Tinta Negra Mole. The first Rainwater came from a consignment of wine that was left unbunged on the beach by mistake and got topped up by the rain. This watery wine appealed to the 18th-century American palate, and has been a popular export to the USA ever since.

two in the decanter – but Madeiran wine seems to relish standing around exposed. Some couples on the island open a magnum when they get married, then sip a glass each on every wedding anniversary, to the 50th and beyond.

After its torrid experience in the *estufa*, the wine is filtered and left to cool and recover for another 18 months or so, then it is put into barrels of American white oak – some of them over a hundred years old. Much of the flavour of the wine derives from these barrels, and, although wine-makers have experimented with other woods, none can rival American white oak. Unlike other wines, madeira enjoys the air, and the barrels are not tightly bunged. This means that, as the wine matures, around 10 per cent of the total volume in a barrel is lost annually by evaporation. This must be topped up, so after the wine is barrelled some is set aside as a shipping *lote* (the wine that will eventually be bottled) and the rest is a stock *lote* (wine used to top up the shipping *lote* barrels). Eventually the shipping lote will consist of vintage wines, 'special growths', *soleras* and common brand names (such as 'Duke of Clarence' or 'Old Reserve').

Vintage wines may only be topped up with stock *lotes* of the same year and grape type. Predicting which wines are to become vintages is one of the most difficult tasks of the winemaker, as it can take decades before a vintage is declared. The winemaker has to assess in advance which barrels should be kept 'pure'. Vintage wines are sold under the name of the grape type, and the year of the vintage, e.g. 'Blandy's 1888 Malmsey'. Vintage wines must remain in the cask for at least 20 years and be allowed to stand in the bottle for two years before going on sale.

Special growth wines are made from the same grape type (such as Sercial or Malmsey). These must be topped up with matching types from the stock *lote*, though the year may differ. When the wine is bottled, it is given the name of the grape type and an age category dependent on the youngest wine that was added to the shipping *lote*. So 'Miles 5-year-old Sercial' will have been made from a blend of Sercial *lotes*, the most recent of which is five years old.

Soleras are a sort of halfway house, and can produce some of the best wines of all. This is done by blending an established vintage wine with top quality 'new blood', or sometimes by mixing vintages. This may be done to expand diminishing stocks of an old vintage, sometimes to pep up a vintage, or to make an entirely new creation of the blender's skill. The *solera* gets its date from that of the *matriz* (mother wine), so a *solera* founded in 1902 on the basis of an established 1890 vintage would become an 1890 Solera.

The various brand-name madeiras are **blends**, sometimes of more than one grape variety, and from different years.

Madeira should be at least three and preferably five years old before you drink it. All the wines continue to improve for decades, even centuries, although as they get older annual changes may not be so marked. 'Madeiran wines are like brothers,' said one winemaker: 'when they are both newborn it may be difficult to tell them apart. If one is two and one is eight years old, then there is a lot of difference between them. If one is five and the other is 20, the difference is even stronger. But if one is 50 and the other is 60, they begin to look like each other again.'

Walking

Suggested routes for individual walks are at the end of each chapter.

Undoubtedly, walking on Madeira is the way to get the most out of your stay. The network of ***levadas*** (irrigation sluices) spreads for hundreds of kilometres over the island. Following paths along the sides of the *levadas* will take you to places inaccessible by any other means of travel. In the course of one afternoon's hike you could be sweltering through semi-tropical undergrowth, then standing on a barren mountaintop nearly 2,000 metres above the sea. One moment you are walking through misty pine forests, the next you come out in a lush, spectacularly sunny valley. You can easily find yourself utterly alone, with not a sound except birds and rippling water – no distant motorway, no occasional jet, not a clue that the 21st century even exists.

Be warned, though: these are seldom gentle afternoon strolls. Increasingly, the authorities are putting up signposts to help walkers on their way, but the paths you take are essentially not tourist routes but those used by farmers and *levada* workers. The terrain is often precipitous, and there are no comforting safety barriers. You might find yourself walking along a 40cm-wide wall with a 200m sheer drop on one side and swiftly flowing *levada* waters on the other.

What to Take

- Wear strong, comfortable, preferably waterproof **shoes** with a good tread on the sole. Lace-up **boots** with firm ankle support are the most advisable, especially for the steeper walks. Leather and hard plastic soles can be treacherously slippery. Don't even think of wearing high heels.
- Take as detailed a **map** as you can find. A **compass** is a good idea for more isolated walks, and the cautious might like to take a **whistle** in case they get lost or hurt.
- A **rucksack** is more convenient than a carry-bag. You will need your hands free for holding torches, grabbing on to branches when you fall and sign-language when asking directions.
- A **jersey** and some sort of **waterproof clothing** (a light mac or cagoule) is essential. Weather changes can be sudden and unpredictable, especially in winter. Mists can envelop you in minutes. Also, some walks take you through a variety of altitudes. Though you might start off in semi-tropical heat, it can get chilly as you climb higher. For the same reason – and also because you might find yourself crashing through the undergrowth at points – it is advisable to wear long trousers rather than shorts or a skirt.
- Pack a bottle of **water** – a litre per person if you can manage it. A light **picnic** is also a good idea. There are seldom shops along the way.
- The sunlight on Madeira can be intense. Take **sunglasses** and **sunblock cream**. If you have a sensitive skin, or are worried about the disappearing ozone layer, you might like to add a **sunhat** and wear a **long-sleeved shirt**.
- If your *levada* takes you through a tunnel it is imperative that you take a good **torch**. The tunnels are bored out of the rock, have irregular walls and are completely unlit. For much of the time you might have to walk hunched up keeping one eye on where you are putting your feet, and another looking out for rocks jutting out at head level. Sometimes you can't even see the other end when you enter, and, even if you can, the length of the tunnel can be appear deceptive. You will need a torch for each person, and it is wise to pack one even if you don't intend to go through a tunnel. Plans could change, or you could get lost. In a pinch you could try the local shepherds' method of navigating in the dark: cut yourself a sturdy **stick**, about 30cm long. If you hold one end in front of you and run the other along the side of the tunnel, you will know that you are keeping an even distance from the wall and are not going to step off the path into the *levada*. You will not know, however, if there are any holes or boulders in your way, or get any warning that you are about to hit your head.

What to Do Before You Set Out

- **Check with the tourist office in Funchal that the route you intend to follow is passable. Landslides sometimes block the way on mountain paths.**
- **Find out what the weather is like where you want to walk, especially if you will be at high altitudes. Madeira has numerous microclimates. It may be sunny in Funchal while Santana is drenched with rain (*see* pp.80–81).**
- **Tell somebody (even the hotel receptionist) where you are going and when you expect to be back. It is very unwise to go walking alone, but, if you do, it is especially important that someone knows where you have gone.**
- **Practise or note down a few Portuguese phrases for asking directions (*see* p.211). Corner a native speaker to make sure that you can pronounce important place names in the area correctly.**
- **Check on bus times at your end destination. Having to wait beside a road in the middle of nowhere for an hour or two can make a boring end to a good walk. You could even end up stranded.**

It is absolutely imperative that you go walking well prepared. People have died falling down the steep inclines. If you have an accident in this rough terrain, it can be a good eight hours before you see a hospital. There are some walks that will paralyse anyone with vertigo, and stiff climbs that will exhaust all but the super-fit. You can quite easily find yourself two hours away from the last evidence of habitation and with a good two hours to go on until the end of the walk – with no comfy cafés along the way. But if you are properly prepared and plan your walk sensibly, it is this very isolation and hint of danger that makes the experience so exhilarating.

Don't let this put you off. There are plenty of easier routes too (though even for these you should never go tripping off in skimpy clothes and silly shoes). All the walks mentioned in this book come with an indication of the degree of difficulty and the time it will take to do them.

Many tour companies offer **guided walks** (*see* p.76), which are a good option for people nervous about setting out alone. Also, as the starting and finishing points of many walks are inconvenient or impossible to reach by bus, these organized jaunts can solve problems of transport.

The Flora of Madeira

The first settlers on Madeira, attempting to clear spaces for building and frustrated at the sheer size of the trees, set fire to the forests they found here. Madeira lost giant trees that had been growing for centuries, but the ash combined with the island's volcanic crust to create an extraordinarily rich soil. Add mild temperatures, plentiful sunlight and soothing rain, and the result is Garden of Eden abundance.

Madeira bursts at the seams with giant-sized versions of plants that northern Europeans are more accustomed to seeing in pots. Camellias grow into 9m-high

Fish, Fruit and Flowers in Season

	Game Fish in Season	Fruit in Season
Jan		Bananas, Custard Apples, Guavas, Loquats, Mandarins, Oranges, Tangerines
Feb	Long Fin	Bananas, Custard Apples, Guavas, Loquats, Mandarins, Oranges, Tangerines
Mar	Swordfish	Bananas, Custard Apples, Loquats, Oranges
April	Swordfish, Blue Shark, Hammerhead, Barracuda, Bonito	Bananas, Custard Apples, Loquats, Strawberries
May	Big Eye Tuna, Blue Fin	Bananas, Cherries, Loquats, Pawpaws, Strawberries
June	Big Eye Tuna, Blue Fin, Blue Marlin	Apricots, Bananas, Cherries, Loquats, Pawpaws, Peaches, Plums, Strawberries
July	Big Eye Tuna	Apricots, Bananas, Grapefruit, Melons, Pawpaws, Peaches, Plums, Pomegranates
Aug	Big Eye Tuna, Swordfish	Bananas, Grapefruit, Grapes, Melons, Pawpaws, Passion Fruit, Peaches, Pomegranates
Sept	Big Eye Tuna, Blue Marlin, Barracuda, Bonito, Swordfish	Apples, Avocados, Bananas, Grapefruit, Grapes, Mangoes, Melons, Nectarines, Pawpaws, Passion Fruit, Peaches, Pears, Pomegranates, Prickly Pears, Quinces, Walnuts
Oct	Blue Fin, Yellow Fin, Blue Shark, Hammerhead	Apples, Avocados, Bananas, Grapefruit, Grapes, Guavas, Mangoes, Passion Fruit, Peaches, Pears, Prickly Pears
Nov	Long Fin	Apples, Avocados, Bananas, Chestnuts, Guavas, Mandarins, Mangoes, Pears, Tangerines
Dec	Yellow Fin	Apples, Avocados, Bananas, Chestnuts, Mandarins, Mangoes, Pears, Tangerines

Flowers in Bloom

Arum Lily, Camellia, Camel's Foot Tree, Cymbidium Orchid, Golden Shower, Mimosa, Poinsettia, Pride of Madeira

Arum Lily, Camellia, Camel's Foot Tree, Cattleya Orchid, Cymbidium Orchid, Golden Shower, Mimosa, Poinsettia, Pride of Madeira, Tree Rhododendron

Arum Lily, Broom, Camellia, Camel's Foot Tree, Cattleya Orchid, Cock's Comb Coral Tree, Cymbidium Orchid, Jasmine, Mimosa, Pride of Madeira, Tree Rhododendron

Angel's Trumpet, Arum Lily, Australian Flame Tree, Bamboo Orchid, Broom, Camellia, Camel's Foot Tree, Canna, Cattleya Orchid, Cock's Comb Coral Tree, Cymbidium Orchid, Jacaranda, Jasmine, King Protea, Passion Flower, Red Passion Flower, Wistaria

Agapanthus, Angel's Trumpet, Arum Lily, Australian Flame Tree, Bamboo Orchid, Broom, Canna, Cattleya Orchid, Cock's Comb Coral Tree, Cymbidium Orchid, Jacaranda, Jasmine, King Protea, Madeiran Orchid, Madonna Lily, Magnolia, Oleander, Passion Flower, Pride of Madeira, Red Hot Poker, Red Passion Flower, Rock Orchid, Snowball Tree

Agapanthus, Angel's Trumpet, Australian Flame Tree, Bamboo Orchid, Broom, Canna, Cattleya Orchid, Cock's Comb Coral Tree, Frangipani, Hydrangea, King Protea, Madeiran Orchid, Madonna Lily, Magnolia, Oleander, Passion Flower, Prickly Pear, Pride of Madeira, Red Hot Poker, Red Passion Flower, Rock Orchid, Snowball Tree

Agapanthus, Angel's Trumpet, Australian Flame Tree, Bamboo Orchid, Broom, Canna, Cattleya Orchid, Cock's Comb Coral Tree, Frangipani, Golden Trumpet, Hydrangea, Lady's Slipper Orchid, Madeiran Orchid, Magnolia, Oleander, Passion Flower, Prickly Pear, Pride of Madeira, Red Hot Poker, Tulip Tree

Agapanthus, Angel's Trumpet, Australian Flame Tree, Bamboo Orchid, Canna, Cattleya Orchid, Cock's Comb Coral Tree, Dragon Tree, Frangipani, Golden Trumpet, Hydrangea, Oleander, Passion Flower, Prickly Pear, Red Hot Poker, Tulip Tree

Agapanthus, Angel's Trumpet, Australian Flame Tree, Belladonna Lily, Canna, Cattleya Orchid, Cock's Comb Coral Tree, Dragon Tree, Frangipani, Golden Trumpet, Guernsey Lily, Hydrangea, Passion Flower, Prickly Pear, Red Hot Poker

Belladonna Lily, Cattleya Orchid, Frangipani, Golden Trumpet, Guernsey Lily, Poinsettia, Tulip Tree

Arum Lily, Belladonna Lily, Frangipani, Golden Shower, Golden Trumpet, Guernsey Lily, Passion Flower, Poinsettia

Arum Lily, Camellia, Golden Shower, Lady's Slipper Orchid, Poinsettia

Plants that flower all year: Anthurium, Begonia, Bougainvillaea, Cape Honeysuckle, Hibiscus, Morning Glory, Popcorn Bush, Strelitzia, Tibouchina

trees; the ferns you remember Grandad lovingly tending in the front room come in thickets that you have to hack through like explorers in a Hollywood jungle; arum lilies are slain in their thousands to feed pigs and provide bedding for cattle. In Funchal the flower-sellers beam at you from behind banks of orchids, protea, agapanthus, strelitzia and daisies five inches wide.

This luxuriance is home-grown, but by no means indigenous. Travellers from all over the world brought bulbs and seeds to Madeira, and the plants flourished. Many escaped beyond garden walls and have become what botanists term 'sub-spontaneous', growing quite happily in the wild. Garden-crazy Brits were responsible for a lot of the imports. The big *quinta* gardens they laid out in the 18th and 19th centuries became nurseries for the whole island. Plants from Australia, Brazil and especially South Africa thrive in the Madeiran climate. There are South African protea and cycads (prehistoric tree ferns) growing here that horticulturalists had previously found impossible to cultivate outside their original environment.

But Madeira also has its fair share of unique species. Of the 700 or so genuinely wild plants on the island, nearly 200 are Macaronesian (i.e. occur naturally only in Madeira, the Canaries, the Azores and the Cape Verde Islands). Around 120 of these are specifically endemic to the Madeiran archipelago. You can find these plants all over the island, but the most prolific indigenous habitats are the laurel forests in the north. Madeira's most famous endemic plant, the **Dragon Tree** (*Dracaena draco*, *see* p.156) now rarely occurs in the wild, but is still grown in gardens and parks.

Climatic Zones

Madeira has three distinct climatic zones: a temperate littoral zone that rises to 200m (or to 300m or even 400m in protected, sunny areas such as the Funchal basin); a cooler mountain zone, between 600m and 1,300m; and an upper zone (1,300m–1,900m). The littoral zone is part of a broader sub-tropical belt that extends as high as 700m or 800m. This is where the really flashy flowers grow, though they prosper best below the 300m line. The upper zone is a stark world of thistles, gorse and twisted tree heather, but here and there, pushing out of the rocks, you'll see tough plants with tiny flowers, such as the **Madeira violet** (*Viola maderensis*) or the brilliant yellow **eyebright** (*Odontites holliana*). The mountain zones are covered in lush woodland – indigenous laurel forests or fragrant plantations of eucalyptus, wattle and pine, most of which come from Australia.

The Laurels

Laurel woods such as those around Portela, Queimadas and Faial (*see* p.176) are the survivors of the giant forests burnt down by Madeira's first settlers. Trees that managed to grow again after the blaze were plundered for their valuable hardwood, but recently the Madeiran government has put vast tracts of the island under protection as a nature reserve.

Most of the trees in the forest are evergreens, with vigorous tangles of branches and waxy, spear-shaped leaves. The **laurel** (*Laurus azorica*), which supplies cooks with bay leaves, is the most common, but you'll also find Madeiran **mahogany** (*Persea indica*, locally called 'Vinhático'), **til** (*Ocotea foetens*), which has an attractive, light wood, and the **Ironwood Tree** (*Apollonius barbujana*). Two types of holly grow in between the stouter trunks, as do various tree heathers, great bushes of yellow **sowthistle** (*Sonchus fruticosus*) and the startling purple brushes of **Pride of Madeira** (*Echium candicans*). If you poke about at ground level you could try to spot the delicate mauve **Madeira orchid** (*Dactylorhiza foliosa*), wild geraniums, and knots of succulent herbs.

Flowering Trees

Flowering trees add dash and spectacular bursts of colour to many a Madeiran view. From April to June Funchal's wide avenues become streaks of mauve as the Brazilian **jacaranda** (*Jacaranda mimosifolia*) breaks out in bloom. From June to September streets may be shaded by masses of yellow blossom as the **Pride of Bolivia** (*Tipuana tipu*) flowers.

During the first part of the year, **Camel's Foot Trees** (which got their name from the odd shape of their leaves) sprout delicate purple-pink flowers. The driveways of *quintas* are lined with ancient and enormous **magnolias** and **camellias**. **Frangipani** flowers perfume the summer air, though the yellow panicles of the **Popcorn Tree** (*Cassia didymobotria*) are somewhat less pleasing to the nose. The dubiously named **Kaffir Tree** (*Erythrina lysistemon*) from South Africa sprouts cockscombs of scarlet flowers before producing little red Lucky Beans. Its cousins, the various Coral Trees, all produce beautiful deep-red flowers. But the queen of this end of the spectrum is the **Tulip Tree**, or **Flame of the Forest** (*Spathodea campanulata*). First brought to Madeira by Captain Cook, the Tulip Tree opens clusters of big, bright orange cup-shaped flowers from July to September.

Flowers, Shrubs and Creepers

Cut flowers put hundreds of thousands of euros into Madeira's coffers every year. Thousands of orchids, especially varieties of **Lady Slipper** (*Paphiopedilum*) are exported annually, mainly to Germany and Switzerland. Other money-spinners include shiny, plastic-looking **anthuriums**, and the spectacular spiked **Bird of Paradise flower** (*Strelitzia reginae*), originally from South Africa. Another South African immigrant is the **agapanthus** (*Agapanthus praecox*), whose blue-mauve ball-shaped blossoms line the roads throughout the summer. **Hydrangeas**, **belladonna lilies** and torch-like **Red Hot Pokers** (*Kniphofia uvaria*) are also wayside favourites, while on the rocky outcrops of some *miradouros* (viewpoints) you can find all sorts of fleshy-leafed flowering **aloes**.

Careful gardeners might have success with a few **king protea** (*Protea cynaroides*) – pink-shelled, artichoke-shaped, rather dry flowers that otherwise grow almost exclusively around Cape Town. Even the least capable will probably manage a **poinsettia** for Christmas and a **hibiscus** bush or two. From April to September the branches of the **Angel's Trumpet** bend with the weight of giant pink bells, or white but in less dramatic profusion. **Golden Shower** creepers (*Pyrostegia venusta*), **jasmine**, **passion flower** vines, **honeysuckle** and a whole spectrum of **bougainvillaea** trail over walls and trellises.

'Flowers,' wrote the 19th-century traveller HN Coleridge, 'are a dialect of Portuguese which is soon learnt.' In Madeira the lesson is by total immersion.

Food and Drink

Menus at most Madeiran restaurants are so similar that they could be photocopies of one another. But although the same dishes appear again and again, you're unlikely to get bored. Fish, salads and fruit are fresh, and seem to explode with flavour on palates jaded by frozen food and greenhouse vegetables. You can quite happily eat the same thing night after night. (Having said that, you'll find that this guide has rootled out restaurants that do include less common regional dishes on their menus.)

Types of Eating Place

The dividing line between restaurants, bars and cafés is not rigid. Most cafés offer meals and many restaurants are quite happy to serve you with just coffee and a sandwich. A *churrascaria* specializes in grilled meats and a *marisqueira* serves mainly seafood. It is very rare to find a restaurant, even in remote parts of the island, that does not have a menu in English – though, of course, howlers abound: 'Green Garbage Soup' and 'Funny Fish Salad' are two that spring to mind.

Madeiran Specialities

Starters are not a Madeiran menu high point. In tourist restaurants you'll find the usual run of prawn cocktails and melons with ham. The tastiest traditional options are the **soups** – especially *açorda*, which combines garlic, bread, egg and oil into a whole that is definitely greater than the sum of its parts. *Caldo verde* (a tasty cabbage broth), or a delicious tomato and onion soup (also sometimes with an egg poached in it) are ideal tummy-warmers after a walk in the mountains.

As can be expected, **fish** is hard to beat as a main course. Many restaurants have big platters of fresh fish of all hues, shapes and flavours. You take your pick, and it comes back grilled (with garlic) in a mound of salad and potato. Sometimes you'll even find live crabs and lobsters in tanks, awaiting your personal selection. Tuna crops up on every menu – not the mushy tinned variety but large, pungent steaks from fish caught off the coast. The local speciality is *espada* (scabbard fish). You can see them at the market – long, sleek, black fish with enormous eyes, sharp beaks and a fearsome set of jagged teeth. They come from a murky world fathoms beneath the surface of the ocean, and are still a bit of a mystery to biologists because they live too deep to be studied properly. Their flesh is white, soft and succulent and can stand up to combination with quite strong flavours – *espada* with banana is an inescapable feature of island cuisine. Prawns, squid and shellfish – especially limpets – are delicious cooked simply and served as a starter or main course. More adventurous chefs may try a *caldeirada*, a mouthwatering combination of all sorts of fish and shellfish into a soupy stew, rather like bouillabaisse; or *cataplana* – a feast of seafood baked with herbs and rice. Dried cod (*bacalhau*) is a mainland dish that has caught on in Madeira. It comes in a variety of guises: grilled, after being reconstituted in milk, and mixed up with olive oil, herbs, eggs and potatoes are the enduring favourites.

Grilled meat, especially chicken, is particularly flavoursome, as most restaurants have natural wood grills. That and a dash of the ubiquitous garlic can turn the simplest chop into something special. After *espada* with banana, the great Madeiran speciality is *espetada* – skewered beef cooked on an open grill. Traditionally, laurel sticks are used for the skewer, but often the meat is poked on to an enormous metal rod that is then hung from a hook that towers a metre or so over your table. With your knife and fork you ease off a few cubes on to a plate below, then transfer them to your own. Often *espetada* is sold by the kilogram, so the price on the menu can appear high. Reckon on about 400g per portion. The skewers might not be brought to the table all at once – you all tuck into the one that is there, and a fresh one arrives as soon as you finish.

In chillier mountain regions you may find *feijoada*, a thick bean casserole, or *cozido*, stew, though if you're squeamish be warned – both may be cooked with black pudding, tripe and odd bits of pig (such as the ears). At inland restaurants you are also more likely to find hunter's fare such as rabbit or quail, simmered in delicious stocks laced with madeira wine. *Carne de alhos* – meat cooked with madeira wine vinegar, bay and garlic – finds its way on to menus all over the island. If you feel that you might still be peckish despite the potatoes and salads that come with your main course, try a side-dish of sweet potatoes, or *milho frito* – delicious cubes of deep-fried cornmeal.

Desserts tend to be quite simple. There will probably be a variety of *pudim*, ranging from passionfruit blancmange to crème caramel with a mouthwatering hard crust. Ice-cream on the island is excellent, with many exotic flavours such as pineapple or passion fruit. Gooey **cakes** are less easy to come by, though there are good pastries and creamy island cheesecake. The local speciality is *bolo de mel*, a heavy, spicy molasses cake, rather like rich gingerbread.

Given the variety and abundance of fresh **fruit** on the island, a fruit salad is always a delight. Bananas are slim and bitingly sweet, unlike their fat, pale cousins that end up in European supermarkets. 'The Bonanoe,' wrote an 18th-century visitor to Madeira, 'is, with them, in singular esteem and even Veneration, being reckoned, for its deliciousness, the Forbidden Fruit.' (Though it turns out that this special status was awarded as much for the extent of the leaves as for the taste of the banana; they were 'of a size fit to make aprons for Adam and Eve'.) Other fruits in the island's cornucopia include figs, peaches, crunchy apples, passion fruit, prickly pears, fleshy custard apples, oranges, plums, mangoes, cherries and all sorts of berries and, of course, grapes. In autumn, fat chestnuts are roasted on the streets in large earthenware jars.

Even **fast food** is healthy and interesting. Try a *prego* – a thin slice of grilled steak in a bun. The best ones have salad inside too, and a *prego* special will have a slice of ham and possibly cheese thrown in for good measure. Portable clay ovens are often set up at festivals to bake *bolo de caco* (*see* below), which are then served warm with *chouriço* (tangy sausage). Even hotdogs from snack bars come replete with a fat frankfurter and a lining of salad. Sandwiches (*sandes*) are filled with either cheese (*queijo*) or ham (*fiambre*). Occasionally someone will branch out to include tuna or chicken sandwiches on the menu – but even then a *sandes mista* (mixed sandwich) will be ham and cheese.

Menu Reader

Restaurant Phrases

the menu *a ementa*
fixed price menu *menu de preço fixo*
the wine list *a lista dos vinhos*
I'd like a table for two, please *Desejo uma mesa para dois, por favor*
May I have the bill, please? *Pode dar-me a conta, por favor?*
bread *pão*
butter *manteiga*
salt *sal*
pepper *pimenta*
olive oil *azeite*
vinegar *vinagre*
breakfast *pequeno almoço*
lunch *almoço*
dinner *jantar*

Ways of Cooking

assado roasted
cozido boiled
estufado stewed
frito fried
fumado smoked
grelhado grilled
no forno baked
mariscos shellfish
amêijoas clams/cockles
camarões shrimps
caranguejo crab
chocos cuttlefish
gambas prawns
lagosta rock lobster/crawfish
lagostins crayfish
lavagante lobster
lulas squid
mexilhões mussels
polvo octopus
vieiras scallops

Peixe (Fish)

atum tuna
bacalhau dried cod
carpa carp
espada scabbard fish
espadarte swordfish
linguado sole
pargo seabream
pescada hake
robalo sea bass
salmonete red mullet
carapau mackerel
sardinhas sardines
savel shad
salmão salmon
truta trout

Breads can also be scrumptious. The village bread, *bolo de caco*, is flat and softly chewy, rather like an English muffin. For a little extra you can have your *prego* or hamburger on *bolo de caco*, or have *bolo de caco* suffused with garlic butter in place of ordinary bread before a meal. *Pão de batata*, a brown bread made with sweet potatoes, is a tasty alternative for picnic sandwiches.

Drinks

See also 'Madeira Wine', pp.52–7.

In the same way as you wouldn't simply order 'a beer' in a British pub, you have to be more specific about **coffee** in Madeira. The most common brew is a *bica*, a small cup of strong black coffee. Ask for a *café grande*, and you'll get it doubled in size. If this is all too much for your pulse-rate, then a *carioca* has water added to dilute it. A *chinesa* (literally 'Chinese lady') is a large cup of very milky coffee. A *garoto* ('little boy') is a small cup with just a dash of milk. *Café branco* or *café com leite* is boring old British-style, medium-strength white coffee. **Tea** (*chá*) comes black, unless you specifically order milk (*leite*).

Carne (Meat)
anho lamb
bife steak
coelho rabbit
fiambre ham
fígado liver
língua tongue
lombo fillet
porco pork
rins kidneys
vaca beef
vitela veal

Aves (Poultry)
codorniz quail
frango/galhina chicken
pato duck
peru turkey

Legumes (Vegetables)
alcachofras artichokes
alho garlic
arroz rice
batata/batata doce potato/sweet potato
cebolas onions
cenouras carrots
cogumelos mushrooms
ervilhas peas
favas broad beans
feijão beans
salsa parsley

Frutas (Fruit)
alperces apricots
ameixas plums
ananás pineapple
anona custard apple
figo fig
laranja orange
limão lemon
maçã apple
maracujá passion fruit
melão melon
morango strawberry
pêra pear
toranja grapefruit
uvas grapes

Bebidas (Drinks)
vinho branco white wine
vinho tinto red wine
vinho verde fresh, *pétillant* white wine
vinho rosada rosé
vinho de mesa house/table wine
cerveja beer
café coffee
chá tea
água (com gás/sem gás) water (fizzy/still)

Apart from madeira (*see* p.52), local **wines** are something of a disappointment. The only commercially bottled wine, Atlantis, is a bland rosé not really worth the price. Some country restaurants might serve their own home-made wines – those on Porto Santo can be most pleasant, with a slaty, volcanic tang, rather like wines from the Greek island of Santorini. Wines from mainland Portugal, on the other hand, are abundant, inexpensive and delicious. A good, crisp *vinho verde* makes the perfect accompaniment to fresh fish. In a restaurant, ordering a *garrafa* of wine will get you a bottle; if you want a jug of the house plonk you should ask for a *jarro*.

The favourite local **beer** is a light dry lager made by the Coral brewery. The same company makes *Tónic*, Madeira's answer to Guinness. Up in the mountains you'll find a tasty scrumpy **cider** (*sidra*), and there is also a good selection of sticky fruit **liqueurs**. Look out especially for home-made cherry liqueur from Jardim da Serra or Curral das Freiras. The local **rum**, *aguardente*, has quite a kick and is often flavoured with herbs, fruit or spices. There are still moonshine distilleries around the island that produce *aguardente* with a proof way over any EU accepted level. Some of this finds its way into bottles of home-made *ponche*, **punch** made with sugar, honey and lemon. A sip after a hike in the rain will zap your body temperature up a degree or two. A glass or so more, and you won't be able to walk home.

Top of the list of **soft drinks** is *brisa maracujá*, a thirst-quenching passionfruit nectar that is so deliciously addictive that you'll find yourself packing bottles to take home. *Brisol maracujá* is similar, but without a fizz.

Tap water is not only drinkable, but soft and pure (though on Porto Santo tap water comes from desalination plants, and it is better to go for bottled). Supermarkets and grocery stores sell bottled water for fizz addicts and the extra-cautious. Spring water from Porto Santo is said to work wonders with dicky kidneys. In the countryside women still do the weekly wash in *levada* water, in much the same way as they have done for centuries – except that they now use bleach. Crystal-clear as it may appear, it isn't advisable to drink *levada* or spring water unless you are very high in the mountains.

Travel

07

Getting There

I do not know a spot on the globe which so astonishes and delights upon first arrival, as the island of Madeira.

Captain Marryat, 19th-century novelist and British naval officer

By Air

Most people these days arrive in Madeira by air. Both Madeira and Porto Santo have **airports**, though the one on Porto Santo is served mainly by charter flights and short-hop connections from the main island. Madeira's

Airlines

TAP

London: 38–44 Gillingham Street, **t** (020) 7828 2092.

Dublin: 54 Dawson Street, **t** (01) 679 8844.

Newark: 399 Market Street, **t** (973) 344 4490.

Los Angeles: 9841 Airport Bvd, Suite 1104, **t** (973) 344 4490 or **t** (310) 3229 222.

Montreal: 1801 McGill College, Suite 1410, **t** (0514) 849 4217.

Toronto: 151 Bloor Street West, Suite 450, **t** (0416) 364 7042.

Funchal: Avenida das Comunidades Madeirenses 8–10, **t** 291 239 211.

Other Airlines

GB Airways (Air Gibraltar), Iain Stewart Centre, Beehive Ring Road, Gatwick Airport, **t** (01293) 664239, booking on **t** 0845 77 333 77 or via the British Airways website, *www.ba.com*.

Transavia Airlines, *www.transavia.nl*.

Websites

www.airtickets.co.uk
www.cheapflights.com
www.ebookers.com
www.expedia.co.uk
www.flightcentre.co.uk
www.flights4less.co.uk
www.lastminute.com
www.travelselect.com

Discount Agencies and Youth Fares

From the UK and Ireland

Budget Travel, 134 Lower Baggot Street, Dublin 2, **t** (01) 631 1111, *www.budgettravel.ie*.

STA, 6 Wright's Lane, London W8 6TA, **t** (020) 7361 6161; 86 Old Brompton Rd, London SW7 3LQ, or 85 Shaftesbury Avenue, London W1V 5DX, plus Bristol, Leeds, Manchester, Oxford, Cambridge, and other branches, **t** 0870 160 0599. *www.statravel.co.uk*.

Trailfinders, 215 Kensington High Street, London W8 6BD, **t** (020) 7937 5400, *www.trailfinders.com*.

USIT Now, 19–21 Aston Quay, Dublin 2, **t** (01) 602 1600, and other branches in Ireland, *www.usitnow.ie*.

From the USA and Canada

Airhitch, 481 8th Avenue, Suite 1771, New York, NY 10061-1820, **t** 877 247 4482 or **t** (212) 736 0505, *www.airhitch.org*.

Council Travel, 205 E 42nd Street, New York, NY 10017, **t** 800 2COUNCIL, **t** (212) 822 2700, *www.counciltravel.com*. Major specialists in student and charter flights; branches from Arizona to Wisconsin. Can also provide Eurail and Britrail passes.

Last Minute Travel, 132 Brookline Avenue, Boston, MA 02215, **t** 800 527 8646.

Now Voyager, 315 West 49th St, New York, NY 10019, **t** (212) 459 1616, *www.nowvoyager travel.com*. For courier flights.

STA, toll free **t** 800 329 9537, *www.statravel.com*. Branches at most universities and also at 10 Downing Street, New York, NY 10014, **t** (212) 627 3111,and ASUC Building, University of California, Berkeley, CA 94720.

Travel Cuts, 187 College St, Toronto, Ontario M5T 1P7, **t** (866) 246 9762, **t** (416) 979 2406, *www.travelcuts.com*. Canada's largest student travel specialists; branches in most provinces.

Websites

www.airhitch.org
www.bestfares.com
www.expedia.com
www.flights.com
www.smarterliving.com
www.travelocity.com

airport balances on a rocky outcrop, and rests at one end on stilts. Your arrival is likely not only to astonish and delight, but to be spiced with a measure of sheer terror (passengers burst into relieved, spontaneous applause as the plane lands). There is little to worry about. Pilots who land here get special training and, if there is any hint of a dangerous cross-wind, all planes are grounded.

TAP, the Portuguese national airline, virtually monopolizes direct flights to the island. This means that either you fly TAP, or take another flight to Lisbon and transfer. Two other companies have scheduled services to Madeira: **GB Airways** offer one flight a week from London Gatwick; **Transavia Airlines** fly twice a week from Amsterdam, and can sometimes do a special deal with onward flights from London. You can also pick up last-minute charter flights from bucket shops, but these are hard to come by; check the travel pages of the Sunday papers or *Time Out*, or try the agencies or websites in the box opposite, especially if you are under 26.

If you're flying from the USA, you're likely to find it much cheaper to travel to London and buy a ticket to Madeira from there.

In Funchal, **Blandy Travel**, Avenida Zarco 2, **t** 291 200 691, *www.blandy.com*, act as agents for Transavia, GB Airways and many charter airlines as well.

Transport To and From the Airport

Taxis from the airport into Funchal cost between €18 and €22. The officially approved rates for taxis to Funchal and other island destinations are displayed on a screen above the baggage carousels (but bear in mind that there is a surcharge at nights and over weekends).

Aerobus, the official airport bus, runs around once an hour. Tickets cost €4, and take around 45 minutes. Departure times are shown on a screen above the baggage carousel.

First and Last Buses between Funchal and the Airport

Funchal *dep.*	Airport *arr.*	Airport *dep.*	Funchal *arr.*
8.30am	9.15am	9.45am	10.30am
10am	10.45am	11.45am	12.30pm
midnight	00.30am	00.30am	1.15am

HeliAtlantis, **t** 291 232 882, *see* p.76, can whisk you by helicopter from the airport to anywhere on the island.

By Boat

There is little to beat arriving in Madeira by sea. At night the lights of Funchal twinkle magically, as if suspended above the water. In the daytime you can see the mountains jutting dramatically above the surface of the ocean, sometimes wreathed in mists and cloud, and looking every bit like the Mouth of Hell feared by ancient mariners. Sadly, though, there is no longer a regular passenger service to Madeira, though cruise boats do call by. Your local travel agent should have details of cruise holidays that include Madeira.

Entry Formalities

Passports and Visas

Citizens of EU member states may visit Madeira for up to 90 days without going through any special formalities. Visitors from the USA or Canada can stay for 60 days without a visa. *See* box, p.74.

Customs

Arrivals from non-EU countries have to pass through Customs. For travellers entering the EU from outside, the duty-free limits are 1 litre of spirits or 2 litres of liquors (port, sherry or champagne), plus 2 litres of wine, 200 cigarettes and 50ml of perfume.

Duty-free allowances have now been abolished within the EU, and much larger quantities – up to 10 litres of spirits, 90 litres of wine, 110 litres of beer and 800 cigarettes – bought locally and provided you are travelling between EU countries, can be taken through Customs if you can prove they are for private consumption only and that taxes have been paid in the country of purchase. Under-17s are not allowed to bring tobacco or alcohol into the EU. **Pets** must be accompanied by a bilingual Certificate of Health from your local vet. You may not bring meat, vegetables or plants into the UK. Canadians can take home $300-worth of goods in a year, plus their tobacco and alcohol allowances.

Portuguese Embassies and Consulates

UK: 11, Belgrave Sq, London SW1 8PP, **t** (020) 7235 5331, **f** (020) 245 1287, *Portembassy-London@dialin.net*.

Republic of Ireland: Knocksinna House, Knocksinna, Foxrock, Dublin 18, **t** (01) 289 4416, **f** (01) 289 2849.

USA: 630, 5th Ave, Suite 801, New York, NY 0111, **t** (212) 246 4581, **f** (212) 262 2143, *cgprtny@aol.com*.

Canada: 438 University Avenue, Suite 1400, 14th Floor, Toronto, Ontario M5G 2K8, **t** (416) 217 0966, **f** (416) 217 0973, *mail@cgtor.dga.ccp.pt*.

Australia: Level 9, 30 Clarence Strett, Sydney NSW2000, **t** (02) 9262 2199, **f** (02) 9262 5991, *info@consulportugal.sydney.org.au*.

Germany: Zimmerstrasse 56, 10117 Berlin, **t** (030) 5900 63500, **f** (030) 5900 63600.

Residents of the USA may each take home US$400-worth of foreign goods without attracting duty, including the tobacco and alcohol allowance. For more information, US citizens can telephone the US Customs Service, **t** (202) 354 1000, or look at *www.customs.gov*.

Getting Around

Addresses

Madeirense usually write the house number after the street name and often follow it by an indication of the storey: Avenida Arriaga 22–4° would be an apartment on the fourth floor at No.22 Avenida Arriaga. Storeys are numbered according to the British, rather than the American, system (i.e. ground level is called the ground floor, and the one above that the first floor). The letters 'Ed.' before a name are short for *Edifício*, meaning office or apartment block. Often addresses are given as a street only, and in smaller villages all you get is a postcode and the village name.

Rua (road) is abbreviated as R., and Av. is for *avenida*. If you wander down side streets you might also encounter the odd *beco* (alley) or *travessa* (cross-street). *Largo* and *praça* both refer to squares. *Estrada* means 'highway' (and usually thunderous traffic day and night). A *caminho* (literally 'way') is generally a country road. Watch out for *calçada*, which indicates a steep hill.

By Car

The easiest way to see Madeira, and the only way of travelling to some spots, is by car. Driving on the island has been made much simpler by a number of new highways and tunnels. Laying these roads out has been done with some sensitivity – and tunnels don't make much impact on the natural landscape. In most cases, the option is still open to follow the old roads, which will provide you with material for postcards home and a good repertoire of hair-raising holiday anecdotes.

Apart from the new highways, Madeiran roads follow the contours of the countryside. Narrow ledges, barely a car wide, are notched out of cliff faces and disappear into rough-hewn, rocky tunnels. In places waterfalls tinkle on to your roof from somewhere high above you, bounce off and splash into the sea below. You might descend from a mountain-top on a road as convoluted as an intestine, then climb out on the other side of the valley through a series of blind hairpin bends that have you praying for second sight.

Among the hazards you will encounter are cars (or, horrors, a coach) coming the other way. This entails a hastily negotiated squeeze with little space to spare, or one of you reversing to a wider spot in the road. There are no pavements. As you round a bend, be prepared to meet a clutch of old folk on the way to Mass, a family walking four abreast or a woman whose legs only are visible as she totters beneath a gigantic pile of bracken. Have sympathy. This is the only route there is between many villages and it can't be much fun flattening yourself against a wall, or balancing on the concrete barrier above a 200m drop, every time a car comes past. In built-up areas cars may stop suddenly, without pulling over, so that the driver can talk to a friend, unload passengers outside their door, or pop into a shop.

Learner drivers in Madeira pick up their skills in cars that not only have dual pedal controls, but two steering wheels as well. Once the instructor has rescued them from a few sticky situations, they develop a confidence that amounts to sixth sense and whizz about the island, overtaking on corners, in a way that quite bewilders the foreign novice. Don't despair. After the first tense hour or two (which will probably involve at least one row with your partner and the resolution not to drive another centimetre), you too begin to get the hang of things. Soon you may even begin to enjoy the experience.

Some tips about the local **highway code** may help. In Madeira people drive on the right (where possible) and give way to traffic coming from the right. The **speed limit** on a few of the newer roads around Funchal is 80kph (100kph for a few brief, heady strips). Generally, however, the limit is 60kph. On most roads this would seem more like a reckless goal than a limit, as you seldom get out of second gear. It is a good idea to hoot as you approach an especially sharp bend, or just before you overtake someone (a short toot-toot is accepted as polite). The onus would appear to be on the approaching traffic and the vehicle being overtaken to slow down in order to avoid an accident.

Petrol stations are located in most of the larger towns, and petrol costs around €1 per litre. **Parking** is seldom a problem: within Funchal there are open car parks along the Avenida do Mar and a more expensive covered car park beneath the Marina shopping centre; and around the island you can usually pull off the road somewhere near to where you want to be. The only place that gets busy is the popular resort of Porto Moniz on the north coast.

Car Hire

To hire a car you will need to show your passport and a current EU or international driving licence. Most companies will only hire cars to drivers who are over 21 and who have a minimum of two years' driving experience.

The major international car hire firms all have offices on the island, but you can get cheaper deals from local companies, most of which are based in Funchal. Travel agencies and hotel receptionists can often arrange to hire cars for you. Tariffs are reduced if you hire cars for periods of longer than two days. If you plan to hire a car for a week, budget on a minimum rate of about €25–35 a day. When comparing prices it is important to make sure that the figure you are quoted includes tax and insurance and to check on what your personal financial liability would be in case of accident. Fees for insurance are likely to be nearly as much again as the basic rental charge. Most companies prefer you to pay by credit card, and most require that you pay in advance and settle up any outstanding payments (such as traffic fines) when you return the car. Dropping the car off at the airport on your way out costs €10–15 extra. If you return the car after the time written on the hire agreement, there is usually a stiff excess charge for every hour that it is late.

Car Hire Companies in Funchal

Avis, Largo António Nobre 164, **t** 291 764 546; airport, **t** 291 524 392.

Budget, Estrada Monumental 239, **t** 291 766 518, **f** 291 765 619.

Futuro, Centro Comercial Infante, Loja G, Avenida do Infante, **t** 291 220 721/291 220 633, **f** 291 222 220.

Hertz, Com. Monumental Lido, 1st Floor, **t** 291 764 410; airport, **t** 291 523 040.

Strawberry Autos, at Strawberry World, Monumental Lido, **t** 291 762 421, **f** 291 762 889, *www.discount-rent-a-car.com*. Friendly service, highly competitive rates and well-maintained cars.

By Taxi

If you would rather hand over the wheel to somebody else, it is possible to hire taxis for long journeys, or by the day or half-day. The rate for a day is around €85, or €70 for a half-day. A list of suggested prices for various island destinations is posted up in the tourist office in Funchal. It is important to set the price before you leave, and to bear in mind that on a full day's outing you could end up buying the driver lunch. One advantage of taking a taxi is that, if the driver speaks English, you can get a guided tour thrown in. Pop down to the local rank and negotiate a price with someone whose car looks comfortable and well maintained.

By Bus

Travelling on local buses is a cheap, though not always very efficient, way of seeing the island. Buses do tend to run on time, but are very much geared to local rather than tourist needs. If you are using buses for transport at either end of a walk, you sometimes have to be careful about planning your day. One of the main drawbacks of bus travel is that there is often a long mid-afternoon siesta gap, and unless you plan your journey carefully you can end up marooned between 1pm and 3pm. Also, services are drastically reduced on Sundays and public holidays. If you are travelling with three or four other people at these times, you might find that a taxi saves you much time and bother for little extra cost.

Funchal's **yellow city buses** travel quite far afield, so can be used for visits to spots around the outskirts of town. For travel on these city buses it is cheaper to buy **blocks of tickets** beforehand (*see* **Funchal**, 'Getting Around', p.96). The rest of the island is served by **private bus companies**. On these buses you need to buy a ticket from the conductor after you have boarded. Confusingly, the yellow city buses may have similar numbers to island buses going to completely different destinations.

Funchal is the hub of island transport. The main departure points for destinations around the island are **Rodoeste Bus Station** in Rua Ribeira João Gomes, the **S.A.M. Bus Station** on Rua Dr João Brito Câmara, and bus stops on the **Avenida do Mar** (*see* map, opposite). You'll find additional bus stops (*paragem*) on the main roads out of town, but be sure to check on the sign that the company you want stops there.

In smaller villages, buses stop on the main square. If there is no timetable in sight, try asking for information at a café. On country roads there is sometimes no *paragem* sign. Look out for a slight widening in the road and a cluster of people who seem to be standing about for no apparent reason.

Timetables

The Funchal tourist office can help with a summary of routes and times.

Tips for interpreting timetables: 'Monday' in Portuguese is *segunda-feira* (literally 'second holiday'). The countdown goes on until Friday – *sexta-feira*. Days are abbreviated not by letters, but by numbers. Thus Monday is written as 2°, Tuesday is 3°, and so on. Saturday (*sábado*) is S, and Sunday (*domingo*) is D. Months are written with Roman numerals. So, 1.V–30.IX, 2°–6° will mean that a bus runs Mon–Fri from the beginning of May until the end of September.

By Helicopter

HeliAtlantis offers sightseeing trips around the island by helicopter, flights to specific destinations (including Porto Santo), hops to the airport and a one-way hiking drop-off service. Prices start at €50 for a ten-minute trip around the bay.

HeliAtlantis, Heliport, near the Marina, **t** 291 232 882, **f** 291 232 804,

Boat Trips and Guided Tours

Travel agencies all over the island offer guided tours and cruises.

Blandy Travel, Avenida Zarco 2, **t** 291 200 691, *www.blandy.com*. Madeira's most respected agency offers coach trips, boat trips, *levada* walks and even nights out on the town.

Strawberry World, Monumental Lido shopping centre, **t** 291 762 429, *www.strawberry-world.com*. Walks with good, experienced guides, and also a range of island tours in nine-seater buses.

Terras de Aventura, Caminho do Amparo 25, **t** 291 776 818, *www.terrasdeaventura.com*. The place to go for jet-ski, paragliding, canyoning and other more adventurous experiences.

Turivena, **t** 291 766 109, **f** 291 763 898 (offices off Av. Infanta, near Quinta Perestrelo hotel), *www.madeira-levada-walks.com*. Good organized walks along the *levadas* and in the mountains.

Viewed from the sea, Madeira's coastline can be most impressive, especially in the early evening. A number of specialist cruise companies operate from the Funchal marina. There are twilight cruises, half-day and full-day

Island Buses (S.A.M. / Rodoeste)

1 Câmara de Lobos
2 Caniço
4 Câmara de Lobos, Ribeira Brava, Ponta do Sol, Madalena do Mar
6 Ribeira Brava, Encumeada, São Vicente, Ponta Delgada, Boaventura
7 Ribeira Brava
23 Santa Cruz
27 Câmara de Lobos
29 Camacha
53 Santa Cruz, Machico, Portela, Faial
77 Camacha, Santo da Serra
78 Faial
81 Curral das Freiras
96 Câmara de Lobos, Estreito de Câmara de Lobos
103 Poiso, Ribeiro Frio, Faial, Santana, Arco de São Jorge, Boaventura
107 Câmara de Lobos, Ribeira Brava, Calheta, Jardim do Mar, Ponta do Pargo
109 Caniço
113 Santa Cruz, Airport, Machico, Caniçal
115 Câmara de Lobos, Ponta do Sol, Jardim do Mar
123 Câmara de Lobos
137 Estreito de Câmara de Lobos
138 Ribeiro Frio, Faial, Santana, Ponta do Pargo
139 Câmara de Lobos, Ribeira Brava, São Vicente, Seixal, Porto Moniz
142 Ponta do Sol, Calheta, Ponta do Pargo
146 Câmara de Lobos, Ribeira Brava, Ponta do Sol
148 Câmara de Lobos
155 Ponta da Oliveira
156 Airport, Machico

City Buses (yellow)

20 Monte
21 Monte
22 Monte (Babosas)
30 Botanical Gardens
35 Tourist Zone/Praia Formosa
36 Palheiro Gardens

Connections (outside Funchal)

154 Câmara de Lobos-Cabo Girão
150 São Vicente-Ponta do Pargo
80 Ponta do Pargo-Achadas da Cruz

Tour Operators and Special-interest Holidays

UK

Abreu Travel Agency Ltd., 109 Westbourne Grove, London W2 4UW, **t** (020) 7229 9905, **f** (020) 7229 0274. Portugal's oldest operator.

Airtours, **t** 0870 238 7788, *www.airtours.com*. Package tours: special offers and late deals.

Arblaster & Clarke Wine Tours, Clarke House, Farnham Rd, West Liss, Hampshire GU33 6JQ, **t** (01730) 893344, **f** (01730) 892888, *www.arblasterandclarke.com*. Wine tours for the Sunday Times Wine Club.

British Airways Travel Shops, **t** 0870 240 0747, **f** (01293) 722702, *www.baholidays.co.uk*. Golf.

Cadogan Holidays, 37 Commercial Road, Southampton SO15 1GG, **t** (02380) 828300, **f** (02380) 228 601, *www.cadoganholidays.com*. Walking holidays.

Caravela Tours Ltd., 38/44 Gillingham St, London SE27 0SH, **t** 0870 443 8181, *www.caravela.co.uk*. TAP's tour arm; *pousadas* and fly/drive packages.

Cosmos, Wren Court, 17 London Rd, Bromley, Kent BR1 1DE, **t** 0870 901 0790, *www.cosmos-holidays.co.uk*. Flowers in springtime.

Exodus Travel, 9 Weir Rd, London SW12 0LT, **t** (020) 8675 5550, **f** (020) 8673 0779, *www.its.net/exodus*. Walking holidays for all levels of fitness.

First Choice, First Choice House, Peel Cross Rd, Salford, Manchester M5 2AN, **t** 0870 750 0465, *www.firstchoice.co.uk*. All-inclusive.

HF Holidays Ltd., Imperial House, Edgware Rd, London NW9 5AL, **t** (020) 8905 9556, **f** (020) 8295 0506, *www.hfholidays.co.uk*. Walking in spring and autumn.

Ramblers' Holidays, Box 43, Welwyn Garden City, Herts AL8 6PQ, **t** (01707) 331133, **f** (01707) 333276, *www.ramblersholidays.co.uk*. Special walking tours of the island.

Thomson Holidays, **t** 0870 165 0079, *www.thomson-holidays.com*. All-inclusive 7–14-day package holidays, holidays for couples.

USA

Abreu Tours, 350 Fifth Avenue, Suite 2414, New York, NY 10118, **t** (212) 760 3301, **t** 800 223 1580 toll free, **f** (212) 760 3306, *www.abreu-tours.com*.

Festive Travel, **t** (954) 523 9984, **f** (954) 467 3443, *www.festivetravel.com*. Short trips to Madeira as part of tailored Portuguese mainland holidays for independent travellers.

Golf International, 14 East 38th Street, New York, NY 10016, **t** (212) 986 9176, **t** 800 833 1389, *www.golfinternational.com*. Holidays for golfers.

Homeric Tours, 55 E. 59th St, 17th Floor, New York, NY 10022, **t** (212) 753 1100, **t** 800 223 5570 toll free, **f** (212) 753 0319, *www.homerictours.com*.

Odysseys Adventures, 535 Chestnut St, Cedarhurst NY 11516, **t** (516) 569 2812, **f** (516) 569 2998, *www.vacation-planner.net*. Individually tailored holidays on such subjects as flowers, wine, walking and embroidery.

Websites

www.strawberry-world.com. Personalized online travel consultancy – good hotels, resorts, self-catering apartments, etc.

www.madeira-holiday.co.uk.

www.ownersdirect.co.uk.

options, and some cruises include a meal and a deep-Atlantic dip. All return to Funchal. Prices for a round trip start at €22.50.

Albatroz, Funchal Marina, **t** 291 223 366. Takes you out in a 1938 replica of King Edward VII's yacht *Britannia*.

Santa Maria de Colombo, Funchal Marina, **t** 291 220 327. Eclipses all competitors by offering cruises in an island-built replica of Christopher Columbus' sailing ship.

Getting Around the Archipelago

Even in Funchal you will find Madeirense who have never in their lives been to Porto Santo, let alone Lisbon or the world beyond. A look at ticket prices for travel between the islands gives you some idea why. In season a crossing on the inter-island ferry will cost around €35–40 return. Crossings by helicopter and aeroplane cost at least double that. *See* **Porto Santo and the Desertas**, p.202.

Practical A–Z

08

Children

Unless they are sturdy little walkers, preternaturally interested in flowers or don't mind spending hours splashing about in shallow water, your children are unlikely to rate a Madeiran holiday as the best they've ever had. It takes long legs and stamina to get the most out of the island, and what rocky beaches there are will batter buckets and bend spades. On the other hand, public swimming baths often have pools and playgrounds for smaller fry. The inhabitants of Funchal's murky aquarium, and their stuffed brethren upstairs in the Municipal Museum (*see* p.127), might provide welcome diversion on a rainy afternoon. A visit to the whaling museum in Caniçal (*see* p.160), a day on an old sailing boat (*see* p.76), or (if the budget can stretch that far) a flight over the island in a helicopter (*see* p.76) might also add spice to their stay.

Eating out should present no problem. Restaurants are usually happy to have children at any time of day or night.

Climate, When to Go and Packing

'It is an island to which you go for the flowers and the climate,' said Sacheverell Sitwell. Madeiran seasons 'are the youth, maturity and old age of a never-ending, still beginning spring,' gushed one 19th-century writer as he joined the trail of consumptives who came here for their health.

Climate

In general, Madeira has a mild, sub-tropical climate that offers a cheering escape from grey northern European winters. The Gulf Stream keeps water temperatures between 17°C and 22°C, so swimming can be pleasant the whole year round. Statistics paint a picture of a paradisiacally temperate isle, but generalizations about Madeiran weather can be misleading. True, the average temperature seldom rises above 23°C or falls below 16°C, and Funchal gets almost no rain from May to September, but the island has a multitude of microclimates. While you are flat out in the sun in Funchal, friends could be shivering in misty forests above Monte, half an hour's drive away, or trudging through rain in Santana, just 20km across the island.

The **southern coast**, protected by a ridge of mountains, is the warmest and sunniest part of the isle, especially in the basin around Funchal. The **northern side** is more exposed to Atlantic winds, and gets more rain – sometimes around 200cm a year. Relatively much flatter and lower than Madeira, **Porto Santo** escapes all these climatic quirks, and tends to bask in sunlight the whole year round – though it can be windy.

On still days, **coastal areas** can be clammy, but breezes eddying off the Atlantic usually make the humidity more bearable. Also, moist air from sea-level rises rapidly up to the mountain tops, cools and condenses. Often this ***capacete*** ('peaked cap') of cloud descends to the coast during the late morning and retreats back up the mountainside by mid-afternoon. Cloudy days are most frequent in June, when you can set your watch by the arrival of the *capacete*.

Sometimes during the summer a searing, dry wind – the ***leste*** – blows across from the North African deserts, often for three or four days. Humidity drops to around 10%, the temperature soars into the 30s and everything gets covered in a fine reddish dust.

It is essential that you check a **weather report** before setting off on a walk, and advisable to do it before any excursion. Your destination may be only a few kilometres

Average Temperatures in °C/°F

Jan	Feb	Mar	April	May	June	July	Aug	Sept	Oct	Nov	Dec
18/64	17/62	17/62	17/62	18/64	20/68	21/70	22/72	23/75	22/72	20/68	19/66

Average Monthly Rainfall in Millimetres/Inches

Jan	Feb	Mar	April	May	June	July	Aug	Sept	Oct	Nov	Dec
100/4	90/3.5	75/3	45/1.8	25/1	10/0.4	0	5/0.2	30/1	75/3	100/4	75/3

away, but weather conditions can change drastically along the way. The local newspaper, *Diário de Notícias*, has an illustrated weather chart that is easy to understand even if your Portuguese is non-existent. The tourist office can also help with weather reports.

Locals will tell you that you can predict the weather by looking out to sea. Sometimes the Desertas islands are clearly visible and look close enough to swim to. This means rain. If they are hazy, then Funchal may be dull, though the rest of the island will probably be clear. Often you see no Desertas at all – not even a smudge on the horizon. Then it is the time to get out the suntan lotion.

When to Go

With such an equable climate, Madeira is worth a visit pretty much all year round. Choosing when to come will probably depend on which flowers you wish to see in bloom, what fruit you'd like to eat or whether you want to catch (or miss) the grape harvest or some local festival (*see* pp.60–61 and 84–5). In June coastal areas are most prone to spend much of the day under the cloudy *capacete*, but then this is the month when you can be sure of a fine view over the clouds from the mountain-tops. In the upper reaches, mists can suddenly close in on unsuspecting walkers at any time of the year, but do so more frequently in the winter. If you plan to do a lot of walking, it is worth bearing in mind that the rainiest months are late September/ October and March/April. Locals call October 'illness month' because the sudden sharp variations of temperature bring on bouts of flu and sniffles.

Porto Santo can be very bleak in dull weather, and if you intend to spend any length of time there, it is best to make it a summer visit.

What to Pack

'Flannel underclothing should not be forgotten,' warns a 19th-century 'handbook for the invalid and other visitors'. Though you won't need coats and heavy jerseys, you will have to pack for all seasons. The sun can be fierce, so a hat and sunglasses are a good idea – but a sweater is a must too. Tourists who jump aboard a bus in shorts and T-shirts in Funchal can be goose-pimpled and uncomfortable half an hour's drive out of town. Funchal's cobbled streets wreak havoc with high heels and hard soles, and if you are walking further afield it is essential to be properly prepared (*see* **Wine, Walks and Wildflowers**, pp.57–9). Dress codes are fairly informal – though you will need to smarten up for a visit to Reid's Hotel.

Mosquitoes can be a problem in the hotter months. Research has shown that the fiends home in on the warmth and air movement caused by our breathing. Holding your breath is unlikely to be a very satisfactory long-term deterrent. Rather pack a bottle or two of insect repellent.

Consulates in Funchal

British: Avenida Zarco 2–4°, **t** 291 221 221.
US: Rua da Alfândega 10–2°A/B, **t** 291 235 636.
South African: Rua Pimenta Aguiar, Ed. Torise, Bl.3–3°, **t** 291 742 825.
French: Avenida do Infante 58, **t** 291 225 514.
German: Largo do Phelps 6–1°, **t** 291 220 338.
Dutch: Rua da Alfândega, 1–2°, **t** 291 223 830.

Crime and the Police

'Murder is here in a kind of reputation,' writes an early visitor to Madeira, 'and it is made the characteristic of any gentleman of rank or fashion to have dipped his hand in blood.' Thankfully, fashion has changed, though in many ways a visit to Madeira puts the clock back rather agreeably. There are no drug-dazed youths hanging about on street corners, and mugging and street crime are almost unheard of, despite the aching poverty on the island.

The main **police stations** are in Funchal at Rua Carmo 49, **t** 291 221 021, and Rua de João de Deus 7, **t** 291 222 022. Report any theft at once and get a written statement for your insurance claim. If you end up on the wrong side of the law yourself, phone your consulate (*see* above) as soon as you can.

Damaging trees can land you in a lot of trouble. A law passed to stop developers surreptitiously setting fire to protected forests so that they can build on the land means that

Organizations for Disabled Travellers

UK

Holiday Care Service, **t** 0845 124 9971, *www.holidaycare.org.uk*. Information on accessible accommodation, transport, equipment hire, services, tour operators and contacts.

Irish Wheelchair Association, Blackheath Drive, Clontarf, Dublin 3, **t** (01) 818 6400, **f** (01) 833 3873, *www.iwa.ie*. Publishes guides with advice for disabled holidaymakers.

RADAR (Royal Association for Disability & Rehabilitation), 12 City Forum, 250 City Road, London EC1V 8AF, **t** (020) 7250 3222, **t** (020) 7250 4119 (minicom), *www. radar.org.uk*. For information and books.

Royal National Institute for the Blind (RNIB), 105 Judd St, London WC1H 9NE, **t** 0845 766 9999, *www.rnib.org.uk*. Its mobility unit offers advice for visually impaired people travelling by plane. Also advises on finding accommodation.

Tripscope, The Vassall Centre, Gill Avenue, Bristol BS16 2QQ, **t** 0845 758 5641, **f** (01179) 397 736, *www.tripscope.co.uk*. Expert practical advice and information to people with impaired mobility on every aspect of travel and transport. Information can be provided by letter or tape.

In the USA and Canada

American Foundation for the Blind, 11 Penn Plaza, Suite 300, New York NY 10001, **t** (212) 502 7600, toll free **t** 800 AFB LINE, **f** (212) 502 7777, *www.afb.org*. The best source of information in the USA for visually impaired travellers.

SATH (Society for Accessible Travel and Hospitality), 347 5th Avenue, Suite 610, New York NY 10016, **t** (212) 447 7284, **f** (212) 725 8253, *www.sath.org*. Travel, travel insurance and accessibility information. The website has excellent links, tips and a comprehensive list of relevant on-line publications for travellers with impaired mobility.

Internet Sites

Can Be Done, **t** (020) 8907 2400, **f** (020) 8909 1854, *www.canbedone.co.uk*. Tailor-made accessible tours for travellers with disabilities: they can book accommodation, flights or organize a complete itinerary.

you can be fined from €5,000 to €100,000 per tree for any that you 'destroy'.

Disabled Travellers

People with mobility problems may find Madeira difficult to cope with. Few public buildings are adapted for wheelchair users. In Funchal, the streets are cobbled and steep and the going is tough.

Eating Out

See **Food and Drink**, pp.65–70, for a discussion of Madeiran food and eating habits. Also *see* 'Madeira Wine', pp.52–7.

Prices are reasonable: you can quite easily get a hearty main course for €7 or less, and an accompanying carafe of house wine won't make much of a dent in your budget either. Even in more upmarket restaurants you'll find inexpensive omelettes and even hamburgers (also with piles of salad and potato) on the menu for around €4.50. Many restaurants offer a dish of the day (*prato do dia*) for €5.50–6.50, though this is often available at lunchtime only, as it is aimed more at the local market and lunch is the main meal of many Madeirense.

You'll invariably get a basket of bread on the table, even if you don't ask for it. The charge for this can be as much as €3 per table, though in non-touristy places it is around €1.50. It is seldom listed on the menu. Some restaurants also bring you portions of soft cheese and fish paste with the bread. Dipping into these while you're waiting for your food to arrive adds up on the bill too.

Restaurants that depend entirely on the tourist trade (most of those in the west of Funchal and the ones at beauty spots) tend to be €2–5 more expensive. While you are unlikely ever to have a really bad meal on Madeira, you can certainly enjoy more subtle cooking and get better value for money at places with more of a local clientele.

Restaurant Price Categories

expensive	over €30
moderate	€18–30
inexpensive	under €18

Restaurants in this book are grouped into three price categories, according to what it would cost one person to eat a full three-course meal (with soup as a starter, a low-range main course, and half a bottle of wine). Service charges are not normally included – a tip of 10%–12% is usual.

Some snack bars, pastry shops and fast-food outlets will display a sign that says *Pré-pagamento*. This means you must decide what you want, pay the cashier first, then take your receipt to the counter to place your order.

Electricity

The **voltage** on Madeira is 220 AC, which is compatible with the UK. US equipment will need a transformer. Wall **sockets** take continental two-pronged plugs.

Adaptors are available from some local electrical suppliers, though it would be cheaper to buy one from a specialist travel or electrical shop before you leave.

Emergency Numbers

The **national emergency number** for ambulance, police or fire is **t** 112 (*see also* 'Health and Insurance', pp.84–6).

Etiquette

Madeiran manners might strike you as being a little formal, though they are not so much stiff as charmingly old-fashioned. Men and women shake hands when they meet. Continental cheek-pecking takes place only between relatives and good friends, and never between two men.

Senhor and *Senhora*, used before the surname, are the equivalent of 'Mr' and 'Mrs', and are used frequently. However, these titles once denoted a person of lower rank than the speaker (just as a British mistress of the house called her char 'Mrs Brown', and was herself referred to as 'Madam'). It is safer to err on the side of formality and address strangers or acquaintances as *Don* or *Dona*, followed by their first name. So you would call Ana Ribeira 'Dona Ana', and not 'Senhora Ribeira'. In Portuguese it is polite, on speaking to a stranger, to use the third person – '*O senhor*' or '*A senhora*' – rather than a form of 'you'.

Festivals

The Madeiran calendar is crammed with festivities, from the official parades put on mainly for the benefit of visitors, to local parish and small village celebrations tinged with pagan ritual. The bigger beanfeasts can be somewhat artificial, with straggles of glum locals in traditional dress and coachloads of pink-legged tourists dancing tipsily in the streets. Harvest festivals and saints' days are much more fun.

You can spot the latter by the bunting. Coloured flags and white banners with a red cross (the design on Zarco's sails) go up some days before. Then come the women, who disappear into the church laden with flowers. Energetic young men string fairy-lights between the trees and across the street, and often outline the church itself. Thickets of laurel and other greenery are brought down from the mountains to decorate arches and to mask the trails of electric flex. On the day of the festival (often two days) church doors are flung open to reveal a galaxy of candles among the flowers, Mass is broadcast through crackly speakers and invisible daytime fireworks (whoosh, bang and a puff of smoke) explode to the accompaniment of church bells. Householders may lay out long carpets or make up mosaics of flowers and petals on the cobbles outside their front doors, ready for the procession. This consists of clouds of young girls in their first-communion whites, the clergy in its glad rags, a brass band, and various parish notables carrying whatever relics or religious paraphernalia the festival is all about. Sometimes onlookers throw down herbs in front of them as they crush the petal carpet underfoot, mingling aromas of rosemary and thyme with the incense. That night there will be a band, a bar, food stalls and maybe a tombola in the churchyard. Sometimes there is a mini funfair too.

Calendar of Events

January

St Amaro (Santa Cruz).
St Sebastian (Câmara de Lobos).

February

End of month: ***Cortejo Trapalhão*** (or People's Carnival). Locals turn out in parade for a big, if tacky, fancy dress competition. The official **Carnival**, a day or two later, is a far more spectacular affair. The beachfront promenade in Funchal is the scene of Brazilian-style revelry: elaborate floats, bands, schools of dancers and people in breathtaking costumes such as giant iridescent butterflies or birds.

April

Day after Pentecost (sometimes May): ***Espírito Santo*** (Camacha).

End of month: **Flower Festival.** On the first day, children fix posies into a Wall of Hope outside the city hall in Funchal and make a wish. On the second day there is a parade of Madeiran blooms – in bouquets, in conical baskets and decoratively fashioned into floats. Local bands and folk dancers also turn out in force.

June

13: **St Anthony** (Santo da Serra).
24: **St John** (Funchal); **St Peter** (Ponta do Pargo).
29: **St Peter** (Câmara de Lobos, Ribeira Brava). Three of the most vigorously celebrated saints' days. On the eve of St John's feast it is traditional to eat salted tuna with boiled potatoes and pickled onions. If you see anyone peering over the end of the pier in Funchal at midnight on St John's Eve, they are probably looking for their reflection in the water. If they can't see it, goes the tradition, they will die within the year. A little more cheery is the schoolgirls' superstition that if three men's names are written on separate pieces of paper and scrunched up, then the last one picked out of the palm (or any one to unfold if left overnight in a bowl of water) shows the name of their husband to be. St Peter (the patron saint of fishermen) is most rousingly honoured in the seaside villages. St Anthony is the patron saint of Portugal, as well as being regarded locally as the lovers' saint. The ancient fertility rituals associated with his name day seem to have spilled over into the other saints' feasts as well. On all three days fragrant bonfires of pine-wood and rosemary branches are lit after sunset. Lovers take turns to leap over the flames; the higher they jump, the stronger their love.

Early in month: **Cherry Festival** (Jardim da Serra). The little village of Jardim da Serra northwest of Funchal is the scene of this good local bash with hardly a tourist in sight (*see* p.191).

Most of month: **Festival of Music** held at various venues around Funchal. Although the organizers often land some fine international talent, they seem to rely on island bush telegraph for publicity. Apart from the odd wind-tattered poster around town, the only way you'll find out what is going on is to ask at the tourist office or at the box office of the municipal theatre.

Most churches manage to find two or three excuses a year for a festival. Keep an eye open for flags and tell-tale puffs of smoke and you are sure to catch at least one during your stay. Exact dates of religious festivals may change from year to year, but the tourist office in Funchal will be able to tell you of any that happen during your stay. The 'Agenda' page in *Diário de Notícias* is an even more useful source of tips. Saints' days may be celebrated in more than one village at the same time. The villages in the box above are where the main festivities take place.

Health and Insurance

Ambulance t 112.

EU nationals are entitled to free medical care in Madeira – but you must carry a validated form **E111** (available from post offices). Theoretically you should organize this two weeks before you leave, though you can usually do it over the counter in one visit. Citizens of other countries have no such privileges, and the E111 does not insure personal belongings, or cover expenses arising from flight cancellation. For these reasons, all

July

17: ***Nossa Senhora*** (Arco da Calheta, Santa Cruz).

22: **St Maria Madalena** (Madalena do Mar, Porto Moniz).

31: **St Beatrice** (Água de Pena); ***Santissimo Sacramento*** (Caniço) – the slopes surrounding the village are decorated with small fires arranged to form symbolic designs.

August

21: **St Lawrence** (Camacha).

28: **St Francis Xavier** (Porto Santo).

Last Sun: **Festival of Our Lord** (Camacha, Porto da Cruz).

Assumption: Celebrated island-wide, with the festivities at Monte going on for a full three days.

Mid-month: Long sections of Madeira's winding roads are closed down for hours on end during the **Madeiran Wine Rally**. Skilled drivers from the international rally circuit whizz around at great speed, and give local road-maniacs delusions of grandeur for weeks afterwards.

September

Some time in month: ***Nossa Senhora do Livramento*** (Caniço).

1st Sun: ***Bom Jesus*** (Ponta Delgada).

7/8: ***Nossa Senhora do Loreto*** (Loreto, Arco da Calheta).

3rd Sun: ***Nossa Senhora da Piedade*** (Caniçal). In an interesting twist to the usual festival, the statue of the Virgin is taken from a chapel on the cliffs to the village by fishermen in a procession of boats.

Mid-month: **Grape Harvest**. Funchal has a week-long festival and a series of special exhibitions. At Estreito de Câmara de Lobos and other villages around the island, tourists jump into pressing vats to squelch bare-footed in the grapes, *borraccheiros* (wine transporters) shoulder their pig's bladders and call to each other in ringing nasal chants, and there is plenty of folk dancing, Madeiran music and feasting.

October

1st Sun: ***Nossa Senhora do Rosário*** (São Vicente)

9: ***Senhor dos Milagres*** (Machico)

Also in month: ***Nossa Senhora do Livramento*** (Ponta do Sol). The little village of Ribeira Brava braces itself for the annual **Meeting of Regional Philharmonic Bands**.

December

Christmas is celebrated with relentless verve on Madeira, starting on 8 Dec with the switching on of the Christmas lights, and lasting through to 6 Jan. Three-quarters of a million light bulbs strung along the streets give Funchal the appearance of a giant illuminated spider's web. There are bell designs, Christmas trees and life-size galleons. At midnight on New Year's Eve it is traditional to switch on all the lights in the house and throw open the windows, and the entire city erupts in a magnificent firework display. Best view of all is from the deck of one of the luxury passenger liners that make a beeline for Madeira especially for the festival – so many that the harbour soon fills up and latecomers have to anchor at sea.

travellers are advised to take out some form of **travel insurance**. Consult your insurance broker or travel agent, and shop around for a good deal. Also check out any existing home policies you have, as you might already be covered for holidays abroad. If you suffer flight cancellation, lost luggage, theft or illness, check the small print of your policy for what documentation – police reports, medical forms or receipts – you will be required to produce when making a claim. If you do fall ill in Madeira you should present your E111 as soon as possible at **Centro de Saúde do Bom Jesus** (*Serviço de Migrantes*), Rua das Hortas 67, Funchal, **t** 291 229 161 or **t** 291 208 700.

Standards of medical care are generally quite high, and there are a number of **English-speaking doctors** (especially in Funchal). The island's major **hospitals** are in Funchal, but many villages have a local clinic (*Centro de Saúde*) that can help with emergencies (*see* separate listings under each chapter).

Hospitals

Hospital Cruz Carvalho, Avenida Luís Camões, Funchal, **t** 291 705 600.

Hospital dos Marmeleiros, Estrada dos Marmeleiros, Funchal, **t** 291 705 730.

English-speaking Doctors

Dr Urbalino Gomes, Rua do Bom Jesus 9-3°, Funchal, **t** 291 755 137 or **t** 291 227 373.

Dr Luis Bicho, Rua Câmara Pestana 24-1°, Funchal, **t** 291 200 390 (*after 4pm*).

Pharmacies

Dois Amigos, Câmara Pestana 10, Funchal, **t** 291 225 547. Pharmacies (*farmácia*) take it in turn to offer an emergency service. You can find the address of the duty pharmacy on the door of any other chemist's, or in the back pages of the *Diário de Notícias*. Pharmacists can be asked for advice about minor health problems and prescribe common remedies.

Dentistry

Dr Johnny Bjelkarøy, Infante (Marina) shopping centre, 3rd Floor, Room 304, **t** 291 231 277.

Emergency dental service (*Sundays and holidays*), **t** 291 207 676.

Laundry

In rural areas you can still see women beside the rivers and *levadas* thumping and twisting the weekly wash. In bigger towns, houses may be furnished with indoor concrete tubs, or even a washing machine. Madeirense do their own washing at home – or take it back to mother. Self-service **launderettes** are unheard of, though there are some that wash clothes for you – often charging per item. Unless you are willing to use (and usually pay handsomely for) your hotel's laundry service, you'll be forced into stamping on your dirty washing in the bathtub or doing it piece by piece in the hand basin. **Dry cleaners** are somewhat easier to find, in Funchal at least (*see* p.98).

Living and Working in Madeira

Madeira, as part of Portugal, is a member of the European Union. Theoretically, this means that there should be no barriers against EU citizens living and working here. In practice, an attempt to settle here or stay longer than the three months officially allotted to EU tourists could bring you up against the defensiveness and bloody-mindedness of island mentality at its worst. If you are not a citizen of the EU, you should buckle down for an even bumpier ride. The Madeirense are terrified of even their own émigrés returning – and not without reason. If all the Madeirense who live in South Africa should suddenly decide to come back (and they threaten to now that life is not so privileged over there), the island's population would triple, and its infrastructure would probably collapse.

Be prepared for long and frustrating tangles with petty bureaucrats. Take with you all the documentation you can lay your hands on, a Valium and a copy of Kafka to cheer you up. It is not unknown for the issuing of a residence permit to be delayed for so long (by complications seemingly invented by the officials themselves) that the time that it would have run for expires anyway, and applicants are threatened with a fine or told that they have to start all over again. You could try to sort out the necessary permits before you leave, at your local Portuguese consulate. Here you will probably be told that you have to go through the formalities on Madeira itself. (Of course, when you get to Madeira you'll be told that you should have done everything at the consulate.) Stamp your feet and stand your ground – though bear in mind that even through the consulate the procedure can take ten months.

You will need both a **work** and a **residence permit** (from the *Departamento dos Estrangeiros* in the government offices on Avenida Arriaga). If you want to work in the catering trade, you need to undergo a medical examination, and can be heavily fined if you do not. You must get a Portuguese **driving licence** (which may also involve a medical examination) within six months of getting your residence permit. If you don't, the penalties if you are caught are the same as if you were driving without a licence at all.

Maps

Islanders know their way about. Those maps that do exist are aimed at the tourist market, and publishers seem to be of the opinion that tourists don't really need an accurate idea of where they are going. There is no street-indexed map of Funchal, and the most detailed map of the island – a 1960s ordnance map, updated in the 1990s – is expensive and a little eccentric (available from the English Bookshop on Rua da Carreira in Funchal).

Few maps, even the decorative 3-D ones, give a clear idea of how steep the terrain can be. Straight-line distances, even across town in Funchal, can be very deceptive. Set out on what appears from the map to be a ten-minute walk, and you could still be puffing uphill half an hour later. It is most important to bear this in mind when planning a walk in the country.

You can buy maps before you go at:

Stanford's, 12–14 Long Acre, London WC2E 9LP, **t** (020) 7836 1321.

The Travel Bookshop, 13 Blenheim Crescent, London W11 2EE, **t** (020) 7229 5260.

In the USA try:

The Compleat Traveller, 199 Madison Avenue at 36th, New York, NY 10016, **t** (212) 685 9007.

Media

You can find most leading **British and American papers** at news kiosks around Funchal the day after publication.

A number of **English-language freebies** aimed primarily at tourists are brought out monthly. They provide topical titbits, odd stories about the island and screeds of ads for restaurants and souvenir shops. You'll find them handed out free at hotels and tourist information offices.

Of the local rags *Diário de Notícias*, which has been going since 1876, is the most informative. At the back you'll find reports, current museum opening times, TV listings and all manner of other useful bits and pieces – all easily comprehensible, even if your Portuguese isn't up to much.

Larger hotels have **cable or satellite television** and so offer some international fare. RTP, the Portuguese television company, seems to exist on a diet of Brazilian soaps, but sometimes screens British or American films with Portuguese subtitles.

Money and Banks

Portugal is part of the **euro** zone. There are 100 cents to the euro. Notes come in denominations of 5, 10, 20, 50, 100, 200, and 500 euros though the three-figure ones, and even sometimes 50s, may be hard to cash. There are 2 euro, 1 euro, 50 cent, 20 cent, 10 cent, 5 cent, 2 cent and 1 cent coins.

Restaurants and shops all over the island have at least one eye on the tourist market. Even rather humble, out-of-the-way establishments will often accept **credit cards**, though it is always a good idea to check first. Petrol stations and hotels are also usually happy to take plastic, and you will certainly need a credit card to hire a car.

Most banks have **cash-dispensing machines** (ATMs) that are compatible with a wide range of cards, not only those normally affiliated to the bank – look out for signs reading '*Multibanco*'. Your bank or credit card may slap fairly steep handling charges on machine withdrawals made abroad, so it is worth a quick phone call to check up before you leave, and worthwhile drawing out largish amounts at any one time.

Local bank charges are also high. If you are cashing **traveller's cheques** or exchanging money, it is a good idea to do so in large amounts, as there is a hefty minimum charge per transaction.

Opening Hours

Banks

Open from 8.30am to 3pm. A *bureau de change* at the tourist office in Funchal stays open until 5pm on weekdays and from 9 to 1 on Saturday mornings.

Shops

With the exception of larger supermarkets, most shops close for lunch. Hours are generally Mon–Fri 9–1 and 2 or 3–6 or 7, Sat 9–1. Some shops close for lunch as early as 12.30, and others stay shut until 3. Supermarkets tend to stay open until 7 or 8pm, and shops in the big shopping centres in Funchal may also stay open in the evenings and on Saturday afternoons. Some of the bigger supermarkets

National Holidays

1 January New Year's Day
February Shrove Tuesday/Ash Wednesday (dates vary)
March/April Good Friday (date varies)
25 April Day of the Revolution
1 May Labour Day
June Corpus Christi (varies)
10 June National Day
1 July Regional Day
15 August Feast of the Assumption
21 August Funchal Day
5 October Republic Day
1 November All Saints' Day
1 December Restoration of Independence Day
8 December Feast of the Immaculate Conception
25 December Christmas Day

in Funchal don't shut their doors until 10pm, and are also open on Sundays (*see* p.97).

Museums

Opening hours and admission prices vary (*see* individual listings), but the general pattern is Tues–Sun, 10–12.30 and 2–6. Sometimes a museum will have free admission over weekends and on public holidays, though this usually means that the security staff are on the beach and that part of the collection is shut off.

Most **public gardens** stay open from 9 to 6 (with the important exception of Quinta Palheiro, which closes at 12.30pm). Many also close on Mondays.

Tourist Offices

The tourist office in Funchal is open Mon–Fri 9–8, Sat and Sun 9–6.

See individual listings for other tourist office opening hours.

Churches

These are a problem. The authorities don't seem to have tumbled to what gems they have tucked away around the island – or they don't want to encourage people to poke about. Most churches – even those in Funchal – remain tightly shut for much of the day.

This doesn't mean that you can't get in. Come just before or after Mass (around 4.30pm or 6.30pm), or on a Saturday afternoon when the cleaning ladies are in, or someone is arranging the flowers. In villages there is often a priest or caretaker living around the back of the church, who will let you in. Failing that, knock on the nearest door; sometimes the neighbours keep the key, or at least know where it can be found.

Post, Telephones and the Internet

You can spot post offices by their red and white signs reading CTT (for *Correios* (mail), *Telégrafos* and *Telefones*). The main **post office** in Funchal is on Rua Dr João Brito Câmara, next to the SAM bus station. More central (and less of an uphill struggle) is the old head office on Avenida Zarco. Both are open Mon–Fri 8.30–8 and Sat 9–12.30.

At both offices a separate hall of **public telephones** stays open until 10pm. To use one of these phones, you first get a token from the attendant, who will direct you to the relevant booth. You pay after the call when you give back your token. **Fax** facilities exist here too.

Normal **payphones** accept all coins from 2 cents upwards. Some payphones take only phonecards, which you can buy (for €3, €6 and €9) at post offices and some news kiosks. You can make international calls from more modern street payphones, but the telephone hall at the post office offers comfort and relative quiet at no extra cost, and so is probably preferable.

The **international access code** from Madeira is 00, so to telephone the UK dial 00 44 then the city code (minus the first nought). To telephone the USA dial 00 1 then the city code (minus the first zero).

Calls to Madeira from abroad go through the Portuguese network. The **international code for Portugal** is 351. The regional code for every number on the island, and on Porto Santo, is 291 (include the code even when phoning from within Madeira to other Madeiran numbers). Towns and villages do not have their own codes. Many numbers have changed recently to cope with an increased load; if you are having trouble getting through to a six-digit number, try putting a 291 in front of it.

You can reach the **local directory enquiries** on **t** 118. The **international operator** is on **t** 172 for collect calls and **t** 177 for international directory enquiries.

Letters and postcards to EU destinations cost 54¢, and to the USA 70¢. If you are writing to Madeira, don't forget to put 'Madeira, Portugal' on the envelope. It is extraordinary how many post office workers think Madeira is in Spain, and incompletely addressed letters can go astray for months.

Global Net Café, Rua do Hospital Velho 25, near the market, **t** 291 280 671, *open Mon–Fri 9–7, Sat 9–1, €2.50 per hour*, is a comfortable, well-equipped Internet café with friendly owners (and home-made Norwegian waffles).

Religious Affairs

The **English Church** in Funchal has a long and at times scandalous history (*see* pp.129–31). The Anglican Church of the Holy Trinity (to give it its official title) is part of the Diocese of Gibraltar in Europe – though you're unlikely to meet the bishop. He is based in London, and his diocese includes parishes as far afield as Finland and Romania.

You will, however, meet the core of Madeira's long-standing British community, more recent expats and other English visitors at the Sunday morning services. Afterwards the chaplain hosts a reception in the church gardens. Here you will get a warm welcome, as well as coffee, soft drinks, wine and snacks – and a glimpse of old Madeira.

Services in English

English Church

Rua da Quebra Costas 18, **t** 291 220 674.

Sun	8am	Holy Communion
	11am	Parish Communion Rite B
Wed	10.30am	Holy Communion

Roman Catholic Church

Chapel of Penha de França, Rua Penha de França, Funchal.

Sun	10.30am	Mass

Baptist Church

Rua Silvestre Quintino Freitas 126, **t** 291 552 053.

Sun	11am

Shopping

Leave space in your suitcase for a couple of bottles of good **madeira wine** (*see* pp.52–7). Take your time before deciding what to buy, and sample the wares in the wine houses in Funchal (*see* pp.97 and 116).

Island handicraft to take home with you includes world-famous **embroidery** and **wickerwork** (*see* pp.49–50). Camacha, in the eastern part of Madeira, is the wicker centre of the island, with a large shop and factory, though you can buy wicker products anywhere. If you feel tempted by a laundry basket or armchair, do bear in mind that your airline might be sticky about oversize objects in your luggage and charge you for freight, no matter how little it weighs. It is worthwhile checking up on current regulations at the local airline office or with your tour operator. Women all over the island stitch away at the lace and embroidery on sale in the souvenir shops and 'factories' in Funchal. Quality varies, so shop around. This is one thing that warrants a visit to the more expensive, established shops (*see* **Funchal**, 'Shopping', p.98). A seal from the Instituto do Bordado, Tapeçarias e Artesanato da Madeira (IBATAM) is some guarantee of quality. **Tapestry** and ***petit point*** are also popular, and approved work carries the same seal. Long-lasting **flowers** such as protea and some orchids can be specially packed for you to take home with you.

Barretes de lã, the odd woollen **pom-pom hats** with comfy ear flaps that are part of traditional male Madeiran farmers' dress, are excellent protection against the winters of less hospitable climes. You can get them in sober natural browns and greys, or in gaudy synthetic knits. Souvenir shops treat the caps as novelties and tend to overcharge, but you can buy them more cheaply at ordinary general dealers around town, or from street vendors.

The traditional **ankle boots** (especially those with car-tyre soles, used by the toboggan men) are strong and long-lasting, and the islanders do a fine line in simple, sturdy **handmade shoes**. Again, shoe shops rather than souvenir shops are the place to go (*see also* under **Funchal**, 'Shopping', p.97). Factory-made shoes from the mainland are also good value.

Pack a few ***bolos de mel*** too. The sticky, spicy cake made from molasses is a local speciality. It is delicious and lasts for months – an ideal gift for the great-aunt you forgot, who suddenly drops in to look at your snaps.

You will see brightly coloured **roosters** everywhere. These are part of mainland Portuguese rather than native Madeiran folklore. Other boldly coloured **pottery** from the mainland is also on sale. Local **woodcarving** is relatively cheap and plentiful, but not done with any great skill.

If you are self-catering in Madeira, you'll find almost anything you want at the large **supermarkets** in Funchal. It is more fun, though, to brave the smaller **grocery shops**. Often these have fittings that date back to the 19th century and staff that look as if they only just made it into this one. Shopping this way involves a visit to a number of stores, as each appears to specialize in just a handful of products (coffee, cooking oil, smoked fish and wine is a common combination). **Markets** are abundantly stocked, and fresh fish is always in good supply – often from the fishermen themselves. The one thing you'll be hard put to it to find is fresh milk. The island's few cows just can't come up with the goods. Long-life milk is sold by the carton, but the only time you are likely to see fresh milk on sale is when you get a rare glimpse of a vendor carrying an urn from door to door, and filling up the jugs that are offered to him. Brown bread can also be a bit of a problem to come by. Again, the bakeries in big supermarkets cater for this northern European penchant, but you could try asking for *pão integral* at your local baker's. Some of the traditional village breads make healthy and tasty alternatives (*see* **Food and Drink**, pp.67–8).

Sports and Activities

Football (or *futebol*, as the Portuguese call it) is the island obsession. The main stadium, Barreiros, is off Rua do Dr Pita, to the west of Funchal. The TV sets which are stationed in the corners of restaurants and cafés flicker to life whenever there is a match to be watched, and if the game is an important one you can abandon all hope of quiet conversation. During home games, bands of supporters (of local teams including Maritimo, Nacional and União) draped in club colours, waving banners and singing, hit the streets. But there is never any violence. The whole family may turn out to watch the game, and smaller towns bubble with a fiesta atmosphere on match days.

Many of the larger hotels have **tennis courts** open to non-guests. You can also hire courts at Quinta Magnolia (*see* p.99).

Madeira has two **golf courses**, both of them in splendid settings. Palheiro Golf, Palheiro Ferreiro, São Gonçalo, Funchal, **t** 291 792 116, adjoins the gardens at Quinta Palheiro. The Campo Golfe da Madeira, Santo da Serra, **t** 291 552 321, is high up on a plateau – sometimes above the cloudline.

As an antidote to the rocky shoreline there are **swimming jetties** at most coast towns and swish lidos (mainly in Funchal) where you can sip cocktails and hire sun-loungers, as well as splash about in well-maintained swimming pools. Some of the larger hotels also open their pools to the public. Porto Moniz boasts a series of natural **rock pools**, and the island of Porto Santo has 8km (5 miles) of uninterrupted **white sand beach**. The sea is deep and crystal-clear close to the shore. Except around the Funchal harbour area and at some river mouths, the sea water is clean – though beaches can be drab and littered with plastic. *See* individual listings under town names.

Deep-sea fishing for tuna, blue marlin, barracuda and other big game fish can add a dash of excitement to your holiday. Most companies operate from the Funchal marina, and all provide the necessary tackle (*see* p.99; for fishing seasons *see* p.60). If you prefer to interact more passively with the creatures of the deep, there is ample opportunity for **scuba diving**, even for complete beginners. Some hotels hire out equipment, and there is an approved British Sub-Aqua Club school at the Funchal Lido (*see* p.99). Larger hotels are also the main source of equipment for **windsurfing** and other **watersports**.

Time

Madeira is on Greenwich Mean Time (i.e. the same as London, and five hours ahead of New York).

Clocks go forward by one hour in summer.

Tipping

A 10–12% tip is usual in restaurants and cafés, and for taxi drivers.

Toilets

Most public lavatories are presided over by an attendent who dispenses paper (and appreciates a small tip). A few of them command a realm of impeccable cleanliness, but most allow their dominions to slide into a state of neglect and nastiness. Public toilets, especially outside Funchal, can be quite vile. It is quite acceptable to pop into a hotel or café and use the toilets there, though if you are not a customer it is polite to ask first.

Cavalheiros, *Homens* or *Senhores* means Gents; Ladies is *Senhoras*.

Tourist Offices

Portuguese National Tourist Offices can help you with information about Madeira before you go.

UK: 22–25A Sackville St, London W1X 1DE, **t** (020) 7494 1441.

USA: 590 5th Ave, 4th Floor, New York, NY 10036–4704, **t** (212) 354 4403.

Canada: 60 Bloor St W., Suite 1005, Toronto, Ontario M4W 3B8, **t** (416) 921 7376.

The main tourist office on the island is in Funchal, Avenida Arriaga 18, **t** 291 211 900, **f** 291 225 658 (*open Mon–Fri 9–8, Sat and Sun 9–6*). There is also a small office in the Monumental Lido shopping mall, **t** 291 775 254. A number of other offices, posing as information centres, are branches of time-share companies whose main aim is to get your signature on that dotted line.

The official Madeira website is *www.madeiratourism.org/uk*, but there is better and more up-to-the-minute information on *www.strawberry-world.com*.

Where to Stay

Most of the island's hotels are in or around **Funchal**, and as the transport system centres on the capital it makes a convenient base. If you would prefer to stay a bit more off the beaten track, then the villages of **Jardim do Mar** or **São Roque do Faial** make attractive alternatives.

Although the island is small, travelling on the twisting roads is time-consuming. The routes east and west out of Funchal become especially tedious if you have to travel them day after day. If you plan to spend most of your time walking, it is worth while considering **São Vicente**, **São Roque do Faial** or **Santa Cruz** as bases. If it's a tan you're after, remember that the northern side of the island gets far more rain and mist than the south.

Hotels and Guesthouses

Madeira has more than its fair share of five-star luxury hotels – it still enjoys a reputation as a winter retreat for the well-heeled. You'll find a wide range of other accommodation from classy modern hotel complexes to simple old guesthouses. An explosion of hotel-building over the past few years has led largely to the appearance of big four-star and five-star hotels with their sights set firmly on the upper end of the package holiday market, but EU grants awarded to people who wanted to do up old island homes to accommodate guests have resulted in a number of places midway in style between a B&B and a small hotel. Often these are attractively located, and some offer use of a communal kitchen. The tourist office in Funchal carries a full list, and the homes can be spotted along the road by a blue sign with a little house on it. Most are called 'Quinta...' or 'Casa...' The best are mentioned in the appropriate accommodation sections in this guide. Rumour has it that some unscrupulous people, and those who could pull strings, used the grants to do up their own holiday homes. The blue signs are there (they have to be by law), and telephone numbers are listed, but you'll never find anyone in, or you'll be told there is no room.

An *estalagem* or *albergaria* (inn) usually denotes something in the mid-range of price and comfort. A *residencial*, *residência* or *pensão* (*pension*) will be inexpensive and often fairly simple. Madeira has two *pousadas* – guest houses established by the Portuguese government in particularly beautiful spots (*see* pp.170 and 179). All of these different types of accommodation operate on their own

Hotel Price Categories

very expensive	over €180
expensive	€90–€180
moderate	€45–€90 (Funchal)
	€40–€90 (outside Funchal)
inexpensive	below €45 (Funchal)
	below €40 (outside Funchal)

star system (though only top hotels get five stars) – so a three-star *pension* does not offer the same quality as a three-star hotel. Stars are awarded on the basis of facilities and are not necessarily a guide to the comfort, location or stylishness of a hotel.

Prices given in this book (*see* box, above) are for a double room (usually with breakfast and private bathroom) in high season. Seasonal variations depend very much on individual managements. Many hotels charge lower prices in June and for the first part of July, and for the month of January (after the New Year festivities). Most will bump up prices by at least 20 per cent (over and above the 'high season' rates given here) for the Christmas and New Year period. At other times you can often negotiate a discount if you are staying for over a week.

Self-catering

Apartment hotels offer self-catering options, and there are also holiday apartments to let around the island – a tempting prospect when the fruit and fish markets are so abundantly stocked.

Private Rooms

In addition to hotel accommodation, you can stay very cheaply in private rooms. A local restaurant or café can often tell you where to ask. The tourist office has a list of private accommodation, but seems to have a policy of giving out information only when the *residencials* and *pensions* are full (they employ more staff and so give more of a boost to the economy). Insist, and look as if you are not going to go away, and you might squeeze an address out of the person on duty.

Women Travellers

Visiting women, who do not have to get involved in staunch local notions of family values, can get the best of Madeiran's good, old-fashioned respect. Women can walk alone unmolested, even at night. You won't even be subjected to Mediterranean-style banter.

Madeiran women dress fairly conservatively. Shorts or skimpy tops will mark you out as a tourist, but are unlikely to give offence unless you want to visit a church – then it is better to dress a little more soberly. Topless bathing for women is virtually unknown, apart from around a few hotel pools.

Funchal

09

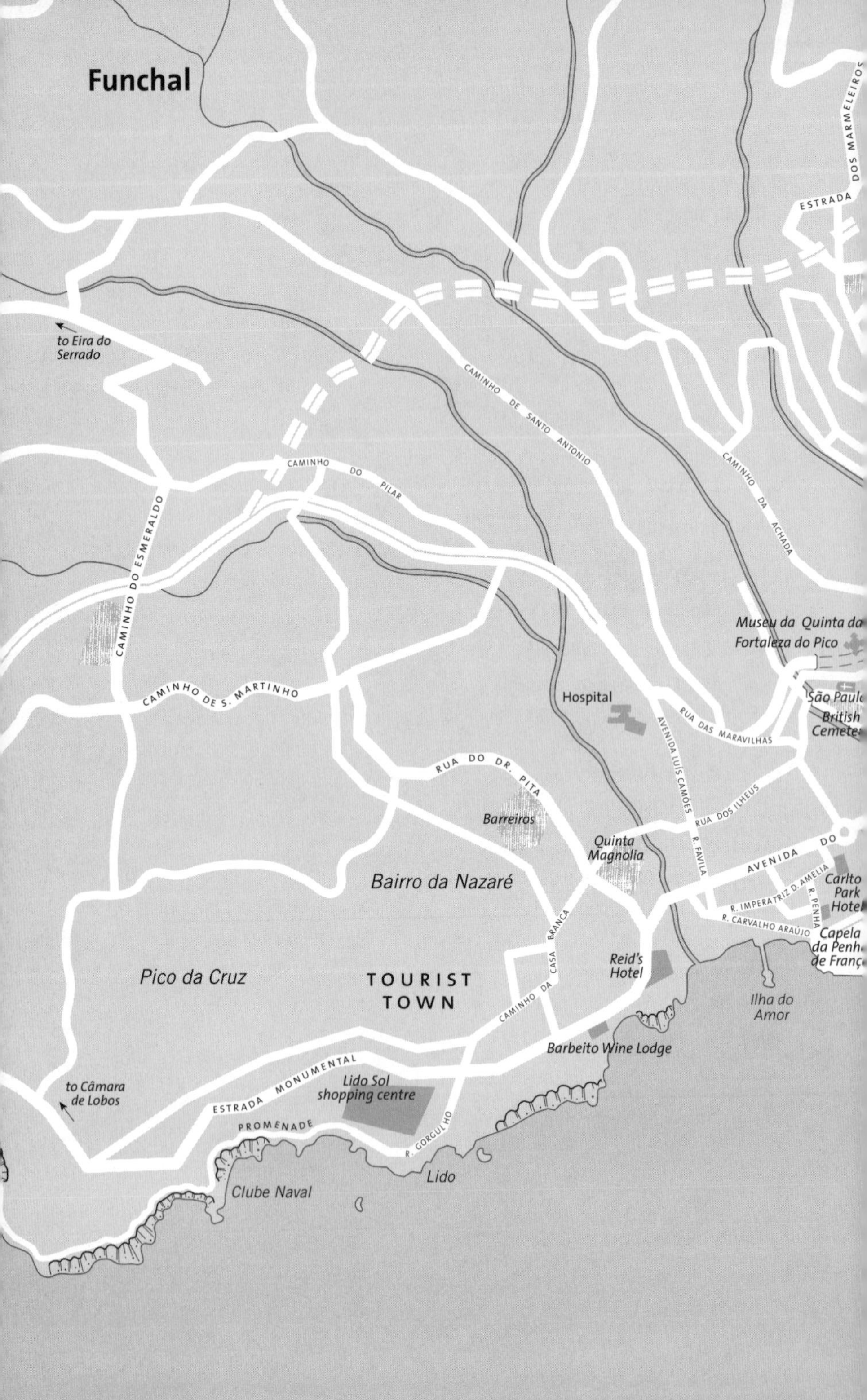

Funchal
to Eira do Serrado
ESTRADA DOS MARMELEIROS
CAMINHO DE SANTO ANTONIO
CAMINHO DA ACHADA
CAMINHO DO PILAR
CAMINHO DO ESMERALDO
CAMINHO DE S. MARTINHO
Museu da Quinta da Fortaleza do Pico
São Paulo
British Cemetery
Hospital
RUA DAS MARAVILHAS
AVENIDA LUÍS CAMÕES
RUA DO DR. PITA
Barreiros
RUA DOS ILHEUS
R. FAVILA
Quinta Magnolia
AVENIDA DO
R. IMPERATRIZ D. AMELIA
R. PENHA
R. CARVALHO ARAÚJO
Carlton Park Hotel
Capela da Penha de França
Bairro da Nazaré
CAMINHO DA CASA BRANCA
Reid's Hotel
Ilha do Amor
Pico da Cruz
TOURIST TOWN
Barbeito Wine Lodge
ESTRADA MONUMENTAL
Lido Sol shopping centre
to Câmara de Lobos
PROMENADE
R. GORGULHO
Lido
Clube Naval

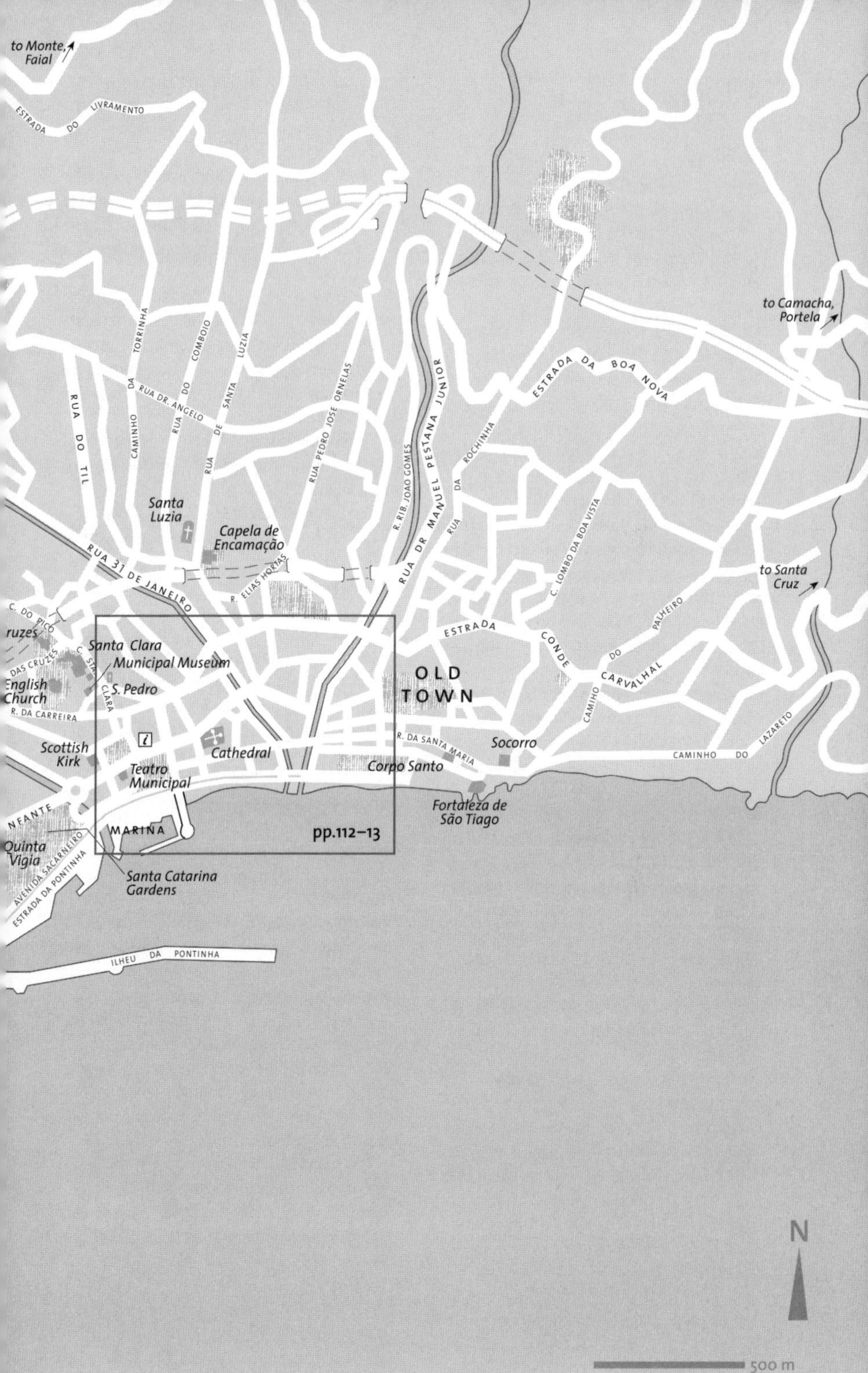

to Monte, Faial
ESTRADA DO LIVRAMENTO
to Camacha, Portela
ESTRADA DA BOA NOVA
RUA DO TIL
CAMINHO DA TORRINHA
RUA DR. ANGELO
RUA DO COMBOIO
RUA DE SANTA LUZIA
RUA PEDRO JOSE ORNELAS
R. RIB. JOAO GOMES
RUA DR MANUEL PESTANA JUNIOR
RUA DA ROCHINHA
C. LOMBO DA BOA VISTA
Santa Luzia
Capela de Encamação
RUA 31 DE JANEIRO
R. ELIAS HORTAS
to Santa Cruz
C. DO PICO
Cruzes
DAS CRUZES
Santa Clara
Municipal Museum
C. STA CLARA
S. Pedro
English Church
R. DA CARREIRA
ESTRADA CONDE CARVALHAL
CAMINHO DO PALHEIRO
OLD TOWN
R. DA SANTA MARIA
Socorro
CAMINHO DO LAZARETO
Scottish Kirk
Cathedral
Teatro Municipal
Corpo Santo
Fortaleza de São Tiago
INFANTE
MARINA
pp.112–13
Quinta Vigia
AVENIDA SACARNEIRO
ESTRADA DA PONTINHA
Santa Catarina Gardens
ILHEU DA PONTINHA
N
500 m
500 yds

Getting Around

Walking

All the streets in Funchal are paved with stones, mostly sharp ones, and there is no causeway, so that walking is neither clean nor agreeable, and as all the streets are either up or down hill, it is a most fatiguing operation...

Isabella de França, in her *Journal* of 1853

Walking in Funchal is still a challenge. Many streets have no pavements. Scrape marks on the walls are testimony to how close cars and buses pass. Pedestrians are left to fend for themselves. In the Old Town especially, the cobblestones are sharp and uneven, so shoes with leather soles and high heels are not a good idea. The sudden, steep hills play havoc with the ratio between the distance apparent on a map and the time you take to travel it.

But walking need not be unenjoyable, and it is really the only way to soak in all that the town has to offer. Take your time, wear comfortable shoes and try to avoid the hottest part of the day (when all the shops and museums are closed anyway). There are wide, shady and even relatively flat avenues as well as precipitous alleys, and plenty of cafés to collapse into along the way.

By Bus

Funchal's bright **yellow city buses** tear up and down the hills and criss-cross town at alarming speeds. You will certainly need them to visit the places listed in 'Around the Centre' below, but routes are not particularly convenient for the other sights. Be careful not to confuse city buses with their multi-coloured counterparts. The number on the window might be the same, but the latter will be headed off across the island (*see* p.77).

The city bus company, **Horários do Funchal**, has three **information kiosks**, one at the eastern end of the Avenida do Mar (near the Open Market), one at the western end (above the Marina) and one midway between the two. These are open to provide information while the buses are running (from around 6am until midnight) and for ticket sales during office hours.

You can buy **tickets** from the driver for a flat fare of €1.30 per journey. You can also buy **books of tickets** in advance from the information kiosks or, after hours, from certain newsagents (such as the magazine kiosks near the Beatles' Boat and on Largo do Município). These tickets should be stamped in the franking machine each time you board. They come in books of five double tickets (use each ticket twice by stamping either end).

Unless your hotel is beyond the Lido, most of your travelling is likely to be in Zone One, so it will probably be more economical to buy Zone One tickets only. If you do cross a boundary, it is perfectly legal to stamp another Zone One ticket to cover the trip.

Seven-day passes costing €15 and valid to all destinations are available at the information kiosks.

You can spot **bus stops** by the yellow Horários do Funchal sign. Most display timetables and a map showing routes and zone boundaries.

By Taxi

There are two types of taxi in Funchal. Smart black tourist or **T taxis** have polyglot drivers, are pricey and are usually used for tours or day trips. Your hotel receptionist will call one, or you can pick up one yourself from ranks near the Lido and behind the Infante Shopping Centre.

Most people settle for the ordinary yellow **city taxis**. These have a minimum charge of €1.50. A journey from the centre out to Hotel Town should cost €3–4. Drivers are entitled to charge 20% more at weekends and after 10pm. You are well safeguarded against being ripped off; a green light shining on the taxi roof reassures any passing policeman that the meter is running; two green lights show that the meter is set at the surcharge rate. For longer trips and island tours you can negotiate a fare with the driver. There is a list of official prices for longer trips on the noticeboard at the tourist office.

The main **taxi ranks** are near the cathedral (**t** 291 222 500), opposite the Municipal Gardens (**t** 291 220 911), on the Esplanade (**t** 291 224 588) and by the market (**t** 291 226 400).

By Car

For information about car hire and local companies, *see* **Travel**, p.75.

Tourist Information

The **tourist office** is at Avenida Arriaga 18, **t** 291 211 900, **f** 291 225 658, *www.madeira tourism.org, info@madeiratourism.org (open Mon–Fri 9am–8pm, Sat and Sun 9–6)*. They have a free map of the island and town plan. There's a smaller branch at the Monumental Lido shopping centre (across the way from Lido Sol), **t** 291 775 254.

You'll find **banks**, all with foreign exchange facilities and most with *Multibanco* machines (*see* p.87) on the streets around the cathedral and in the larger shopping complexes. **Money-changing machines** on the Avenida Arriaga, near the cathedral, offer a 24-hour exchange facility, but are frequently out of order. The only other after-hours *bureau de change* is a small kiosk near the cathedral, open daily until 8pm; commission charges here are good.

Emergency number for ambulance and police: **t** 112.

Police stations: Polícia de Segurança Pública, Rua Infância 28/32, **t** 291 208 400; Rua de João de Deus 7, **t** 291 222 022/**t** 291 230 631.

Hospital: Hospital Cruz Carvalho, Av. Luís Camões, **t** 291 705 600.

Pharmacy: Dois Amigos, Câmara Pestana 10, **t** 291 225 547. Details of the emergency pharmacy on duty are posted on the doors of all chemists.

Post offices: There are main post office branches on Avenida Zarco, Rua Dr. João Brito Câmara and and at the Lido Sol shopping centre on Estrada Monumental (*see* **Practical A–Z**, pp.88–9).

Festivals

Carnival, February.
Flower festival, end April.
St John, 24 June.
Assumption (Monte), Aug.
Grape Harvest, mid-Sept.

Shopping and Services

See also **Practical A–Z**, pp.87 and 88–9.

Four large **shopping malls** are likely to be able to meet your every need, from dry-cleaning to hairdressing, sticky sweets and stationery: the **Lidosol** (west, just above the Lido), the **Marina Shopping Centre** (centre, near the marina), **Shopping Anadia** (east, near the market) and the huge new **Madeira Shopping**, out near the motorway in São Martinho. All are open on Sundays, and there are good supermarkets in Anadia and Lidosol.

But shopping in Madeira can be more fun than this. All over town, understated doorways between shop-fronts lead to warrens of interior arcades lined with small, family-run businesses. There is one halfway up the Rua João Tavira, and another behind the Café Funchal, but the most attractive by far is the **Bazar do Povo** on Largo do Chafariz, built in the 19th century, and still resplendent with a grand staircase and wooden counters.

The Funchalese do most of their day-to-day shopping along **Rua Dr Fernão Ornelas**, which leads from the centre of town down to the **covered market** (*see* p.136). At the market you'll find all manner of fresh fish, fruit and vegetables, as well as wine, baskets and other souvenirs. Prices at the small **open market**, a few blocks closer to the sea, are a little lower.

Designer Clothes and Shoes

Check out the boutiques along **Rua dos Ferreiros** and **Rua das Pretas**. The alleys around the back of the cathedral can be a rewarding hunting ground for all sorts of shoppers.

Wines

Most shops will give you a taste of madeira and advice before you buy. The most recommendable wine stores are:

São Francisco Wine Lodges, Avenida Arriaga 22, **t** 291 740 110. The main outlet for the Madeira Wine Company. Here you'll find the big names, such as Blandy's, Leacocks and Cossart Gordon. The shop in front sells mainly 3–15-year-old madeiras. Older vintages are available from the tasting bar around the back, where you can pick up a bottle of 1908 Bual for just €698 (or taste a glass of it for €43). *See also* p.116.

Artur de Barros e Sousa, Rua dos Ferreiros 109, **t** 291 220 622. A traditional family firm which is a gem (*see* p.122).

Other wine shops include:

Diogos, Avenida Arriaga 48, **t** 291 233 357. An outlet for Barbeito wines.

Garrafeira do Mercado, Merc. dos Lavradores, Stall 15/16, **t** 291 230 479. Stocks Henriques & Henriques and less upmarket brands.

D'Oliveiras, Rua dos Ferreiros 107, **t** 291 220 784. Cavernous and touristy.

Garrafeira Zona Velha, Rua Don Carlos I 48, **t** 291 232 956. A wide range of wines.

Embroidery

Where you shop for tapestries and embroidery will depend largely on your taste. There are a number of *bordados* shops along the Rua dos Murças.

Imperial Hand Embroideries, Rua São Pedro 26, **t** 291 223 282. Has truly excellent quality, and imaginative designs; a cut above most other shops, it offers a change from the run-of-the-mill tablecloths and twee blouses.

Madeira Sun, Avenida Zarco 2, **t** 291 221 318. Good work in traditional designs.

Traditional Boots and Handmade Shoes

A stall to the right of the main entrance of the **Mercado dos Lavradores** sells sturdy boots, sandals and traditional ankle-high *botas*. You can buy them for similar prices, and see the makers at work, at **Barros & Abreu Irmãos**, Largo do Corpo Santo 20–22, in the Old Town.

Sports Equipment

The Best, Rua 5 de Outubro 16–18, **t** 291 211 580. Fashionable sportswear and various sporting equipment.

Imersão, on the Marina, **t** 291 234 815. The place to go for rods, fishing and all you'll need for a deep-sea jaunt.

Pastries

Penha d'Agua, Rua João Gago 6, **t** 291 228 119. Specializes in local pastries and *bolos de mel*.

Health Food Shops

Bio-Logos, Rua Nova de São Pedro 34, **t** 291 236 868. Wholefoods, natural remedies and a small vegetarian/vegan restaurant.

Bioforma, Rua Queimada de Cima 31, **t** 291 229 262. Natural remedies and beauty products.

Souvenirs

Casa do Turista, Rua do Conselheiro José Silvestre Ribeiro 2, **t** 291 224 907. Next door to the Infante Shopping Centre. Piled high with Madeiran mementoes, and not overpriced, despite the unalluring name.

Books

The English Bookshop, Rua da Carreira 43, **t** 291 224 490. Books on Madeira and novels at reasonable prices.

Livraria Esperança, Rua dos Ferreiros 119, **t** 291 221 116. The best Portuguese bookshop, with a wide-ranging Madeiran selection and some books in English.

Photography

Quick-developing shops can be found in all the major shopping malls.

Profissional, Rua Queimada de Cima 15, **t** 291 227 638. Everything from a 30-minute developing service to photocopies, films and equipment – with delightfully helpful, English-speaking staff.

Dry-cleaners and Laundries

There is a reliable dry-cleaner on the basement level of the Infante Shopping Centre – but no self-service launderette in town.

Sports and Activities

Swimming

As Funchal ends in lumpy rocks rather than golden beaches, many hotels have their own swimming pools, but there is also quite a choice of public swimming baths.

Lido, Rua Gorgulho, off Estrada Monumental (*open summer 8.30–7, winter 8.30–5; adm €2.50; bus 6 or 35*). Municipal complex popular with locals and tourists. Terraces of sunbeds, a vast pool, swimming jetties in the sea, a diving school, newsagent, café and upmarket restaurant – all spotlessly clean at non-rip-off prices.

Praia Barreirinha, Rua de Santa Maria, at the eastern end of the Old Town (*open summer, 8.30–7, winter, 8.30–5; adm summer €1, winter free*). A perpendicular lido; small-scale, friendly and almost exclusively local. A lift takes you down the cliff-face, through the equivalent of five storeys, past a café and changing room to the sea below. There are terraces on which to sun yourself, a paddling pool for children and a pebbly beach and diving jetties for the rest.

Quinta Magnolia, Rua do Dr Pita (*open summer, 8.30–7, winter, 8.30–5; adm €1.38 per hour*). Once the British Country Club, now very much Funchalese. Pretty gardens and one of the few freshwater pools in town.

Ponta Gorda, Tourist Town Promenade (*open summer 8–8, winter 8.30–7; adm €2.50*). A smart new lido with a large pool and a children's paddling area.

On the far western edge of town, at the end of the Tourist Town promenade, steps lead down to a cluster of **natural rock pools**, some of them enlarged with concrete walls. It is a quiet spot, well off the tourist track, and a great place for children to have fun snorkelling.

Praia Formosa, reached through a tunnel at the very end of the promenade, or by car along the Estrada Monumental, is a long, rocky **beach** (one could almost call them boulders) that eventually stutters into a series of small coves, spread with sinister black sand. The presence of an oil refinery does not contribute much to the beauty of the setting, but this is a favourite bathing spot among the Funchalese, and there are a couple of bars and kiosks along the edge.

Tennis and Squash

Quinta Magnolia (*see* above) has squash and tennis courts (*squash €1.38 per hour, tennis €1.69 per hour in the day, and €3.37 at night, to pay for the floodlights*).

Grander hotels, e.g. the Savoy and the Cliff Bay, may also open their courts to the public.

Watersports

Terras de Aventura, Caminho do Amparo 25, **t** 291 776 818. Water-skiing, jet skis, windsurfing and other adventurous watersports.

Scorpio Divers, at the Lido, **t** 291 266 977. Hire out diving equipment, and offer training from beginners to advanced levels with British Sub-Aqua Club certified instructors.

Costa do Sol, on the Marina, **t** 291 238 538 (*10am–7pm*). Will take you fishing for tuna, marlin, swordfish and sharks, as will **Xiphias**, **t** 291 280 007, and **Madeira Big Game Fishing**, **t** 291 227 169. Prices start at around €115 per angler for a half-day (4hrs) and €150 per angler for a full day (7hrs). Most companies prefer to follow an environmentally friendly 'tag-and-release' policy with the catch.

Where to Stay

Most of Madeira's hotels are in Funchal. Most of these form part of an outgrowth of look-alike concrete lumps along the busy, noisy, polluted Estrada Monumental. The selection below weeds out the hotels with balconies overlooking the slow lane, and offers instead a bouquet of the choicest places to stay. Should all these be full, the tourist office (*see* p.97) can help out with addresses and information on accommodation around the island.

Very Expensive

2 **Reid's**, Estrada Monumental, 9000-098 Funchal, **t** 291 717 171, **f** 291 717 177, *www.reidspalace.orient-express.com, reservations@reidspalace.com* (*from €275*). Ten acres of garden, private balconies overlooking the Atlantic, and everything in achingly good taste. A Madeiran institution making cautious attempts to liven up its image without losing its style. Some visitors still don a black tie for dinner, and though the possession of a title may no longer be *de rigueur*, a healthy bank balance still helps.

6 **Savoy**, Avenida do Infante, 9004-542 Funchal, **t** 291 213 000, **f** 291 223 103, *www.savoyresort.com, savoy.reservation@netmadeira.com* (*from €280*). The breakfast buffet is spread out in a restaurant on the 8th floor, with views across the ocean. The rooms are large and the lounges classy. Through a quiet private garden you reach the best hotel lido on the island, and, if you tire of lazing about, staff can arrange anything from parasailing to 'banana riding' at discounted prices. Rooms at the front of the hotel, overlooking the Atlantic, are well worth the extra cost.

20 **Choupana Hills**, Travessa do Largo da Choupana, 9050-286 Funchal, **t** 291 206 020, **f** 291 206 021, *www.choupanahills.com, info@choupanahills.com* (*from €250*). High in the forests above Funchal, beside the Levada dos Tornos, and very much in

the mould of a southeast-Asian luxury spa resort. Accommodation is in sumptuous wood and stone bungalows, and all manner of well-being treatments are available. The sense of isolation is intensified by the one-car-wide road that winds up to the hotel, which could prove terrifying if the journey from the airport is your first experience of driving on Madeira.

Expensive

17 **Quinta Bela São Tiago**, Rua Bela de São Tiago 70, 9050-042 Funchal, **t** 291 204 500, **f** 291 204 510, *www.hotel-qta-bela-s-tiago.com, hotel.qta.bela.s.tiago@mail. telepac.pt* (*from €155; sea-view from €220*). Built around a 19th-century mansion in a small garden overlooking the Old Town, but decorated in a fairly bland modern style. Rooms are not large; the best have balconies with views over Funchal and out to sea.

18 **Casa Velha do Palheiro**, Palheiro Golf, 9050 Funchal, **t** 291 794 901, **f** 291 794 925, *www.casa-velha.com, casavelha@mail.eunet.pt* (*from €150*). The poor man's Reid's. Quietly elegant country-house hotel in the 19th-century homestead adjoining the Blandys' gardens at Quinta Palheiro. You get free access to the gardens, and discount on green fees at the golf course.

8 **Carlton Park**, Rua Imperatriz D. Amélia, 9004-513 Funchal, **t** 291 209 100, **f** 291 232 076, *www.pestana.org, cph@pestana.org* (*from €150*). Unforgivably ugly building with a lobby rather like an airport – but the rooms hog some of the best views in town.

5 **Carlton Madeira**, Largo António Nobre, 9004–531 Funchal, **t** 291 239 500, **f** 291 227 284, *www.pestana.org, carlton.madeira@pestana.org* (*from €150*). Towering hotel with views over the sea and back to the mountains. Luxuriously appointed and conveniently close to the centre.

21 **Quinta do Monte**, Caminho do Monte 192, 9050-288 Funchal, **t** 291 780 100, **f** 291 780 110, *www.quintadomonte.com, info@quintadomonte.com* (*from €150*). Beautiful old *quinta* with a large modern extension, set in a rambling garden (complete with its own chapel) in Monte.

15 **Porto Santa Maria**, Avenida do Mar, 9050-029 Funchal, **t** 291 206 700, **f** 291 206 720, *www.portostamaria.com, portosantamaria@ portobay.com* (*from €136*). On a prime site beside the sea. A large hotel designed to resemble a row of low-rise traditional buildings, with comfortable rooms and mod cons from gym to Jacuzzi.

1 **Pestana Palms Hotel**, Rua do Gorgulho, 9000-107 Funchal, **t** 291 709 200, **f** 291 766 247 (*from €126*). An oasis of unassuming luxury in the gardens of a former *quinta* near the Lido. The rooms are modern and all have a sea view and a kitchenette.

3 **Quinta Perestrello**, Rua do Dr Pita 3, 9000-089 Funchal, **t** 291 763 720, **f** 291 763 777, *www.charminghotelsmadeira.com* (*from €112*). Intimate hotel in a 150-year-old *quinta*, run with a family touch and dotted about with antiques. There is a small pool, and a garden terrace separates you from the full impact of the passing traffic.

7 **Quinta da Penha de França**, Rua Penha de França, 9000-014 Funchal, **t** 291 204 650, **f** 291 229 261, *www.hotelpenhaquintafranca. com, info@hotelpenhaquintafranca.com* (*from €53, old house from €110, Penha França Mar from €114*). A lone traditional *quinta* nestling in a protective garden in the thick of the hotel district. Here you'll get a far more pleasant taste of old Madeira than at many hotels that are double the price. A big new extension out the back has less romance. A seaside wing, known as Penha França Mar, has a large pool, ocean views and a more modern air.

Moderate

11 **Hotel Madeira**, Rua Ivens 21, 9000-046 Funchal, **t** 291 230 071, **f** 291 229 071, *www.hotelmadeira.com, hotelmadeira@oninet.pt* (*€67*). Simple, quiet hotel near the Municipal Gardens.

4 **Hotel Quinta do Sol**, Rua do Dr Pita 6, 9000-089 Funchal, **t** 291 764 151, **f** 291 766 287, *www.madinfo.pt/hotel/quintasol, hotel.quinta.sol@mail.telepac.pt* (*from €60*). Next door to the Quinta Magnolia and set back from the busy Avenida do Infante. This is one of the few hotels where the 'mountain view' is any sort of view at all. Rooms are comfortable and most have private sun terraces. Distant traffic noise is compensated for by the friendly staff.

22 **Eira do Serrado**, Curral das Freiras, 9000-421 Funchal, **t** 291 710 060, **f** 291 710 061 (*from €60*). A large, somewhat soulless hotel, but overlooking the magnificent Curral das Freiras.

28 **Residencial da Mariazinha**, Rua de Santa Maria 155, Funchal 9050-040, **t** 291 220 239, **f** 291 241 739, *www.residencialmariazinha.com*, *residencialmariazinha@netmadeira.pt* (*from €60*). Cosy small hotel in the Old Town; stylish décor, friendly staff.

27 **Hotel do Centro**, Rua do Carmo 20–22, 9000-019 Funchal, **t** 291 200 510, **f** 291 233 915 (€59). Newest and smartest of the bunch of hotels sprouting near the Carmo church. Rooms on the top floors at the back of the building overlook red rooftops to the sea. Excellent value for money.

23 **Apartmentos do Castanheiro**, Rua do Castanheiro 27, 9000-081 Funchal, **t** 291 227 060, **f** 291 227 940 (*from €58*). Old villa stylishly converted into self-catering apartments (although the price includes breakfast in the restaurant). You get air-conditioning, TV, a CD player and silence – a rare thing in Funchal. Situated up a quiet street just off the main city square. There have, however, been reports of advance reservations not honoured.

12 **Hotel Monte Carlo**, Calçada da Saúde 10, 9000-221 Funchal, **t** 291 226 131, **f** 291 226 134 (*from €50*). One of the oldest hotels in town, but done up in a simple, modern style. Most rooms in the old part of the hotel have spectacular views across Funchal. Those in the new annexe do not, and are also rather small. It's a steep climb to get there, so be prepared to get fit or fork out for taxi fares.

10 **Residencial Gordon**, Rua da Quebra Costas 34, 9000-034 Funchal, **t** 291 742 366, **f** 291 743 948 (€45). Next to the English Church and as quiet as a graveyard. Heavy wooden furniture and sombre rooms.

26 **Sirius**, Rua das Hortas 29, 9050-024 Funchal, **t** 291 226 117, **f** 291 226 118 (*from €45*). Simple, no-nonsense small hotel, between the Old Town and centre.

Inexpensive

14 **Residencial Santa Clara**, Calçada do Pico 16b, 9000-206 Funchal, **t** 291 742 194, **f** 291 743 280 (*from €43*). Toil uphill past the Santa Clara nunnery, through wrought-iron gates and up the garden path to this old mansion with a *grand perron* staircase. Inside, the wooden floors are polished to a gleam and there is an extraordinary salon, covered in Baroque *trompe l'œil*. Rooms vary in size (some smaller ones in a tower), but most open out to splendid views. From the tiny roof terrace you can see the entire Funchal basin, in all directions. There is even a small swimming pool. A gem – though make sure you get rooms in the old house and not the annexe down the road.

13 **Residencial Colombo**, Rua da Carreira 182, 9000-042 Funchal, **t** 291 225 231, **f** 291 222 170, *www.residencias-colombo.pt*, *rescolombo @telepac.pt* (€40). The main building has rooms with large shuttered balconies or sunny terraces; an annexe around the corner is older, but quieter.

9 **Residência São Paulo e Alegria**, Rua Pimenta Aguiar 2, 9000-026 Funchal, **t** 291 741 931, **f** 291 741 946, *saopauloalegria@iol.pt* (€40). Apartments with private showers and kitchenettes. No vistas from the rooms, but the building is in an attractive, non-touristy part of town, with a nice view from the roof terrace. Good value.

24 **Residencial Monte Rosa**, Rua João Tavira 31, 9000-075 Funchal, **t** 291 229 091, **f** 291 223 563 (€40). Simple, central, silent, spotless.

25 **Pension Astoria**, Rua João Gago 10–30, 9000-071 Funchal, **t** 291 223 820, **f** 291 227 229 (€25). Old-fashioned, down-to-earth, clean *pension* overlooking the flower-sellers beside the cathedral.

Private Rooms

The tourist office does have a list of people who let out private rooms, though you sometimes have to be pretty insistent to see it, as the policy is to direct people to commercial establishments first.

Alternatively, you could bypass the tourist office and head straight for the following recommendations:

16 **Dona Vitorina Côrte**, Rua de Santa Maria 279, 9000-040 Funchal, **t** 291 220 249. Easily the pick of the bunch. In her 19th-century family home in the Old Town you can stay in a flat with private bathroom,

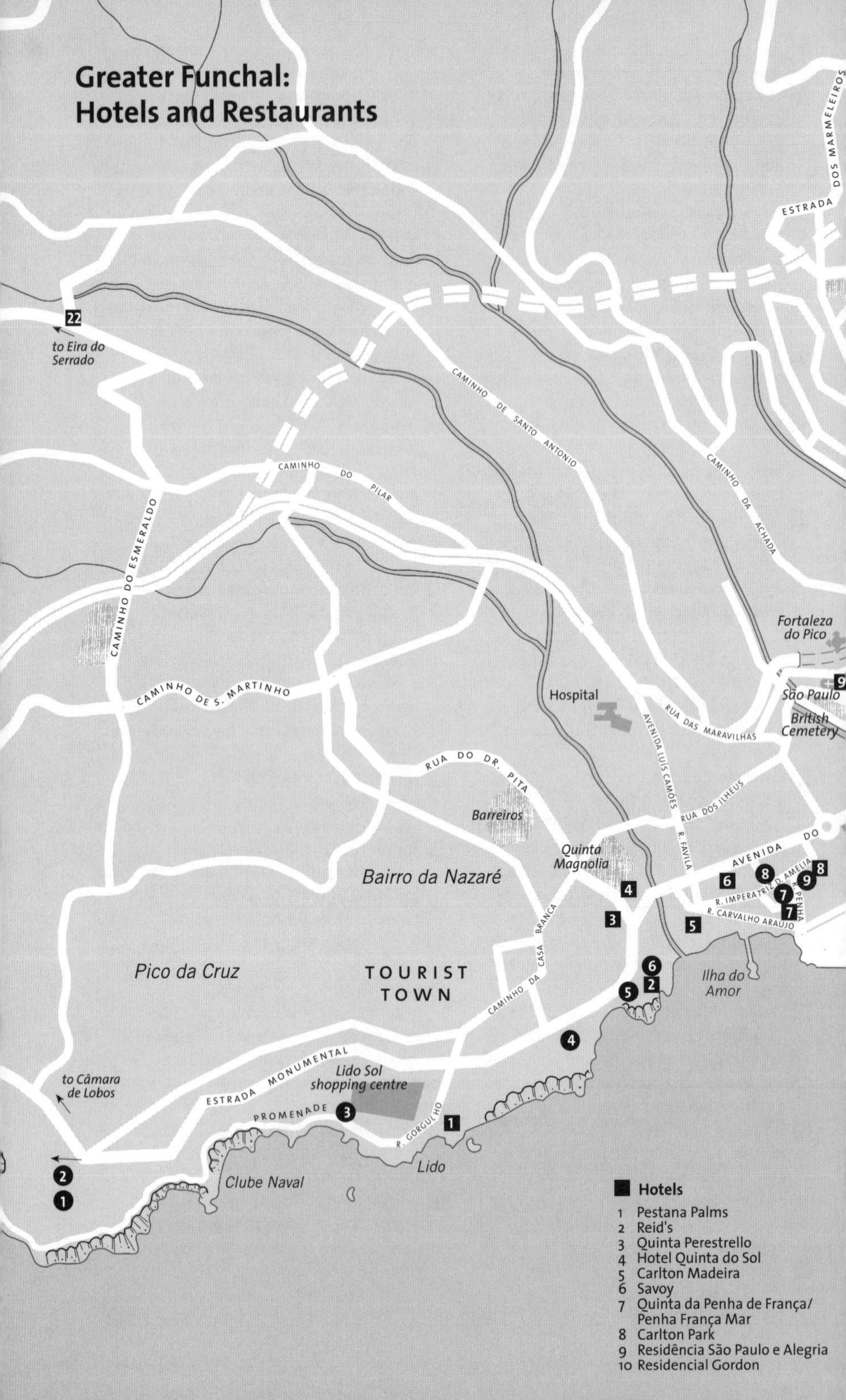
Greater Funchal: Hotels and Restaurants
Estrada dos Marmeleiros
22
to Eira do Serrado
Caminho de Santo Antonio
Caminho do Pilar
Caminho da Achada
Caminho do Esmeraldo
Caminho de S. Martinho
Fortaleza do Pico
9
São Paulo
British Cemetery
Hospital
Rua das Maravilhas
Avenida Luís Camões
Rua do Dr. Pita
Rua dos Ilheus
R. Favila
Barreiros
Quinta Magnolia
Avenida do
Bairro da Nazaré
8
6
8
9
R. Imperatriz D. Amelia
7
R. Penha
7
4
3
5
R. Carvalho Araujo
Caminho da Casa Branca
6
2
5
Ilha do Amor
Pico da Cruz
Tourist Town
4
Estrada Monumental
to Câmara de Lobos
Lido Sol shopping centre
Promenade
3
1
R. Gorgulho
Lido
2
1
Clube Naval
Hotels
1 Pestana Palms
2 Reid's
3 Quinta Perestrello
4 Hotel Quinta do Sol
5 Carlton Madeira
6 Savoy
7 Quinta da Penha de França/ Penha França Mar
8 Carlton Park
9 Residência São Paulo e Alegria
10 Residencial Gordon

Restaurants

1 Doca do Cavacas
2 Marisqueira O Barqueiro
3 Mezanino
4 Casa Madeirense
5 Villa Cipriani
6 Les Faunes
7 Casa de Penha
8 Quinta Palmeira
9 Casa Velha
10 Clube Avenida
11 O Agrião
12 Mar Azul
13 Ducouver
14 Princesa
15 Apolo Mar
16 São Pedro
17 Marisa
18 O Jango
19 Arsénio's
20 Xaramba
21 A Tartaruga
22 Restaurante do Forte
23 Montanha
24 Belomonte
25 Quinta Terreiro da Luta
26 Xôpana
27 Vasco da Gama

Cafés and Bars

A Santinho
B Espirito do Baco
C Jasmine Tea House
D Hortensia Gdns Tea House
E Café do Parque

11 Hotel Madeira
12 Hotel Monte Carlo
13 Residencial Colombo
14 Residencial Santa Clara
15 Porto Santa Maria
16 Dona Vitorina Côrte
17 Quinta Bela São Tiago
18 Casa Velha do Palheiro
19 Trejuno
20 Choupana Hills
21 Quinta do Monte
22 Eira do Serrado

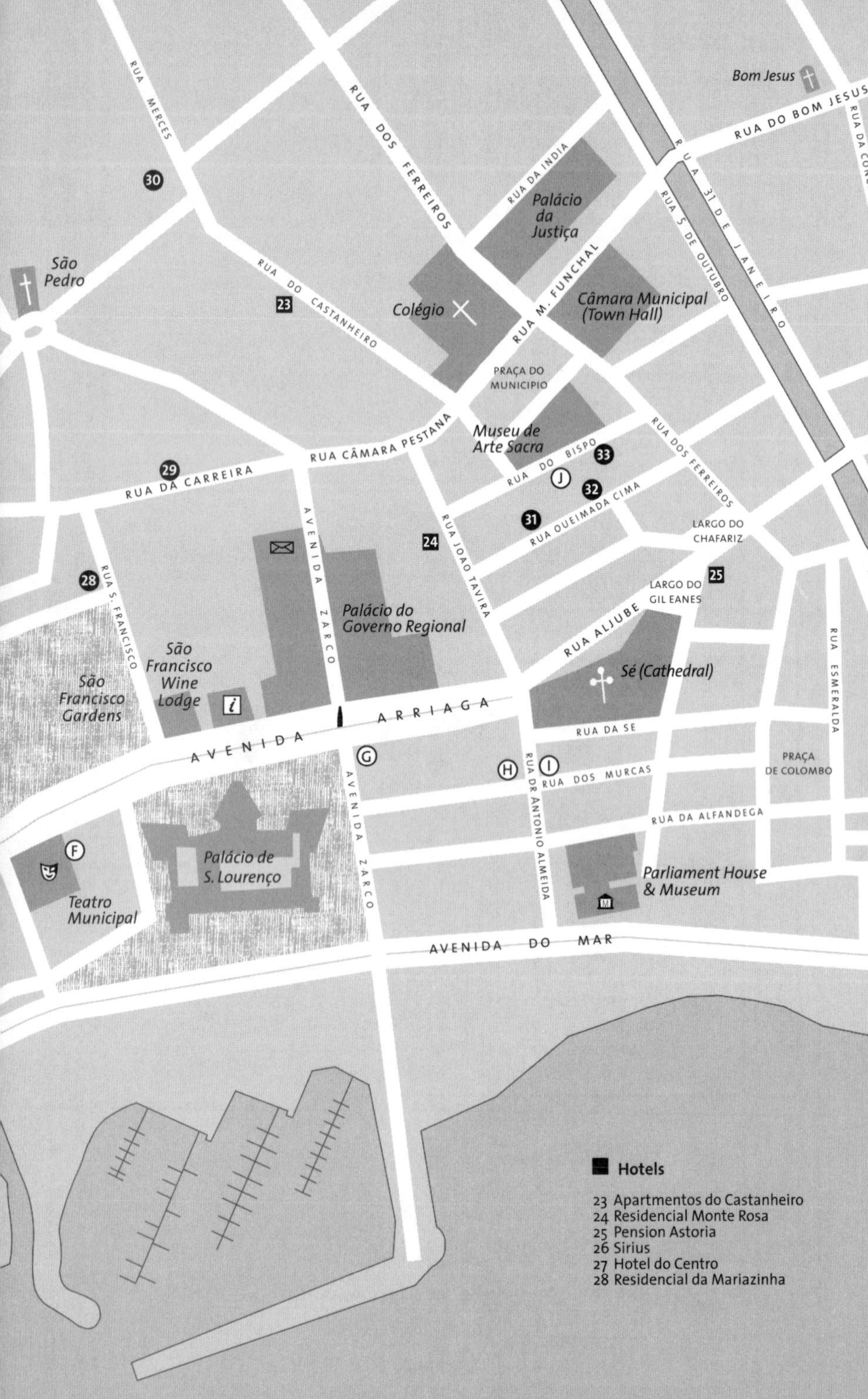

Bom Jesus
RUA DO BOM JESUS
RUA DA CONCEIÇÃO
RUA MERCES
RUA DOS FERREIROS
RUA DA INDIA
Palácio da Justiça
RUA 31 DE JANEIRO
RUA 5 DE OUTUBRO
São Pedro
RUA DO CASTANHEIRO
Colégio
RUA M. FUNCHAL
Câmara Municipal (Town Hall)
PRAÇA DO MUNICIPIO
RUA CÂMARA PESTANA
Museu de Arte Sacra
RUA DOS FERREIROS
RUA DA CARREIRA
RUA DO BISPO
RUA QUEIMADA CIMA
LARGO DO CHAFARIZ
AVENIDA ZARCO
RUA JOAO TAVIRA
RUA S. FRANCISCO
LARGO DO GIL EANES
Palácio do Governo Regional
RUA ALJUBE
RUA ESMERALDA
São Francisco Wine Lodge
São Francisco Gardens
Sé (Cathedral)
AVENIDA ARRIAGA
RUA DA SE
PRAÇA DE COLOMBO
RUA DOS MURCAS
RUA DR ANTONIO ALMEIDA
RUA DA ALFANDEGA
Palácio de S. Lourenço
Parliament House & Museum
Teatro Municipal
AVENIDA DO MAR
Hotels
23 Apartmentos do Castanheiro
24 Residencial Monte Rosa
25 Pension Astoria
26 Sirius
27 Hotel do Centro
28 Residencial da Mariazinha

Funchal City Centre:
Hotels and Restaurants
RUA DAS HORTAS
R. DA FABRICA
RUA DO CARMO
Carmo
LARGO DO PHELPS
RUA DO SEMINARIO
RUA DO RIBEIRINHO
RUA DR. FERNÃO ORNELAS
RUA DO VISCONDE DO ANADIA
RUA BRIGADEIRO OUDINOT
RUA DA INFANCIA
RUA CONSELHEIRO A PESTANA
RUA HOSPITAL VELHO
RUA 31 DE JANEIRO
RUA DIREITA
RUA 5 DE OUTUBRO
R. TANOEIROS
Mercado dos Lavradores
RUA LATINO COELHO
RUA BOA VIAGEM
RUA PROFETAS
RUA DE SANTA MARIA
RUA DOM CARLOS I
Customs House
PRAÇA DA AUTONOMIA
Cable car departure point
Rotunda da Autonomia
AVENIDA DO MAR
Restaurants
28 Restaurante dos Combatentes
29 Jardim da Carreira
30 Tangerina
31 Ponto Final
32 Loja das Sopas
33 O Lampião
34 Qualifrutas
35 Sirius
36 Jaquet
37 Gavião Novo
38 Arco Velho
39 Embaixador Madeirense
40 Tropicana
41 O Tapassol
Cafés and Bars
F Theatre Café
G Golden Gate
H Café Apolo
I Café Funchal
J A Cuba
N
100 m
100 yds

balcony and kitchenette (*from €40*), or in one of the cavernous, high-ceilinged rooms that share a bathroom (*from €30*), or, if you're really lucky (and if Dona Vitorina's son is not in town), in a magnificent tower room with views on all four sides (*€40*). The rooms contain beautiful old Madeiran furniture, and are kept spotlessly clean. The Barreirinha lido is practically on the doorstep, and next door Dona Vitorina's brother runs the family madeira *estufa*.

19 **June and Trevor Franks 'Trejuno'**, Estrada do Livramento 94, 9000-231 Funchal, **t/f** 291 783 268, *www.tjwalking-madeira.com*, *franks@ mail.telepac.pt* (*from €55*). Good if you're a keen walker. The Frankses offer a traditional English B&B atmosphere and considerable knowledge of island walks.

Eating Out: Restaurants

Centre

Moderate

10 **Clube Avenida**, above Infante (Marina) shopping centre, **t** 291 281 282 (*€25*). This is where Funchal business deals are clinched, and where well-to-do local families come for Sunday outings. The menu includes usual Madeiran fare, and some more exotic departures such as stuffed mushrooms and pig's trotters with chickpeas.

13 **Ducouver**, Marina, **t** 291 237 050 (*€24*). Of all the restaurants along the marina, this one is the most stylish and has the freshest fish, though the hard-sell antics of waiters touting for passing custom forms an irritating background soundtrack.

12 **Mar Azul**, Marina, **t** 291 230 079 (*€18*). Once a jolly, chaotic restaurant, Mar Azul has now succumbed to the Madeiran style of bright lights and tables in regimented rows. But the staff in traditional dress are still cheery, and the grilled chicken and seafood good.

16 **São Pedro**, Rua de São Pedro 2, **t** 291 222 217 (*€18*). Large, plain restaurant near the São Pedro church. The menu is almost a photocopy of the one at O Tapassol, *see* p.107.

28 **Restaurante dos Combatentes**, Rua Ivens 1–3, **t** 291 221 388 (*€18*). One of Funchal's oldest restaurants has undergone a makeover. The waiters' crumpled white coats have given way to waistcoats covered with ersatz embroidery, and there's an abundance of bright yellow table linen. But the good, solid, no-risks-taken menu remains the same.

Inexpensive

30 **Tangerina**, Rua Merces 3, **t** 291 221 300 (*€17.50*). From the street it seems no more than a bar, but behind a screen the room opens out into a large restaurant full of local families tucking into hearty meals. Noisy conversations do battle with the TV in the corner (only football can cause a temporary hush). Everything comes with piles of potatoes and salad. The *açorda* (garlic soup) is unrivalled.

14 **Princesa**, Marina, **t** 291 237 719 (*€17*). Busy restaurant on the marina, popular with locals as well as tourists. Good-value Madeiran fare, including *espetada* on laurel sticks rather than metal skewers.

29 **Jardim da Carreira**, Rua da Carreira 118, **t** 291 222 498 (*€17*). Set in a garden courtyard in the heart of Funchal. The menu contains *espada*, *espetada* and all the usual Madeiran dishes. The food is well-prepared, though the staff can be offhand.

35 **Sirius**, Rua das Hortas 31, **t** 291 220 503 (*€12*). Bright restaurant that packs out with locals at lunchtime, but is also open during the evenings. Service is brisk and friendly, and the food is well prepared: anything from a sandwich to local stewed tongue.

Old Town

Expensive

22 **Restaurante do Forte**, Fortaleza São Tiago, **t** 291 235 470 (*from €35*). Stylish restaurant inside the ancient fort, and spilling out on to the battlements, where candles flicker in the breeze, and waves crash on the rocks below. The food is a little different from the Madeiran norm, with wonton pancakes stuffed with shrimp.

Moderate

19 **Arsénio's**, Rua da Santa Maria 169, **t** 291 224 007 (*€27*). Very touristy, but to be recom-

mended for the mixed seafood *espetadas*. Later in the evening there's *fado*, but arrive before 8pm and you'll probably be subjected to 'Love is a Many Splendoured Thing' on electric keyboard.

36 **Jaquet**, Rua de Santa Maria 5, **t** 291 225 344 (*€25*). No windows, wooden stools, formica tables and a cupboard-sized kitchen at one end. The menu (with shellfish priced by the kilogram) is chalked up on the wall. Whatever you order comes with heaps of vegetables simmered in stock with fresh herbs and chilli. Towards the end of the evening unmarked bottles of lethal *aguardente* are liable to make an appearance. Given the rather simple surroundings, the bill can come as a shock.

18 **O Jango**, Rua de Santa Maria 166, **t** 291 221 280 (*€22*). An intimate, family-run restaurant where those in the know come again and again. Dishes such as *espada* with banana, on menus all over town, here somehow garner unique flavours. Owner Firmino Santos buys directly from local fishermen, so the fish is flappingly fresh. There's a whole platter of it to choose from daily, and the *cataplana* (an enormous mixed seafood dish for two) can bring tears to your eyes. The only drawback about Jango's is that once you have eaten here, nearly every other restaurant will be a disappointment.

37 **Gavião Novo**, Rua de Santa Maria 131, **t** 291 229 238 (*€22*). Busy little restaurant in the Old Town that fills up with Funchalese at lunchtimes and tourists in the evenings. Traditional Madeiran cuisine; good fish.

39 **Embaixador Madeirense**, Rua dos Barreiros 10, **t** 291 224 655 (*€21*). A cosy little restaurant, with a charming owner and menu that branches away from the island norm, offering such delights as *espada* cooked with honey and paprika. Everything comes with loads of healthy veg, plus brown rice and sweet potatoes.

17 **Marisa**, Rua de Santa Maria 162, **t** 291 226 189 (*€21*). A quiet restaurant where dad does the cooking, son brings you your food and mum keeps an eagle eye on everything. The *caldeirada* (fish stew) is delicious, and there are other seafood and rice specialities.

41 **O Tapassol**, Rua Dom Carlos I 62, **t** 291 225 023 (*€21*). Swift and cheery service, a rooftop terrace and a menu that includes octopus stew, quail and rabbit set this a notch above most other restaurants in the Old Town. Here the *espada* comes not only with banana, but with passion fruit and mango. Haunt of many British Madeirans.

40 **Tropicana**, Rua Dom Carlos I 43, **t** 291 225 705 (*€19*). Smartest of the stretch of restaurants and cafés on the way up to the Old Town and often overflowing with Funchal yuppies. Specializes in rice with seafood.

Inexpensive

21 **A Tartaruga**, Largo do Corpo Santo 4, **t** 291 280 645 (*€17*). Good Old Town lunchtime stopover, with fresh salads and a range of omelettes as well as an assortment of other meals.

20 **Xaramba**, Largo do Corpo Santo 9, **t** 291 229 785 (*€12*). Snug pizzeria behind the Corpo Santo church. Open late and very popular with younger Funchalese.

Tourist Town

Expensive

6 **Les Faunes**, Reid's Hotel, **t** 291 763 001 (*over €90*). Original Picassos on the wall, *haute cuisine* on your plate, and a hole in your wallet. More informal than the hotel's dining room. In summer months, the restaurant moves on to the veranda as 'Brisa do Mar'.

5 **Villa Cipriani**, Estrada Monumental 139, **t** 291 717 100 (*€60*). Tranquil cliff-top restaurant that serves pastas and other Italian dishes. Starched napkins and starchy waiters; ideal for a cool lunch or romantic sunset supper.

8 **Quinta Palmeira**, Avenida do Infante 5, **t** 291 221 814 (*€60*). A 19th-century *quinta*, still with a patch of garden, in the tourist district, and now with a flash modern extension, with views out to sea. In the Gourmet Restaurant, surrounded by gilt-framed mirrors, velvet drapes and marquetry screens, you can savour such dishes as octopus in rich piquant gravy. There is a good list of South African, French and Portuguese wines.

❸ **Mezanino**, Promenade, **t** 291 763 325 (*from €40*). Chic designer restaurant that is the latest hit with trendy Funchalese – and justifiably so. Think prawns with soft polenta and tomato-garlic sauce, squid with ginger, or lamb with borlotti beans and green olive pesto.

❾ **Casa Velha**, Rua Imperatriz D. Amélia 69, **t** 291 205 600 (*€32*). Converted villa hiding behind the Carlton Park Hotel. Inside, it is an odd mixture of olde-worlde charm and bright green paint. The menu departs from the Madeiran norm into the realms of lobster in red wine and duck with pepper.

❹ **Casa Madeirense**, Estrada Monumental 153, **t** 291 766 700 (*€30*). Crammed with folksy bric-a-brac and tourists. Besides the usual Madeiran fare, the chef tries his hand at prawns with pineapple and steak with bacon and cheese.

Moderate

❷ **Marisqueira O Barqueiro**, Promenade, **t** 291 765 226 (*€29*). At the very end of the Tourist Town promenade, just before it disappears down steps to the rocks. Live lobsters and crabs live out their last moments in large tanks; the home-made fishcakes are delicious.

❶ **Doca do Cavacas**, Estrada Monumental, **t** 291 762 057 (*€25*). This little restaurant on a cliff face, at the end of a row of fishermen's huts, was much recommended in the first Cadogan guide, but proved deeply disappointing in a subsequent update. The restaurant was closed for vacation while this edition was being researched, but local word has it that standards have improved. Nevertheless, it may be worth comparing fish on offer with the excellent **O Barquiero**, almost next door.

❼ **Casa de Penha**, Rua Penha de França, **t** 291 225 182 (*€25*). Ordinary food at a reasonable price on a small cobbled terrace under the bougainvillaea.

Out of Town

Expensive

㉖ **Xôpana**, at Choupana Hills hotel (*see* p.99), Travessa do Largo da Choupana, 9050-286 Funchal, **t** 291 20 60 20 (*from €40*). High in the hills over Funchal, with something of the atmosphere of a large, hip London or New York restaurant and the sort of menu city slickers delight in, from shrimp ravioli stuffed with coriander to duck caramelized in sugar-cane honey and almonds.

㉕ **Quinta Terreiro da Luta**, Sítio do Terreiro da Luta, Monte, **t** 291 782 476 (*€30*). The old rack-and-pinion railway station above Monte has been restored as a Belle Epoque restaurant. You can stroll about the gardens, have a sundowner in the station bar, then enjoy fine international cuisine.

Moderate

㉓ **Montanha**, **t** 291 793 182 (*€28*). On the slopes overlooking Funchal along National Road 101, about 15mins by car; bus 38. Large restaurant subject to 'folkloric dancing' and *fado* evenings, but a favourite for its tasty *espetada* and panoramic view.

㉗ **Vasco da Gama**, Estrada do Livramento 93, **t** 291 784 005 (*€21*). Tops among the restaurants-with-a-view. Up where the air is clean, in the centre of a ridge just below Monte. The lights of Funchal twinkle below you, and friendly staff ply you with delicious food. Try the cod stuffed with shellfish and tomatoes, or the smoked *espada*. The fish soup is full of taste and surprises you with explosions of herbs and chilli. Bus 19 stops outside and runs till late.

Inexpensive

㉔ **Belomonte**, Monte, **t** 291 741 444 (*€17.50*). Near the toboggan station. The first-floor snack bar fills with toboggan drivers and is cheap. Above it, the restaurant serves tasty, if unadventurous, Madeiran fare.

Nun's Valley, Curral das Freiras, **t** 291 712 177 (*€16*). Dimly lit and often crowded with villagers eating chestnut soup. Chicken dishes are also a speciality. A new rooftop terrace offers views down the Curral.

Snacks and Cheap Meals

Many restaurants in Funchal have a *prato do dia* for €4.50–5.50, though you usually have to visit at lunchtime to get it. Two alleys parallel to Rua Aljube (Rua da Queimada de Cima and Rua da Queimada de Baixo) are lined with bars that sell inexpensive food.

At the **Anadia Shopping Centre** (near the covered market) there is a food mall that offers a range of cheap eating possibilities, from hamburgers to pizzas and more exotic island nibbles.

31 **Ponto Final**, Rua da Queimada de Cima 43, **t** 291 223 867. Best bet along here, where you can get tasty home cooking.

33 **O Lampião**, Rua do Bispo 30A, **t** 291 225 015. Good filling meals during the day.

38 **Arco Velho**, Rua Dom Carlos I 42, **t** 291 225 683, in the Old Town. Good daily specials, usually with fish, for around €6.

15 **Apolo Mar**, on the marina. You can get away with a meal for €6 here (usually sausage, egg and chips and a drink).

32 **Loja das Sopas**, Rua da Queimada de Cima 17, **t** 291 227 063. Big bowls of freshly made soup – some traditional, some with inventive combinations of ingredients – for around €4. Just the thing for one of those unexpectedly chill, rainy Madeiran days.

11 **O Agrião**, Infante (Marina) shopping centre, **t** 291 236 797. Great source of healthy, home-made quiches and salads for when you need a quick lunch.

34 **Qualifruitas**, Rua de Coperative Agricola, **t** 291 222 715. Break for lunch on a pleasant square just off the Rua de Conceicão. Mounds of bright fruit turn into freshly squeezed juices and fruit salad, and there are also good quiches and cakes.

Eating Out: Cafés and Bars

Centre

(A) **Santinho**, Marina, **t** 291 228 945. Gathering place for young Funchalese in an otherwise touristy strip of restaurants. Watch local love affairs wax and wane, and slip into the swirling currents of island gossip. Excellent *pregos* and light meals.

(I) **Café Funchal**, Rua Dr António Almeida, **t** 291 234 600. Tourists, locals in their Sunday best and ancient regulars fill the terrace day and night and watch the rest of Funchal go by.

(H) **Café Apolo**, Rua Dr António Almeida, **t** 291 220 099. Opposite the Café Funchal, with a similar clientele but a smaller terrace. In bad weather they all take refuge in the stark 1950s Art Deco interior.

(G) **Golden Gate**, Avenida Arriaga 21, **t** 291 220 053. Careful restoration work has returned the Golden Gate very much to the way it looked when it was the hub of Funchal social life at the beginning of the century. The place to linger over coffee and cakes and watch the world go by.

(F) **Theatre Café**, Avenida Arriaga, **t** 291 249 959. A stylish designer canopy down the side of the municipal theatre shades a small café that buzzes day and night with Funchal's arty set and what there is of the city's gay life. Tasty quiches with salad make it a popular lunching-place.

(J) **A Cuba**, Rua do Bispo 28, **t** 291 220 986. Sit on, eat off (and even in) old wine barrels. Good spot for a drink and a snack, with an imaginative choice of sandwiches than is usual. Popular with students and a young crowd on the way home from work.

(B) **Espirito do Baco**, Largo do Corpo Santo 28, **t** 291 282 159. Tiny bar above a wine shop in the Old Town, offering a good range of Madeiran and foreign wines.

Out of Town

(C) **Jasmine Tea House**, Caminho dos Pretos, **t** 291 792 796. Just above the Palheiro Gardens and a few steps below the Levada dos Tornos. Take a break from your walk to relax in a garden tea house and tuck into cream scones or delicious home-made soups and salads. The friendly English owners are full of tips and stories.

(D) **Hortensia Gardens Tea House**, Caminho dos Pretos, **t** 291 792 179. Tea, scones, salads and waffles in an attractive garden setting just off the Levada dos Tornos.

(E) **Café do Parque**, Largo do Fonte, Monte, **t** 291 782 880. Beautifully situated under the plane trees, beside the *fonte* in Monte.

Viste Alegre, Curral das Freiras, **t** 291 712 157. Rest your weary limbs after a walk, or sit here building up strength beforehand with chestnut cake or delicious home-made cherry liqueur.

Entertainment and Nightlife

Isabella de França was most amused to see Madeira's convalescents whirl their way through a series of society dances: 'The most remarkable thing at these balls is to see the invalids, who in England would be confined to their beds, polking as if they went by steam, and that not once, but at a succession of balls throughout the winter.' These days a stroll along the pier and a gossip in one of the cafés near the seafront is more the Funchalese idea of a good night out. On a balmy Madeiran evening, after dinner in a local restaurant, you will probably feel inclined to agree with them. But if you are in search of a little more excitement, there is plenty to choose from.

Clubs and Discos

Vespas, Avenida Carneiro, near the container dock. Perennial vortex for the 18–30s. You'll probably meet the waiter who served your dinner and your hotel receptionist.

Copacabana, Casino Complex, Avenida do Infante. Big, sleeker than Vespas, and edging into the 30+ end of the spectrum.

O Molhino, Funchal Port. Popular weekend disco atop the Loo rock in Funchal docks.

Do Fa Sol and **Momge**, adjacent music cafés below the São Lourenço shopping centre (across the way from the Marina), where Funchal's hip young things hang out and listen to acid jazz and other music (sometimes live) till very late.

Fado

Fado – that yearning music some way between flamenco and the French *chanson* – is more a mainland than a Madeiran form, but there are some *fado* clubs in town. You can eat in all of them, though it is also possible just to nurse a drink or two. There is no entrance fee and prices are not inflated, though there is usually a minimum charge of around €5. Hotels may put on *fado* nights for guests and sometimes lay on folk dancers as evening entertainment. 'Folkloric dancing' also breaks out along the marina in the evenings – but the clubs are a more atmospheric place for *fado*, and village festivals a more appropriate place to catch the folk dancers.

Arsénio's, Rua de Santa Maria 169, **t** 291 224 007. Big and touristy. The singers keep up a gallant fight against the sounds accompanying the demolition of *espetadas*.

Marcelino '*pão e vino*', Travessa das Torres 22, **t** 291 220 216. The shutters are closed, the lights go out. In the candlelight an old woman in black stubs out her fag, takes a breath, and fills the tiny room with her gravelly voice. From time to time the artistes nip around the corner to do a set for the tourists at Arsénio's, but they end up back here where the audience not only appreciates the music, but sometimes even joins in the singing.

Theatre, Music and Cinema

A 19th-century visitor – who was evidently unamused by balls – complained that one was 'likely to be devoured with *ennui* long before the time for leaving the island comes round'. Madeira still doesn't have a glittering cultural calendar, though there is a **music festival** in June that attracts international artists, and the local Orquesta de Câmara da Madeira gives occasional **chamber music recitals** at the municipal theatre or in the Sé.

Cinemas are to be found in the Marina and Anadia shopping centres. Films are often shown in their original language with Portuguese subtitles, though it is worthwhile checking first.

From time to time local bands stage **open-air concerts** in the amphitheatre in the Municipal Gardens. The programme is displayed on a board on the Avenida Arriaga.

Teatro Municipal Baltazar Dias, Avenida Arriaga, **t** 291 220 416. A jewel of a theatre, which hosts visiting musicians, dance companies and theatre troupes. From time to time it is used as a cinema for art film festivals.

Late-night Bars

Banana's Pub, Largo do Corpo Santo 20–22. Friendly bar in the Old Town, open long after everywhere else is closed, even unto breakfast. *See also* 'Clubs and Discos', above.

Casino

Casino da Madeira, Rua Imperatriz Dona Amélia, **t** 291 231 121.

Wedged between the sea and a crescent of mountains, Funchal clings to the slopes with claws of steep, cobbled streets and hosts nearly half Madeira's population, most of the island's visitors and far too many of its motor cars. Flowering trees and voluptuous gardens add a dash of colour to the rows of low-rise, cream-painted buildings. Stocky mountain farmers, pink-legged tourists in gaudy shorts and slick young professionals dawdle in the shade of the jacarandas, or sweat their way up the breakback alleys. Cruise ships sail by within swimming distance of the shore and yachts bob gently in the bay.

'Funchal is a town of not much distinction or interest yet that satisfies,' wrote Sacheverell Sitwell from the cloistered luxury of his room at Reid's Hotel. Granted, Funchal doesn't offer up its delights on a plate. Sights are unsignposted, and curious corners of town are often ignored by visitors and tourist office alike. But if you are prepared to poke about and put in a little leg-work, you'll find richly stocked museums, fine old buildings, abundant markets, musty wine lodges, grand churches and gardens that you can get lost in.

History

Funchal gets its name from the wild fennel (Portuguese *funcho*) that the first settlers found growing here when they arrived with Captain Zarco in 1420 (*see* p.36). Soon they had uprooted all of it, planting instead the vines and sugar cane that poured gold into their pockets. At first just a handful of farmers lived in Funchal. Zarco had established Madeira's first major settlement at Machico near the eastern tip of the island, but in 1508 the bulk of the settlers moved to Funchal, which had a larger bay and more room on the land for expansion. The town was awarded city status, and declared Madeira's new capital. For a while it was so prosperous that it was acknowledged as Portugal's third city (after Lisbon and Porto). King Manuel himself paid for a cathedral, and in 1514 Funchal was made a bishopric. Ever since then Funchal has been Madeira's chief harbour, the hub of inland transport, the focus of all commercial activity and the vortex of island society.

The City Centre

The Sé (Cathedral)

Funchal's Gothic cathedral hasn't had a very good press. 'An unsightly pile,' shuddered Isabella de França in her diary; a 19th-century guidebook dismisses it with: 'There is little that can be called remarkable in its structure except the fretted ceiling.' But if you are prepared to spend some time poking about, and are not expecting Notre Dame, the Sé (the name refers to the Holy See) holds some appealing surprises.

Work on the church was begun in 1485 and completed in 1514. King Manuel I dug into his own pocket to pay for it, and sent builders across from the mainland to supervise the construction. The architect Pedro Enes (or Anes) has been identified from the

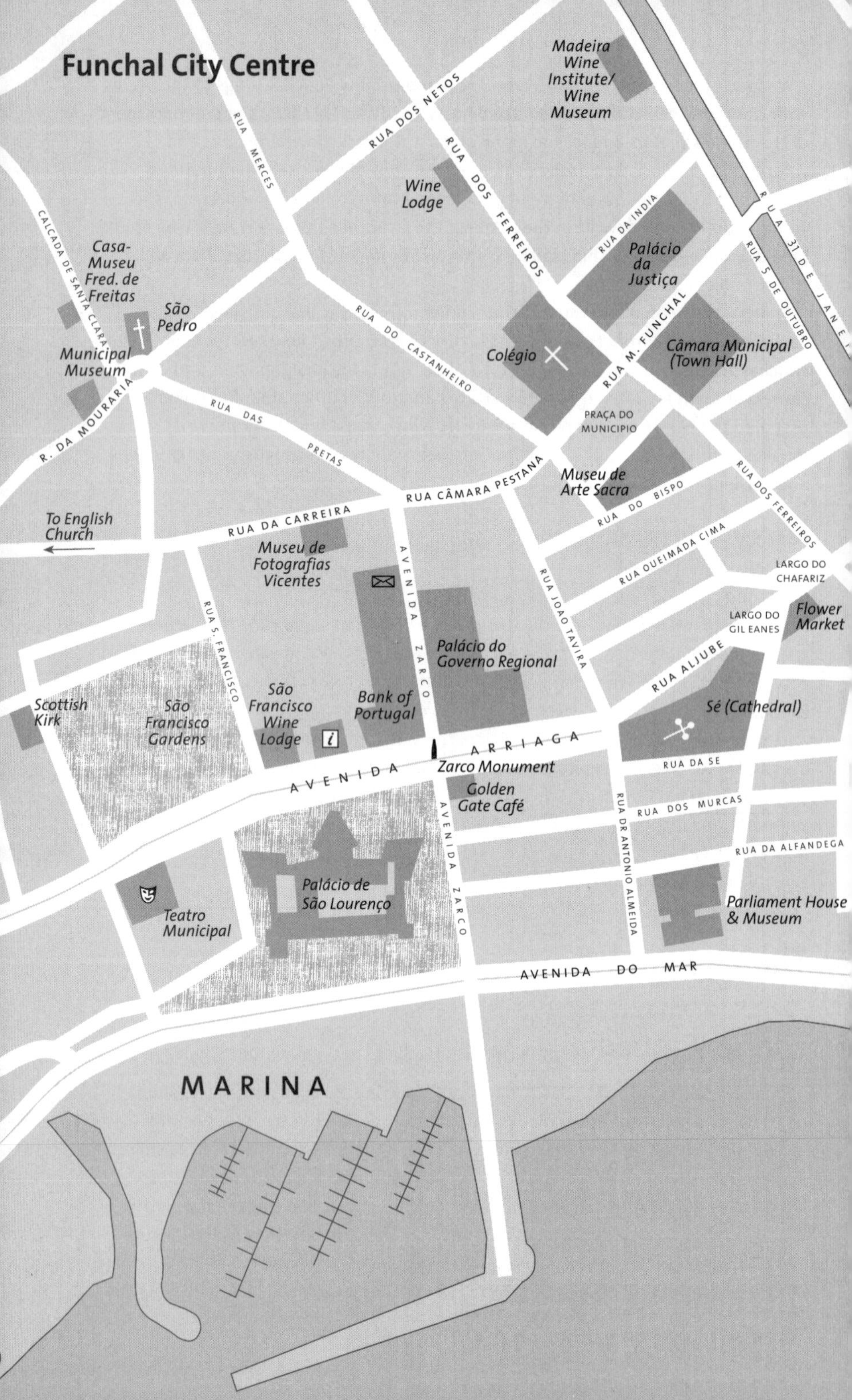
Funchal City Centre
Madeira Wine Institute/ Wine Museum
Rua dos Netos
Rua Merces
Rua dos Ferreiros
Wine Lodge
Rua da India
Palácio da Justiça
Rua 31 de Janeiro
Rua 5 de Outubro
Calcada de Santa Clara
Casa-Museu Fred. de Freitas
São Pedro
Municipal Museum
R. da Mouraria
Rua do Castanheiro
Colégio
Rua M. Funchal
Câmara Municipal (Town Hall)
Praça do Municipio
Rua das Pretas
Rua Câmara Pestana
Museu de Arte Sacra
Rua do Bispo
To English Church
Rua da Carreira
Museu de Fotografias Vicentes
Avenida Zarco
Rua Queimada Cima
Largo do Chafariz
Rua Joao Tavira
Largo do Gil Eanes
Flower Market
Rua S. Francisco
Palácio do Governo Regional
Rua Aljube
Scottish Kirk
São Francisco Gardens
São Francisco Wine Lodge
Bank of Portugal
Sé (Cathedral)
Avenida Arriaga
Zarco Monument
Rua da Se
Golden Gate Café
Rua dos Murcas
Rua Dr Antonio Almeida
Rua da Alfandega
Palácio de São Lourenço
Teatro Municipal
Parliament House & Museum
Avenida do Mar
MARINA

Bom Jesus
RUA DO BOM JESUS
Museu Henrique e Francisco Franco
RUA JOÃO DE DEUS
Instituto da Bordado, Tapeçarias e Artesanato da Madeira
RUA DA CONCEIÃO
RUA DAS HORTAS
R. DA FABRICA
RUA DO CARMO
Carmo
LARGO DO PHELPS
RUA DO RIBEIRINHO
RUA DO SEMINARIO
RUA BRIGADEIRO OUDINOT
RUA DO VISCONDE DO ANADIA
RUA DR. FERNÃO ORNELAS
RUA HOSPITAL VELHO
RUA 31 DE JANEIRO
RUA DIREITA
OLD TOWN
RUA ESMERALDA
RUAS 5 DE OUTUBRO
R. TANOEIROS
Mercado dos Lavradores
RUA LATINO COELHO
RUA BOA VIAGEM
RUA PROFETAS
PRAÇA DE COLOMBO
RUA DE SANTA MARIA
RUA DOM CARLOS I
Customs House
PRAÇA DA AUTONOMIA
Cable car departure point
Rotunda da Autonomia
AVENIDA DO MAR
N
100 m
100 yds

sign of a ruler and compass (the traditional mark of the master builder) after his signature on old documents – though he is often confused with the master stonemason, Gil Eanes (a mistake perpetuated by the city council when they named the small square beside the Sé after Gil Eanes, 'Master of the Cathedral').

At first glance, the label 'Gothic' would appear a misnomer. With its sturdy white walls, stumpy tower and tiny windows the Sé is more in the tradition of heavy, southern-European Gothic than the vast stone symphonies of the north. In sultry Mediterranean and semi-tropical climes, great spear-shaped windows would have meant that the congregation was burned to a frazzle. Here windows are mere chinks in the thick walls, casting pale streams of light across a cool, gloomy interior. Apart from the odd pointed arch and the occasional buttress, there is so little that is familiarly Gothic to the northern European that some art historians doubt the Sé fits into the category at all. Instead they see Moorish touches, designs imported from mainland Portugal and parts that are home-grown Madeiran, with no architectural ancestors at all.

The **tower** is capped with a peak of brightly coloured *azulejos* (*see* pp.46–7). King Manuel himself designed the original spiral of red, green, blue and white tiles, though this was badly damaged in an earthquake in 1748. Below it is a **clock** presented in 1922 by the legendary Dr Grabham (*see* p.163; he had a failing for timepieces and had over 200 of his own). Around the back of the church, on the southeast corner, the sober white walls break out in stylish Manueline stonework. The Sé was built at the height of Madeira's sugar-boom prosperity, yet these ice-cream-cone twirls and filigreed balconies are its only attempt at a swagger. The real treasures lie inside. Highlight of them all is the **ceiling**, carved in indigenous cedar (or juniper; no one is quite clear which), inlaid with ivory and picked out in red, gold and blue. The geometric design and complicated interlocking patterns show a distinct Mudéjar (Hispano-Arabic) influence, and wouldn't look out of place in the Alcázar in Seville; but there are also flourishes of Manueline and Gothic carving, and the overall effect is quite unique. Sadly, natural light barely makes it up this high, and only for concerts and feast days are the chandeliers lit brightly enough for you to really appreciate the sight – but you can get a reasonable view from the transept, or do what one traveller did and lie on your back in the aisle until your eyes have become accustomed to the dark.

The **choir stalls** were carved in the early 16th century in Flamboyant Gothic style. Moses and Aaron join the apostles and a host of unidentifiable saints under elaborate gilded canopies, but the craftsmen obviously had most fun in carving the misericords. Lift the choir seats and you'll find monkeys, pigs and other animals (some in rather rude positions) and touches of local colour, such as a cherub with a bunch of bananas and a carving of a *borracheiro* with his pigskin full of wine.

Much of the interior has suffered from a rather tawdry Baroque facelift. Heavily gilded side altars cling to the walls of the nave, but in the vestry (to the left of the main altar) you can get a better idea of the original simplicity of the church. Look out also for other early remnants, such as the delicately carved rose windows in the transept, the canopied pulpit and (in the chapel to the left of the main portal) the cathedral's first baptismal font and heavy wooden altar. Near the wall in the north-west corner of the nave is an ancient brass grave-plate which dates back to the late 15th century. It depicts a merchant and his spouse thought (as the design is Flemish) to be the rich Belgian trader Esmeraldo and his wife (*see* p.119).

Along the Avenues

Stretching in front of the cathedral is the **Avenida Arriaga**, lined with jacaranda trees and paved with a mosaic of black and white stones. From April to June the trees are drenched with mauve flowers, which they scatter like confetti over the ground. The limestone and basalt blocks of the mosaic are cut and laid painstakingly by hand. The idea first became fashionable in Lisbon in the mid-19th century, and soon spread to Madeira. Today you can find similar mosaics all over the island, but designs tend to be more sober than their counterparts on the mainland.

Once, the Avenida was the route of the daily promenade, but the streams of traffic that thunder down either side have driven strollers on to the road which runs from the Sé to the sea. Also paved with mosaic, this is closed to cars and is the site of two Madeiran institutions, the Café Funchal and the Café Apolo (*see* 'Eating Out', p.109).

Cutting across the jacarandas of the Avenida Arriaga is **Avenida Zarco**, itself lined with shady tipuana that burst into yellow flowers between June and September. On the northeast corner of the intersection are the administrative offices of the regional government (**Palácio do Governo Regional**), a solid Baroque building with odd, delicate wrought-iron lamps and balconies at each window. Through a grand portico, lined from floor to ceiling with yellow, blue and white *azulejos*, you come to a courtyard that sports a small fountain. Across the road a 19th-century pile houses the local headquarters of the **Bank of Portugal**. Climb up the marble stairs for a peek at the octagonal, wood-panelled banking hall. It would make a perfect setting for a scene from Mary Poppins. The **Golden Gate Café** on the other side of Avenida Arriaga was once nicknamed 'the corner of the world' and was a meeting place for all the town. For decades after the Second World War, a bank occupied the ground floor, and squeezed coffee drinkers somewhat ignominiously upstairs. But in 1996 the old café was restored with much of its former style, and it is once again a stop-off point for promenaders. The fourth corner of the intersection is taken up by the 16th-century **São Lourenço** fortress (*see* p.134), now the Madeiran military headquarters.

A short walk up Avenida Zarco brings you to **Rua da Carreira**. The straightness and flatness of this road is quite a novelty in Funchal, enticing the gentry of yore to hold riderless horse-races there, in imitation of the Romans in the Corso. Spectators would hang out of the upstairs windows, cheering the horses on as they thundered up the narrow alley. At No.43, in one of the most beautiful 19th-century buildings in town, is the **Museu de Fotografias Vicentes** (*open Mon–Fri 10–5; adm €2*). A horseshoe-shaped courtyard ringed by a wrought-iron balcony ends in a double stairway that sweeps you up to the oldest photographic studio in Portugal. You can still see the hand-painted screens that were used to create impressive backdrops for portraits. There

Vicente Gomes da Silva

Vicente Gomes da Silva was born in Funchal in 1827. After a spell as a teacher he took to painting and engraving before becoming intrigued by the fledgling art of photography. He opened his studio in 1848, at first experimenting with daguerrotypes (the Empress of Brazil and her daughter were subjects). By 1856 he was already well established as a professional photographer – the first in Portugal – and nine years later opened a smart new studio on the Rua da Carreira. Soon the Imperial Coat of Arms of Austria and the Coat of Arms of the Portuguese royal family joined that of the Empress of Brazil hanging outside the door. Vicente Gomes da Silva died in 1906, but the studio at Rua da Carreira remained in family hands up until the 1970s, when it was bought by the Regional Government and turned into a museum.

are rows of old cameras, faint daguerrotypes and pictures of some of Madeira's illustrious visitors (such as Empress Elizabeth of Austria). The museum is also a treasure trove of old photographs of Madeira, with over 380,000 negatives in its archives. The walls of the museum are lined with shots of people in traditional dress, landscapes, and pictures of festivals and village life going back more than a century.

Back on Avenida Arriaga, beside the tourist office, is an **art gallery** run by the Madeiran Tourist Authority and hosting temporary exhibitions, often by local artists.

Wine, Flowers and the Fruit of Calvinism

Next door to the tourist office building is the **São Francisco Wine Lodge** (***t** 291 740 110; tours only, Mon–Fri 10.30am and 3.30pm, Sat 11am; adm €3*). The lodge is housed in what remains of a 16th-century convent (the rest, most notably a chapel made entirely of human skulls and bones, was demolished last century after it had fallen to ruin). Legend has it that in 1566 the pirate leader Bertrand de Montluc, who had terrorized the island for 16 days, was swiftly despatched by a shot fired from the convent as he led an attack on the Fortress São Lourenço across the way. Today the old building is the headquarters of all the really big names in madeira wine – Blandy, Miles, Leacock and Cossart Gordon – united under the banner of the Madeira Wine Company. Guided tours start off in the heavily beamed Vintage Cellar, pass barrel upon fragrant barrel of maturing wine, take in a coopers' workshop and end up with a wine-tasting. On the way you get a crash course in the history and making of madeira. The guides are well informed, the setting romantic and the wine delicious. No other lodge on the island quite manages this combination, so this is the place to come if you are a madeira beginner (alternatively, immerse yourself in pp.52–7).

At its western end the lodge opens on to the little **São Francisco Gardens**, hardly the size of a football pitch, yet a jungle of exotic plants from all over the world – headily scented frangipani, shocking blue heads of agapanthus, tulip trees that sprout jagged, scarlet-orange flowers in September and October, swathes of creepers and soft thickets of fern. 'A lilliput of the tropics,' breathed Sacheverell Sitwell, 'of transcendental interest.' In one corner there is a pond replete with black swans and ducks, fountains and a statue of two chubby children dipping their toes in the water. On the other side is a small **open-air theatre** (scene of many a local talent contest and pop concert) and a kiosk that serves milkshakes so thick you can stand the straw upright.

On the far western side of the garden is the neat, rather prim **Scottish Kirk**, built in 1861 and now home to Madeira's small Portuguese Presbyterian congregation.

Across from the garden, on the other side of the Avenida Arriaga is the graceful **Chamber of Commerce**, built at the end of the 19th century and decorated with blue and white *azulejos* showing scenes from island life. The exhibition hall is now a motor showroom, with shiny Japanese saloons looking curiously out of place against a backdrop of original *fin de siècle* fittings. Many of Funchal's most beautiful interiors aren't open to the public; the most you can hope for is a glimpse from the hall or a

The Madeiran Outrage

In the 1840s a series of events, which became known as the Madeiran Outrage, lifted the lid on a seething ferment of discontent between Madeirans and the resident British, and within the British community itself. Relations between the Roman Catholic Portuguese and Protestant Brits on the island had always been a little itchy. Residents usually kept their heads down, but there had been outbreaks of violence between the local populace (supposedly incited by priests) and visiting troops and sailors. Tensions eased a little in the 1820s and 1830s when the Bible Society was even permitted to distribute testaments, on the understanding that it wouldn't try to convert anyone.

The delicate balance of this *status quo* was tipped by the fiery Scots Calvinist Dr Robert Reid Kalley. A wealthy doctor of medicine, Kalley whirled into Madeira in 1838. Soon he was fluent in Portuguese, had requalified in Lisbon, set up a busy practice (where people who couldn't pay were treated free) and established 17 schools, which he financed personally. He was hailed as a great philanthropist, but Kalley had a secret agenda – he wanted to see Madeira converted to Calvinism. He began to hold Sunday meetings at his house, and to preach to the somewhat captive audience in his surgery. In May 1841 the governor of Madeira protested, and Kalley agreed to stop his proselytizing, but a visit to Scotland the following year topped up his zeal. On his return he not only resumed the meetings, but encouraged some locals to take communion following the Calvinistic order of service. A horrified bishop complained to Lisbon and the governor mobilized the police force to try to prevent locals from entering Kalley's house and surgery. His schools were closed. Labelled as an antichrist, a heretic, infidel and agent of the devil, Kalley went on undeterred.

Stoddard, the British consul, began to stir uneasily. Kalley had alienated the resident Church of England British who disliked anything that rocked their rather comfortable boat – especially if it was bad for trade. When the doctor was arrested in 1843, Stoddard had little sympathy. Kalley was charged with heresy and blasphemy and (as these charges carried the death sentence) refused bail. He ground the gears of local politics even more harshly by appointing fellow Scot Henry Veitch (*see* pp.191–2) as his adviser. Veitch, a notorious womanizer, was regarded by local clergy as being 'one of the greatest sinners on the island', nor was there any love lost glance up the stairwell from the first-floor landing. If you do this at the Chamber of Commerce or the **Clube Sports do Madeira** next door you'll be rewarded with a view of splendid stucco ceilings, grand wooden stairways and stylish statuettes and chandeliers.

Next in line comes the **Municipal Theatre** (Teatro Municipal Baltazar Diaz), built between 1884 and 1887 and named after a local playwright. Here is Merchant-Ivory Madeira, a small-scale La Scala with four tiers of boxes, a sea of plush velvet, cherubs, tasteful gilding and an enormous pendant lamp. On the rare occasions when opera or the ballet come to town, the boxes are occupied by the high and mighty and the air seethes with every bit as much gossip and intrigue as it must have done 100 years

between him and Stoddard, Veitch having been sacked as consul some time previously. After much scuttling up and down the diplomatic corridors in Lisbon, Kalley was eventually released. He returned to his preaching with renewed vigour. Again the governor tried to block his efforts, even to the extent of sending a full military expedition of 70 soldiers to close one of his schools. Kalley had several close scrapes, narrowly avoiding arrest, but his followers weren't quite so lucky. By 1844 28 of them were in jail, some facing the death sentence.

Then in 1846 a new governor, Valentin de Freitas Leal, was appointed. Leal was a determined Anglophobe, believing that the British were trying to buy up the island and denude it of its Portuguese population. (Local merchants were lining their pockets by chartering ships to carry Madeiran emigrants across the Atlantic.) He was a great chum of the chief of police. Together with Father Conego Telles, a zealous Jesuit, they incited the local populace to attack houses where Protestant meetings were being held. On 2 August Telles led a group of some 60 people against a den of evil belonging to the elderly Misses Rutherford. With the battle-cry of 'There is no law for Calvinists' the mob invaded the house and beat up the Portuguese they found inside. The chief of police refused help to the Misses Rutherford, and the governor later wrote to Kalley, 'I look upon you to be the cause of all these disturbances. This is the fruit of the tree you have planted in this island, nor will it ever produce anything else but discord and trouble.' On 9 August, after an even more violent attack involving several hundred people, Kalley fled. Disguised as a sick woman, he was carried in a hammock to a British ship in the bay. Over the next few months large numbers of his followers also left the island. Stoddard, feeling that Kalley got what he deserved, did very little to intervene. This impassivity nearly cost him his job. Lord Palmerston, the British Foreign Secretary, admonished that he had 'failed to show the firmness and energy required for an officer of the British Crown' and sent him on extended leave.

Kalley never came back, but went on to found a mission in Brazil. British members of the Scottish Free Church quietly continued to worship, without any attempt to convert locals. The small group of Portuguese Presbyterians went underground, and it wasn't until the beginning of the 20th century that they were able to stop holding meetings in secret.

ago. On other nights (sometimes films are shown here) you can slip past the bored usher, climb the stairs and have a box all to yourself. If you are passing in the daytime, speak nicely to the usher on duty, who may let you in for a look if the theatre isn't being used. The upstairs foyer, which has ceilings painted with colourful sprays of flowers, often houses travelling exhibitions worth a visit.

Avenida Arriaga ends with a busy roundabout, a fountain and an ugly statue to Prince Henry the Navigator, but just before you get there you'll find the small **Christopher Columbus Museum** (*open Mon–Fri, 9–12.30 and 3–6, Sat 9–1; adm €1.50*), which has an exceptionally good array of books and manuscripts about Madeira, and one of the best collections of material relating to Christopher Columbus in the world (most of it, alas, for the eyes of serious researchers only).

Beyond the Sé

Flower-sellers and Explorers

Just behind the cathedral, on the triangular **Largo do Gil Eanes**, is a small **flower market**. Women in bright red traditional dress sit behind buckets of strelitzia, orchids, protea and agapanthus. Their costume – striped skirt, bolero jacket and odd spiky cap – had all but disappeared from everyday use until the Tourist Authority engineered a revival some years ago. Today it pops up everywhere, on flower-sellers, waitresses and 'folkloric' dancers, but is treated with the detachment of a work uniform. At closing time the flower ladies, rather like Kabuki actors, stand up, pull a few strings, and their bright cladding crumples and falls, revealing plain, 21st-century clothes underneath.

Rua Aljube leads eastwards to **Largo do Chafariz**, a pretty little square paved with wavy-patterned mosaic and lined with characteristic Funchal buildings – cream walls, green shutters, wrought-iron balconies, and windows and doors edged with bare volcanic stone. On one corner is the **Bazar do Povo**, a 19th-century shopping arcade that still has long, dark wooden cabinets and a double staircase with fancy wrought-iron banisters leading up to its mezzanine floor.

South of Largo do Chafariz, cobbled alleys of small shops lead to the spacious, eerily silent **Praça de Colombo** where, at No.28, the 15th-century Flemish sugar baron João Esmeraldo (Jean d'Esmanault) had his mansion. At the time it was one of the few two-storey buildings in town. Tradition has it that Christopher Columbus stayed here in the 1480s, while he was working as a sugar trader. Later the mansion was occupied by the wine merchants Gordon Duff & Co. When the Gordon family left the island during the oidium (*see* p.54), the town council used the house as a granary. Later the building fell into disrepair, and in the 19th century it was demolished – though one Manueline window frame was saved. Today this stands in the garden of a private *quinta*, though rumour has it that it is soon to return to grace the square.

Praça do Município

North of Largo do Chafariz, through a gauntlet of smart fashion boutiques on the Rua dos Ferreiros, you reach the Praça do Município. The *praça*, covered in scalloped mosaic (the design is supposed to represent fish scales), boasts some of Funchal's most gracious buildings.

At its eastern end is the **Câmara Municipal** (Town Hall). Designed as a town house by the Conde de Carvalhal in the 18th century, the Câmara has a portico lined with blue and white *azulejos* in a voluptuous Baroque design. Twin staircases run up either side of the entrance hall, and an arch leads through the centre to a neat courtyard, with a marble fountain depicting Leda and her over-amorous swan. The count never lived to occupy his new house, and in the 19th century it was taken over by the municipality and has served as a city hall ever since.

On the northern side of the square the **Colégio Church** raises a façade resplendent with the figures of the founders of the Society of Jesus. The Jesuits began building their church in 1629. Grand yet austere, the original frontispiece was embellished by SS. Ignatius Loyola, Francis Xavier, Francis de Borgia and Stanislav in the 18th century. The interior beats any other that a Madeiran church has to offer. There are priceless multi-coloured *azulejos* from the 17th and 18th centuries, Mudéjar-inspired wall paintings and one of the most splendid arrays of 17th-century gilt carving in Portugal. The ceiling is a witty *trompe l'œil* of painted domes and people peering over balconies draped with fruit and flowers.

The Jesuits on Madeira

When Bertrand de Montluc and his pirates occupied Funchal in 1566, the locals sent off a plea for help to the mainland. The armada sent from Lisbon arrived too late to be of much help, but on board one of the ships was a small band of Jesuits, sent to console the ravaged populace and offer succour. The armada soon headed home, but the priests stayed on, preaching twice a day in the cathedral and wandering around town spreading the word.

To demonstrate their gratitude – and, no doubt, not without some encouragement from the priests themselves – the people of Funchal asked the king to establish a Jesuit college on the island. The first Colégio was on Largo do Chafariz, though around 1578 the Jesuits moved to the site of the present church where they taught theology and the humanities.

In 1599 they bought two *quintas* outside Funchal, farming the land to generate an income for the college. Cashing in on the growing prosperity of the wine trade, they introduced two new grape varieties to the island. Sercial and Verdelho have since become two of the most popular types of madeira, but for a long time bottles were rare. In the words of a 17th-century traveller, 'Those Jesuits there so engross it, that it is a hard matter to get any.'

When the tyrannical Marquês de Pombal was clawing his way to power in Dom José's court in the 18th century, he expelled the Jesuits, whom he regarded as his enemies, from Portugal. Jesuits on Madeira suffered the same fate as their brothers on the mainland, and were forced to leave the island in 1760. Their church and college lay derelict. For a while in the 19th century the buildings served as a military barracks, before becoming a school and later part of Madeira's university.

Next door to the church, in what was the Jesuit College, is a branch of Madeira's fledgling **university**, founded at the end of the 1980s.

Along Rua do Bispo

Across the square from the Jesuit church is a delicate two-storey cloister belonging to the disused **Capela do São Luiz**, built in 1600 by Jerónimo Jorge, who had been sent by the king to direct the building of Madeira's fortifications. If you leave the square by its southwest corner, you can see the chapel's Renaissance-style stone portal.

Below the church, on Rua do Bispo, is an excellent example of a ***torre-mirante*** (belvedere tower). These square towers, usually three or four storeys high, poke up above many of the grander 17th- and 18th-century houses in town. They hark back to a century or two earlier, when the Funchalese lived in terror of pirate attacks and families who could afford it (and who had stashes of valuables to protect) built their own lookout towers to give themselves early warning of any suspicious-looking ships on the horizon. The fierce corsairs were finally eradicated, but the architectural style stuck.

Museu de Arte Sacra (Museum of Sacred Art)

Open Tues–Sat 10–12.30 and 2.30–6; adm €2.24.

Rua do Bispo doubles back parallel to the Praça do Município. The stately Baroque **Bishop's Palace** at the end of the street was built after the earthquake of 1748 had destroyed the original one (built by Jerónimo Jorge). Today the palace houses the Museum of Sacred Art.

During the glory-days of the sugar boom Madeira did a roaring trade with Flanders. Sugar was then a pricey luxury. Flemish merchants often paid the sugar farmers with paintings, and the wealthier plantation holders commissioned their own works, so the island acquired a rich hoard of 15th- and 16th-century Flemish art. Much of it was holed away in village churches and private chapels and forgotten about. It was really only in the 1930s that Madeirans began to realize just how valuable those grimy altar pictures were. Churches were scoured and works sent to Lisbon for restoration. Today most of these paintings, together with other ecclesiastical treasures, are gathered here under one roof – though the experts are still arguing over who the artists were.

The **top floor** is given over mainly to 15th- and 16th-century Flemish painting. Highlights include: a sensitive picture of *St James*, attributed to Dirk Bouts, the first northern European painter to use perspective; a superb *Annunciation*, in the introspective style of Hugo de Goes; and a richly textured diptych on the same subject thought to be by Jan Provost. A touchingly beautiful painting of *Mary Magdalene* (no.3), once attributed to Henry Met de Bless, is now also thought to be by Provost, though the work does have something of Met de Bless's Italianate treatment of light (but no sign of the owl he liked to paint into his pictures). Look out also for a delightful picture of the *Virgin*, painted in 1543, a little later than most of the works in the gallery, and thought to be by Mabuse. The cherubs attendant on the Madonna have colourful parrot-like wings, a sign that they are a notch or two higher in status than their white-feathered brethren. The baby Jesus clutches a bunch of cherries – the fruit of paradise and a traditional gift to the virtuous.

Some of the paintings have an interesting touch of local history, as they include portraits of the patrons who commissioned them. The panels on either side of the triptych of *SS. Philip and James* show the family of Simão Gonçalves de Câmara, Zarco's grandson. The painting of *The Meeting of St Anna and St Joachim* (no.7) in fact shows King Ladislau of Poland and his wife, who owned the land around Madalena do Mar (*see* p.195).

In the rest of the museum you'll find **statues** and **religious artefacts** dating back four centuries. Prize of the collection is the magnificent **gilt processional cross** given to the cathedral by King Manuel I in 1514. There is a good collection of polychrome **carving** ranging from the 16th to the 18th centuries (with some delightfully tacky 19th-century additions), and some richly embroidered **liturgical vestments**, many from the hands of local nuns.

Wine and Old Lace

Cut back across the Praça Município and make your way uphill along the **Rua dos Ferreiros**, past a hat shop whose window display seems not to have changed since the 1930s, and the Esperança Bookshop where, up the narrow wooden stairs, students and old men with skin like parchment wander in the half-light of a maze of bookshelves.

The Rua dos Ferreiros is the address of several **wine lodges**, most open to the public and aimed unashamedly at the tourist market. Tucked between them, at No.109, is a gem – a lodge which has been in the Barros e Sousa family for four generations. Through an unmarked door, up a passage lined with dusty baskets, barrels and cobwebs, you come to a lush courtyard. One of the Barros e Sousa brothers sits bottling vintage wine by hand, the other will emerge from behind piles of books and invoices to offer you a taste of wine. If you're really lucky, Don Edmundo will then take you across the courtyard to the *estufa* where wines are warmed naturally, in tiered attics (not in artificially heated concrete vats as is now the practice of nearly every other winemaker on the island), then aged in oak barrels. Here he unbungs a barrel or two, dips in a long spoon made from a piece of cane, and brings out a drop of the purest nectar. If you want to take home a wine that will remind you of Madeira every time you have a sip, this is the place to buy it.

Leave Rua dos Ferreiros eastwards along **Rua dos Netos**. The Ateneu Comercial do Funchal at No.44 has one of those stately Madeiran interiors that you can glimpse from the entrance hall. Rua dos Netos comes to an abrupt halt on **Rua 5 de Outubro**, one of Funchal's traffic-clotted artery roads. To the right is the yellow and red, faintly oriental home of the **Madeiran Wine Institute**. Originally a *quinta* designed by Henry Veitch (*see* pp.191–2), the building also houses a small **Wine Museum** (*open Mon–Fri 9.30–12.30 and 2–5; adm free*). There are photographs of wine production and pieces of old wine-making equipment, but the museum is not nearly as interesting or informative as the tour of the São Francisco Wine Lodge (*see* p.116).

A bridge crosses the main road to **Rua do Bom Jesus**, named after the 17th-century **convent** which you can still see on the left-hand side. In the 19th century the convent became a home for widows, 'women in an interesting condition' and 'married ladies who have lost for a time the society of their husbands'. Today it is a *residencia leiga* (lay nunnery).

On Rua da Conceição, which leads downhill off Rua do Bom Jesus, is the **House of the Consuls**, a splendid Baroque building with wavy window-ledges and a line of the little four-leafed clover windows which were popular in Madeiran architecture at the time. The local authorities started to build this row of homes for diplomats in the early 18th century, but ran out of money. Only the shell and façade were finished, and for centuries the hollow cavern was used for storage. But in 1994 the government stepped in to prevent the building from gracelessly collapsing into ruin. Restorers got to work and builders began finally to give it an inside, as offices and a shopping mall.

Rua do Bom Jesus leads into **Rua de João de Deus**, where you can see some good examples of ***casas de prazeres*** (literally, 'houses of pleasure'), quaint, typically Madeiran summer houses built on the garden walls of *quintas* and larger homes. Simple and airy, these box-shaped tea houses were usually suroundeded by shuttered windows or trellis-work, and had a door opening into the garden. Inside, they were decorated with Madeiran embroidery and English chintz. Here family and friends would sit in the shade for that great Madeiran institution, five o'clock tea (a habit they developed before the British did – it was Catherine of Bragança who introduced the custom to the English court when she married King Charles II).

Towards the end of the street is the **Museu Henrique e Francisco Franco** (*open Mon–Fri 9–12.30 and 2–5.30; adm €1.50*). The brothers, one a painter and the other a sculptor, are Madeira's most famous artists. They had studios on the island and in Lisbon and hobnobbed with the likes of Modigliani and Picasso. Francisco (1885–1955) was the more talented of the two, and is responsible for many of the statues around Funchal. The museum has a few original works, and also prints and photographs documenting the brothers' lives.

Just around the corner, on Rua do Visconde da Anadia, is the **Instituto do Bordado, Tapeçarias e Artesanato da Madeira** (Institute of Embroidery, Tapestry and Handicrafts; *open Mon–Fri 10–12.30 and 2.30–5.30; adm free*). The museum upstairs has displays of lace and embroidery (mostly made between 1880 and 1915) that put today's work to shame. There is a tapestry self-portrait of the flamboyant master of the craft Gino Romoli, alongside his woollen renderings of Churchill, Queen Elizabeth and Jackie Onassis. On the staircase is a gigantic (20-square-metre) tapestry of Madeiran scenes, designed by Romoli, but painstakingly stitched by the 16 schoolgirls who were brave enough to bear what he termed the 'enthusiasm and discipline' of his supervision. Begun in 1959, it took over two years to complete. Also in the museum is a small collection of the traditional costumes of each of the island's regions, and a cabinet showing, step by step, how some of Madeira's indigenous musical instruments are made.

Rua do Visconde do Anadia leads on down to the market and the sea.

North of the Avenida Arriaga

Convents and *Quintas*

Fashion-conscious Funchalese who can't find what they want on the Rua dos Ferreiros head for the equally classy boutiques on **Rua das Pretas**, before giving up and waiting for their next trip to the mainland. The 'Road of the Negresses', a name with echoes of the slave trade (*see* p.127), leads from the top of Avenida Zarco up to **São Pedro**, a pretty little church built at the end of the 16th century. Inside, 17th-century *azulejos* cover the walls with a simple crisscross pattern that is spoiled by rather vulgar Baroque gilding. There is an attractive side chapel with a false Italianate loggia, and some curious choir stalls covered in rococo tendrils.

Running past the left side of the church, the **Calçada de Santa Clara** is a hill to be taken seriously, but up it lie three of Funchal's greatest attractions. As each could easily detain you for an hour, it might be a good idea to visit them one day at a time.

The pink **Casa-Museu Frederico de Freitas** (*open Tues–Sun 10–12.30 and 2–6; adm €2*), with a flimsy *casa de prazer* balancing on its corner wall, is the sort of museum that could keep you browsing for most of a rainy afternoon. The recipe for success is a common one – the idiosyncrasies, good luck and fine taste of one man and his family.

Isabella de França

Poking about a London bookshop in the 1930s, Dr Frederico de Freitas came across a clothbound folio containing some 300 pages of neat handwriting. On the dust-jacket the bookseller had written '*Journal of a Visit to Madeira and Portugal, with 24/5 (one double page) drawings to illustrate it*' (they turned out to be watercolours, not drawings). After scouring the text and digging through archives in Madeira and England, a picture of the authoress began to emerge, and with it hints of a rather charming love story. The *Journal*, which is written with lively wit and sharp perception, was published in 1969, together with the illustrations, under the name of Isabella de França.

Isabella came to Madeira on her honeymoon in 1853. She was born Isabella Hurst, the daughter of a London architect. Her new husband was Joseph Henry (or José Henrique) de França, and it would seem that they had met when both were living in Kensington. Joseph Henry had an English mother, but his father was a Madeiran merchant and *morgado*, with estates around Estreito da Calheta. He had been born in England, but kept his Portuguese passport, and had even served in the Funchal Militia. The youthful verve of Isabella's style, the descriptions of jaunts around the island and the glimpses she gives of her passion for her new husband seem very much those of a young and accomplished English rose on her first trip abroad. Yet Isabella was 58 when she wrote her diary, and her husband a mere stripling of 50. He had looked after his widowed mother for decades, and married only after she had died. The de Franças returned to England in 1854. Isabella died in 1880 at the age of 85, and Joseph Henry six years after that. They are buried together at the Roman Catholic Cemetery in Southampton.

Dr Frederico Augusto da Cunha e Freitas moved into this 18th-century mansion in the 1940s, and went on to fill it with beautiful objects from all over the world. When he died in 1978, he left house and contents to the Madeiran State, and today the museum is run by his son. The magnificent, high-ceilinged rooms cluttered with English and Portuguese furniture, priceless carvings, paintings and old fortepianos have somehow kept a comfortable, lived-in atmosphere. The museum also has a collection of Persian, Turkish and Moorish tiles and *azulejos* of inestimable value, as well as the original manuscript and illustrations of the 19th-century diary of **Isabella de França**.

The road climbs even more steeply after the de Freitas museum, past the erstwhile Hotel Santa Clara (now government offices) much favoured by 19th-century visitors for its big triangular veranda, and on to the **Convent of Santa Clara** (*open 10–12 and 3–5; although there is no charge, a donation of €2–4 per person is appreciated*). Ring the bell at the gate, and someone will appear to show you around. Santa Clara is still a convent, though the number of nuns has dwindled to just a handful.

The convent was founded in 1496 by one of Zarco's grandsons, João Gonçalves de Câmara, who installed his sister Dona Isabel as abbess. Zarco and a generation or two of his descendants are buried in the church. Built on the site of a chapel originally put up by the old Squinter himself, the convent is today a straggle of buildings of different periods, hardly distinguishable from the rest of the street but for the cupola clad in bright tiles that pokes up from behind the outer wall. Beyond the Gothic doorway lies a quiet cloister and orange garden, where in an open niche you can see the remains of Zarco's original chapel, with a 15th-century Flemish altar. Nearby, the tiny Chapel of the Resurrection has a richly painted ceiling and a gilded altar thick with cherubs. The main church was finished in the 16th century and is covered from floor to ceiling in blue and yellow 17th-century *azulejos*. There are also some extremely rare monochrome green tiles. In the 1980s work on the floor of the choir uncovered more rare tiles, apparently laid at random. These are slowly being cleaned and replaced in the positions in which they were found. Later Baroque additions are quite muted (by Madeiran standards), with some skilfully marbled cedar pillars.

The nuns were a reclusive order, drawn from the best families on the island. At the back of the church is an iron grid behind which they had to sit during services and on the rare occasions that they were allowed visitors. The flowers they made of feathers, and their sweets, were favourite souvenirs for visitors to Madeira well into the 19th century. They were also famed for sculpting sugar, and once sent the Pope a sugar model of the sacred college, complete with tiny cardinals. (History doesn't record whether or not His Holiness ate them.) One young visitor coming to buy flowers and sugared melon in the 1830s records his frustration at not being able to glimpse the nuns, as business was conducted via a wheel that rotated through the wall, keeping both parties invisible from each other. It seems, though, that this seclusion from the outside world had its lapses. Isabella de França, who lived nearby during her stay on Madeira, noted, with some amusement, the nuns 'at their balconies and windows, with their veils thrown off for coolness, and pointing their telescopes in all directions to watch their neighbours'.

Sister Maria Clementina

Sister Maria Clementina was Santa Clara's most famous inhabitant. Maria was the youngest daughter of a large family, and something of a Cinderella. With her blue eyes, brown hair and fair skin she was quite different from her sisters and (for reasons about which we can only speculate) her parents developed an antipathy to her from the start. But Maria grew into one of the most beautiful young girls in Funchal. By the age of 13 she had already had countless offers of marriage, which she passed on to her sisters. When she was 18 her father despatched her to the nunnery, and at 19 she took the veil. A year or two later, in 1820, the Portuguese Cortes (parliament) passed the new Constitution, promising to abolish convents and allow nuns to marry. Maria met and fell in love with a handsome young lieutenant of the Portuguese navy, but fell ill just before her wedding day. The ceremony was postponed, but before Maria got well the king had revoked the Cortes' decree and she was whisked back to the convent and celibacy.

When the writer HN Coleridge visited her in 1825, he was bewitched. Meeting Maria at the grate at the back of the church, he handed her a bunch of violets. 'She took them, curtsied very low, opened the folds of a muslin neck kerchief, and dropped them loose on her snowy bosom'. When he asked her if she was happy, she replied, '*O sim, muito feliz* (Oh, yes, very happy),' but when the abbess turned away she put her hand through the grating, pressed his hand tightly and murmured '*Não, não, não: tenho dor do coração* (No, no, no: my heart aches).' Then, as he left, she raised one of his violets to her lips behind her service book, and kissed it. When Isabella de França met her, some thirty years later, she was no less enchanted – though a little surprised by her dress that was 'in the most elegant and recherché style that the garb of a Nun will admit of'. Lionized by British visitors in particular, Maria Clementina held court at Santa Clara until her death at the age of 64.

Behind the convent, **Rua das Cruzes** runs west to a terrace with a fine view over Funchal. Opposite, a short walk down **Rua das Capuchinhas** leads to the **Capelhina das Almas**, a tiny chapel carved out of the rock-face in 1781.

Continuing up the Calçada de Santa Clara, you come to the **Museu da Quinta das Cruzes** (*open Tues–Sun, 10–12.30 and 2–6; adm €2*). The *quinta* grew up in fits and starts from the 16th to the 19th century. It has a large garden dotted with odd bits of architecture rescued from buildings around Funchal – a Manueline window-frame being the most striking. Larger and grander than the de Freitas house, the Quinta das Cruzes lacks the smaller museum's cosy atmosphere, but the exhibits are just as impressive. Upstairs, the rooms are arranged thematically. The Oriental Room (room 4) has some especially beautiful inlaid cabinets, and the French Room (room 6) has porcelain especially commissioned in China in honour of Louis XVI and Marie-Antoinette. The collections of English furniture and Flemish and Italian paintings are also impressive. Downstairs, you'll find indigenous pieces, with some particularly good *caixas de açúcar* (sugar boxes). There is also a glittering treasury full of old pewter and finely worked silverware – including beautiful 18th-century children's rattles made of silver and coral.

Make your way back down the Calçada de Santa Clara, and turn right into the **Rua da Mouraria** (road of the Moorish Quarter, once crammed with dormitories for slaves, *see* box, below). The **Municipal Museum** in the Palácio de São Pedro (*open Tues–Fri 10–6, Sat and Sun 12–6; adm €2*) comprises mainly stuffed birds and a few fearsome preserved sharks. In the small, murky aquarium downstairs you can see fat, sulky sea bream, ugly moray eels, one or two turtles, and sprinklings of brightly coloured tropical fish. The building itself, a stolid 18th-century pile, was once the town house of the Conde de Carvalhal (*see* p.145).

The British, Alive and Dead

Rua da Mouraria continues downhill to Rua da Carreira. A short walk to the right brings you to **Rua da Quebra Costas** ('Break-back Street' – until recently the street was called Rua Nova da Bela Vista, but the authorities finally relented and allowed it the name it had popularly held for centuries). Halfway up the street, set back from the road in a lush garden, is the **English Church**. Until the early 19th century local Brits worshipped at their consulate. Visiting ship's chaplains officiated, and were rewarded with a box of preserved citrons for their services. Then in 1810 the British Factory (an association of the leading merchants, *see* p.39) bought a piece of land on which to build a church – something that was only recently permitted by a treaty with Portugal. A voluntary levy was put on wine exports to raise money for the project, and a subscription fund attracted such illustrious donors as King George III, Lord Nelson

Slavery in Madeira

Slavery and the sugar trade went hand in hand. The first slaves were brought to Madeira in the mid-15th century for the perilous, often fatal task of cutting the *levadas* through the precipitous valleys and for the back-breaking labour of harvesting sugar cane. By the middle of the 16th century there were almost 5,000 slaves on the island. They were treated as human stock, sold by weight and even subject to bills of lading when they were shipped. Portuguese law allowed masters to brand their slaves (to prove ownership), cut their ears off for minor offences, and, on Madeira, subjected slaves to an evening curfew. Even when public opinion began to turn against slavery in the 18th century, those working on the sugar plantations were among the last to benefit. Most families were just beginning to be able to afford sugar, and were not keen on anything that might mean a rise in price. The poet William Cowper put it neatly in 'Poor Africans':

I pity them greatly, but I must be mum,
For how could we do without sugar and rum?

After slavery was finally abolished, the Madeiran slaves assimilated completely with the local population, though today there are still traces of Moorish and African culture in Madeiran music and local folk dances (*see* p.48).

and the Duke of Wellington. Every penny was to be needed. The new church, designed by Henry Veitch – British consul, talented amateur architect and notorious high-liver – cost £10,000, 'an unconscionable sum of money' (according to HN Coleridge, writing five years later). Because of the time it took to raise the money, and because Veitch was so often obstinately locked in conflict with other Factory members about the design, the church opened only in 1822. Under the foundation stone Veitch placed the gold coins he had received after giving a pipe of madeira to a hapless Napoleon, who had stopped by on his way to exile in St Helena (*see* p.53).

The story goes that, when working on the design, Veitch was constricted by a Portuguese law that forbade non-Roman Catholic places of worship from having the external appearance of a church. It is more likely that the consul, who was very much in touch with fashion, simply wanted the most up-to-date building on the island. He came up with an elegant neoclassical design, in his own words: 'a handsome building, a square outside with a circular colonnade inside, supporting a gallery from which rises a fine dome and cupola to give light to the church'. A large all-seeing eye glares down from the dome. Some say this is a Masonic symbol, though it does also have antecedents in Italian churches. Airy and attractive, the Holy Trinity has pews of Madeiran til, with painted palms and lilies. The gargantuan organ that was installed in 1841 was palmed off onto the Sé in the 1930s when the son of the music-loving Dr Michael Grabham (*see* p.163) donated a more modest instrument in memory of his father. Perhaps the celebrated doctor, who was an excellent organist, had complained to his family about the quality of the music in the church – the donor's plaque ends with the cautionary words:

Sing to the Lord a new song
Play skilfully with a loud noise.

Outside, in the garden, there is a bust of **Philippa of Lancaster**, the daughter of John of Gaunt who, as wife of King João I, became Queen of Portugal in 1386. The first discoverers of Madeira were voyagers sent by her son, Prince Henry the Navigator (*see* p.35). There is also a small **library** where, while browsing through books on Madeira, you can eavesdrop on the local gossip. (You can take books out after paying a small membership fee of €3, valid for one month.) The English Church is still a focus of British community life on Madeira, and after the service on Sundays the garden fills with locals and visitors alike, sipping wine or coffee, chatting and nibbling snacks. For details of services, *see* p.89.

Back on Rua da Carreira, but a little further up the hill, you come to the **British Cemetery** (*open Mon–Fri 9–5; adm free*). Ringing the bell at the big wrought-iron gate will have no effect at all. Rather, walk a little further on to the green door at No.235. Here the caretaker will answer your summons (she has some trouble in getting about, so you might have to wait a while). Up until 1764 the bodies of dead Protestant heretics were simply thrown into the sea. Even after the Portuguese government allowed them to be buried on Madeiran ground, a guard of soldiers was for a long while needed to protect Protestant funeral processions. In 1764 the British consul received a permit to buy land for what became known as 'The Nations' Burying Ground'. During the second British occupation in 1808 an adjoining plot was bought (even in peace time the British Army had a high mortality rate), and in 1809 part of this military burial ground was taken over for civilian use, as the old cemetery was becoming overcrowded. This New Burial Ground was extended in 1851, and in 1887 became the repository for bones from The Nations' Burying Ground, which was getting in the way of the town council's road-building plans. The New Burial Ground was divided into sections for Residents and Strangers. Residents were buried free, but Strangers (or their survivors) had to pay. As so many visitors to the island were invalids in the final stages of tuberculosis, the income from the Strangers' burial fees

Lowe and High Church

The young Reverend Richard Lowe arrived on Madeira with his ailing mother in 1826, at the age of 25. 'His appearance,' writes Roy Nash in his chronicle of the scandal, 'gave him the air of an ascetic – a tall gangling frame surmounted by a thin, high-cheekboned, almost monkish face [and] deep-set ice-blue eyes.' He was possessed of a furious energy, yet was a pitiful hypochondriac, and his relationship with his mother was 'close, almost to the point of suffocation'.

Lowe had read mathematics at Cambridge and been ordained in the year of his graduation. His chief interest, however, was natural history, a field he had been introduced to by the brilliant young mineralogy don, John Stevens Henslow. When Lowe's mother was diagnosed as having TB, they decided to come to Madeira and he secured a university scholarship to study the island's plant and animal life for a year.

When the Lowes arrived, the English Church was just four years old, yet it was already having a bit of a bumpy ride. Having designed the new church and spent great energies in raising funds for the construction, Consul Veitch saw himself pretty much as a dictator in church affairs, and wasn't the only one to feel that he 'owned' the English Church; the leading British merchants in Funchal had all worked hard at raising funds to build it. It was a situation that virtually guaranteed the resident chaplain a difficult time.

The Reverend Mr Lowe, however, blissfully went about his sample-gathering activities, learned Portuguese and made great friends of the fishermen at Câmara de Lobos. He made quite a name for himself with the papers he published back in England. In 1831 he stood in as locum for the chaplain, Reverend Mr Deacon. Deacon had gone on leave to consider his future after Veitch had wielded the weapon of reducing his stipend. Lowe let it be known that he would happily accept the post permanently. Veitch approved, and by 1833 Lowe – largely through the machinations of Mr Stoddard, a local businessman – had got what he wanted. He didn't get off to a very good start. First he complained when he found out the reduction of his predecessor's stipend was to be regarded as permanent, then he (rather pedantically) wouldn't accept Consul Veitch's word for his appointment, and refused to start work until approval arrived from London. Veitch was furious and tried to sack him immediately, but Stoddard intervened and Lowe backed down.

proved to be a nice little earner. Consul Veitch burned his fingers by redirecting burial ground funds to pay for the upkeep of the English Church. After a stiff letter from the Foreign Office, residents were also made to pay, and strict government control was kept over the account.

Today the cemetery is filled with flowers and trees, and is a quiet retreat from the bustle of Funchal. In the Residents' section are graves of the families that have played such an enormous part in Madeira's economic development: names such as Blandy, Hinton, Leacock and Krohn.

A stone from the Strangers' section poignantly tells the story common to so many visitors, who came here hoping to convalesce:

The real trouble started when Lowe began to get interested in the Oxford Movement. The movement was High Church in the extreme. Lowe's espousal of its cause led to such heinous crimes as his unilaterally introducing a Sunday evening service and collection after Holy Communion. This and other brazen displays of independence antagonized Veitch, and he sent a letter complaining about Lowe to the Foreign Office. In his turn, Lowe complained about Veitch to his own superior, the Bishop of London. Against all precedent, Lowe was not invited to the crucible of island power politics, the English Church AGM. But Veitch was in for a shock. Reports of his rampant adultery, complaints from important merchants whom he had antagonized and the rumour that he had addressed the deposed Napoleon as 'Your Majesty' had built up into a Foreign Office decision to dismiss him from his post. His place as Her Majesty's Consul was taken by Stoddard, Lowe's ally.

In 1843 Lowe went on leave to England, returning with a wife, Catherine Guerin, the daughter of a Somerset clergyman. The new Mrs Lowe found that half the British population of Funchal crossed to the other side of the street when she approached. Letters flew back and forth between Lord Palmerston, Bishop Blomfield, Lowe, Stoddard (whom Lowe had by now antagonized) and the group of disgruntled clergy. Formal complaints were lodged. Vicious pamphlets were printed. Unsuspecting new arrivals were collared by both sides as they stepped off the boat. The bishop continued to send separate replies to all the parties, with a (sometimes radically) different slant to his sympathy in each. Lowe's critics boycotted services (and from then on had to rely on secret reports from the pew-opener to fuel their objections). Lowe was presented with an eight-point indictment of his behaviour, which included the devastating complaint that he prayed with his back to the congregation, and copies were sent to the Bishop and Lord Palmerston.

The 1846 AGM passed a motion effectively sacking Lowe by stopping his stipend. Lowe's supporters claimed the vote was rigged (as indeed it was – only people who paid a £20 annual subscription could vote, and the Treasurer, who held sole sway over whether to accept subscriptions, was firmly in the anti-Lowe camp).

Supporters set up a fund in order to continue paying the chaplain. Each side began furiously to accuse the other of Schism. A desperate Blomfield roped in any fellow bishop who happened to be passing Madeira to mediate, but with no success.

Roger Gaskill
Brought hither by his mother for
restoration of his health, and
consigned by her to this foreign
grave on 9th March 1841 in
the 25th year of his age.

Near the gate that leads from the old to the new cemetery, under a simple stone cross, is a barely legible inscription to one Rev Richard Thomas Lowe and his wife, who went missing at sea in 1874. Today Lowe is best known for his authoritative books on

An Emergency General Meeting (with Lowe's supporters disenfranchised) passed a motion to submit a 'memorial' to Queen Victoria accusing Lowe of innovation and change.

It was Lord Palmerston's wisdom, however, that was set to grant relief. There had already been questions at Westminster about the 'un-Christian bickerings' in Madeira that were becoming 'a scandal to our Church'. Benjamin Disraeli, as leader of the Opposition, had demanded that all correspondence on the matter be put before the House. It is unlikely that Palmerston allowed himself to get into any more hot water by allowing the 'memorial' to reach the Queen. He sent a letter to Consul Stoddard that, in so many words, demanded that Lowe be sacked.

Bishop Blomfield was enraged. The chaplain on Madeira acted under his licence. Palmerston had upset one of those delicate balances of understanding and precedent that are the fabric of constitutionless British government. On 15 November 1847 a General Meeting held in Stoddard's house recommended the Reverend Thomas Kenworthy Brown for the chaplaincy. Palmerston immediately confirmed the appointment, and sent a letter dismissing Lowe. Bishop Bromfield refused to grant a licence, saying that Lowe was the only true representative of the Church of England on the island. When the Rev Mr Kenworthy Brown arrived to take up his post in 1848, Lowe hived off, together with his followers and six pieces of 18th-century communion plate, to establish a rival church. The new church, in a Gothic chamber of a mansion in the narrow Rua das Aranhas, became known as the Becco Church (after the Portuguese *beco*, meaning alley). Now Madeira really did have Schism – and so the situation remained until 1852 when Lowe finally resigned and went back to England, and the Bishop felt free to grant the Rev. Mr Brown a licence. Most of the Becco congregation trickled back to the English Church, but the Becco survived for another 45 years. It was only when it shut its doors for the last time, in April 1893, that the communion plate Lowe had taken with him was finally returned to the English Church. (The building that housed the Becco chapel was demolished in the 1980s.)

Lowe continued to visit Madeira, but only for natural history purposes. It was on one of these trips, in 1874, that he and his wife left Liverpool in the new steamship *Libreria*. The ship was never heard of again.

Madeira's flora and fauna, but there was a time when the mere mention of his name could send shudders down spines as far away as Whitehall, Westminster and (it is even whispered) Windsor. He was at the centre of a rumpus that began with the snide backbiting and petty rivalries of an insular expatriate community, and developed into the biggest scandal the Madeiran British have ever known (*see* pp.129–31).

The Seafront

Quinta Vigia and the Gardens

High on a bluff overlooking Funchal's waterfront is the pink Quinta Vigia, official residence of the island's president. Originally, the house was called Quinta das Angústias after the chapel of Nossa Senhora das Angústias (believed to have been the family chapel of a 17th-century *morgado*) around which it was built. The real Quinta Vigia was a short distance further west – a magnificent 19th-century mansion which in later years served as Funchal's casino. It was flattened (together with most of the surrounding garden) in the 1960s to make way for the ugly Carlton Park Hotel complex. In a fit of remorse the government restored the pink villa nearby and renamed it Quinta Vigia in 1982.

The *quinta* has a melancholy history. In the 1850s it was let to the Dowager Empress of Brazil, who came here in the hope of a cure for her only daughter, the Princess Maria Amélia. The young princess, who became a great favourite during her stay, died of consumption in 1853, aged only 22. People on the island were deeply affected by her death and, after the empress left, the *quinta* remained desolate and uninhabited for years.

Towards the end of the century the word went round that the house had been bought by the Comte de Lambert, an *aide-de-camp* to the Russian Empress. For a while it seemed as if the sad old house might live again, but the new arrival proved to be reclusive and depressed. The story goes that he had fallen out with a Russian general over an *affaire de cœur*. The two decided to draw lots, with the agreement that the loser would kill himself. The general lost and committed suicide, and the count was haunted by the belief that he was to blame. He came to Madeira, shut himself away in what became known as Quinta Lambert, and spent most of his time sitting on the veranda and staring out to sea.

The public are usually allowed in to look at the gardens and the chapel, though it is wise to check with the guard at the gate first (*adm free*). The **gardens** are lush, with til trees and giant camellias. Peacocks and parrots hop about in elegant aviaries, and there is a splendid view over the harbour. Car-lovers might like to wander to the far corner of the garden where, in a glass-doored garage, there is a 1930s Hudson Super 6 in mint condition. The **Capela de Nossa Senhora das Angústias**, which forms part of the main house, was virtually rebuilt in the 18th century. The marble altar is exquisitely inlaid with designs of flowers, butterflies and fruit. Blue and white *azulejos* depict saints and biblical stories. On one of the panels, St Francis turns from a meal of dead animals to bless a dog and a rather comically frightened cat at his feet.

Below the *quinta* stretch the **Santa Catarina Gardens**, with terraced walkways overlooking the bay, a children's playground with two ancient steam tractors, lovers' nooks and some giant Alice-in-Wonderland bird-cages and a refreshment kiosk. On Saturday afternoons fleets of cars with large bouquets on their bonnets come toot-tooting up the hill and spill out flouncy brides and their grooms for photographs.

The gardens get their name from the squat white **Capela de Santa Catarina** at the far end. Shut up and disused, the little chapel is on the site of one built in 1425 by Constança de Almeida, Zarco's wife. The present building you see here dates back mainly to the 17th century, but you can see a Manueline holy water bowl just outside the front portal.

On the landward side of the park, set in a beautiful garden off the Avenida do Infante, is the **Hospício Maria Amélia**. A heartbroken Empress of Brazil founded the hospice in memory of her daughter, but she could never bring herself to have anything more to do with it. Instead she asked her sister Josephine, Queen of Sweden, to administer the Trust – so both the Brazilian and Swedish royal coats of arms are to be seen above the entrance. If you are respectably dressed, and if there are not too many of you, you can ask one of the nuns at the door to direct you to the chapel. You'll find it past a grand salon, and up a sweeping wooden staircase. Inside is a beautiful marble Madonna donated by Emperor Maximilian of Mexico, who is said to have been in love with the young princess.

Forts and Fish

The **harbour**, which lies immediately below the gardens, is for the most part a busy container port. But around five o'clock in the evening, behind a shed beyond the containers, you can watch the brightly coloured fishing boats come in and unload the day's catch. Most of it is rushed off to hotels and markets, but you can try a little dock-side bargaining. Soon, though, the quay gets pretty gory as many fish are gutted on the spot, and ugly sharks are chopped up into bits.

On the far side of the harbour is the massive **Loo Rock** on which is perched the 17th-century fortress (nowadays inhabited by customs officers) that was built to protect ships in the bay – though was powerless against the storms that frequently dashed boats against the cliffs below. The Portuguese call the rock *Ilhéu da Pontinha* ('The Islet' or 'The Speck'). Dutch sailors changed *Ilhéu* to *Het Leeuw* ('The Lion'), which in English became The Loo. A tunnel through the rock leads on to a pier built in the 1930s. It's a long walk to the end, but the view you get of Funchal, especially at night, makes a good second-best to arriving by boat.

Along the Esplanade

Steps lead down from in front of the Capela de Santa Catarina on to the **Avenida do Mar** (recently officially changed to the Avenida das Comunidades Madeirenses, but nobody takes much notice). Cars and buses thunder in both directions, but the esplanade has a wide, shady pavement along which tourists and locals saunter day and night. Along its length are quaint green kiosks with oriental domes. Some are news-stands, others small bars that spawn clusters of white wrought-iron furniture and are a favourite meeting place of the Funchalese. Below the level of the street, yachts nudge each other gently in the **marina** – which is lined with restaurants and cafés. A long stone pier takes the strollers out to sea and back again. Beyond it lies a gnarled, rocky and uninviting beach. In the warm Madeiran evenings the street umbrellas fold up like daisies, young couples cuddle on the sea wall and friends and families walk up and down the pier, then gradually fill up the cafés.

Above the marina, across the esplanade, is the **Casa do Turista**, a souvenir shop that is not nearly as awful as the name might lead you to expect. Once this was the home of the German consul. Many of the original fittings, including the moulded ceilings, are still intact. The pebbled arches that once surrounded the garden have been converted into wine-shelves, and a servant's room has been restored and filled with period furniture. On the roof terrace there is a reconstruction of an old *venda* – the tiny shop-cum-bar that is still the centre of social life in many villages on the island. Prices here are not inflated, so it is a good place to gift-hunt.

A few yards further on you come to the **Palácio de São Lourenço**, the sturdy white fortress that was Funchal's first defensive building. Construction began in the first part of the 16th century, but improvements and additions continued to be made up until the 19th century. The turret on the east side is part of the original Manueline design, but most of the southern façade dates from the 18th century, when the fortress was converted into a palace for the military commander (which is still its function today). Around the back of the fort is the entrance to a small **museum** (*open daily 10–12 and 2–6; adm free*), where the history of the building is traced, largely through prints and photographs. There are also pictures of some important visitors, including shots of President Amérigo Tomás and Prime Minister Marcelo Caetano, who spent a night here on their way to exile in Brazil after the 1974 revolution.

Across the way from the fortress, moored alongside the pier, is the **Beatles' Boat**. The *Vagrant*, a 36-metre-long luxury yacht, was built in the USA in 1941 for the millionaire Horace Vanderbilt. In 1966 the Beatles bought it, and later it was owned by the pop singer Donovan and a Greek shipping magnate, before running aground in the Canaries in 1977. Two years later it was bought by a Madeiran businessman, João Bartolomeu de Faria, who in 1982 moored it here and refurbished it as a café and restaurant, a feat for which the government honoured him with the coveted Golden Strelitzia award. It is surrounded by little canopied lifeboats, each with its own table and concreted down in 15 centimetres of water – an exercise in seaside kitsch that is irresistible.

At the entrance to the Beatles' Boat is the **Monument to the Madeiran Emigrant**. For centuries impoverished Madeirans have left their island to seek their fortunes elsewhere – mainly in the West Indies, the USA, Jersey, Britain and South Africa. Money would be sent home to a needy family, and often the emigrants themselves would return, snappily dressed and with a new car and money enough to build an impressively large house and start a business. Some of them made quite a mark. Joe 'Gold' Berado amassed a fortune in South Africa by using modern technology to re-sift old mine-dumps, extracting tons of gold that earlier methods had left behind.

Today he is rumoured to be one of the richest men in the world, has returned to Madeira, opened the Monte Palace Gardens (*see* p.142) and set up a foundation for the protection of the island's environment.

Madeira used to be rather proud of its emigrants – hence the statue – but things are beginning to change. A deep resentment is mounting against returnees who build ostentatious houses and are seen as taking up jobs (rather than creating them, which is more likely to be the case). Since the abolition of apartheid, thousands of Madeirans have returned from South Africa, fearing black reprisal. (The white Portuguese community had a bad name among black South Africans for being harsh and inconsiderate employers.) There are frequent reports in the local press of murders of Madeirans in South Africa. The islanders are understandably jumpy – if all the Madeirans in South Africa were to return, they would outnumber the local population by two to one. Many returnees find that they are given a hard time in their old villages. Local objection and petty officialdom lay obstacles against the returnees' attempts to start a business. Younger South African Madeirans (many of whom were born abroad and speak Portuguese with an identifiable accent) complain of local unfriendliness, and the ex-South African community tends to stick together.

A few metres further on from the Emigrant statue is a circular stump of stone, some three metres high. This is all that remains of **Banger's Tower**. In 1798 John Light Banger put up a tower. It was thirty metres high and three metres in diameter, made of blocks of red basalt from Cabo Girão, and cost a hefty £1,350. A crane and a system of pulleys on top helped swing merchandise from ship to shore (there was no proper harbour at the time). But some years later violent storms brought boulders crashing down the rivers. The debris extended the beach so far that Banger's Tower was left isolated and useless. Later it was bought by the Blandy family and used to signal to their warehouses what merchandise was aboard newly arrived ships, so that the foremen could prepare to receive the goods. For years the tower was a Funchal landmark, and there was enormous protest in 1939 when the government pulled it down to build the Avenida do Mar. The ruin you see today was built out of stones from the tower's foundations, unearthed in 1987, a short distance from the original site.

Back on the landward side of the road is the **Old Customs House** (Alfândega), now the seat of Madeira's parliament, and (to borrow a British Royal phrase) grotesquely disfigured by a carbuncle of modern architecture attached to its front façade. Most of the building dates back to the end of the 15th century, and, though it has undergone several facelifts, luckily none has been so drastically destructive to the tone of the building as the last. There is a ground-floor hall with handsome Gothic arches (which you can see by peering in through the window), but unfortunately you are not allowed upstairs to see a carved ceiling reputed to be one of the finest in Portugal. Around the back of the building, on the left-hand corner, there is a reassuringly small-scale, unmodernized Manueline doorway.

After this the Avenida do Mar becomes less interesting, leading, in succession, to the city sewage works and the Old Town.

The Old Town

You can reach the Old Town (*Zona Velha*) along the Avenida do Mar, but the approach from the centre of town, along Rua Dr Fernão Ornelas, is more attractive. Buses 2 and 12 run along the Avenida and will drop you near the market.

Madonnas and Markets

Rua Dr Fernão Ornelas starts with a small three-sided *praça*, the **Largo do Phelps**, named after Elizabeth Phelps, the daughter of a British wine merchant. Her early efforts with local women started the Madeiran embroidery industry rolling in the 1850s (*see* p.49). A little knot of flower-sellers sits tight in the triangle of traffic.

At the far end of the *praça* is the **Carmo Church**, built in the 17th century for an order of Carmelite monks, though much remodelled since. Even in the context of a heavily gilded Baroque interior, the high altar stands out, encrusted with cherubs, diverse saints, fronds, drapes and swirls. The nave is lined with modern *azulejos*, but there are some fine examples of 18th-century picture-tiles in the chancel. Here too you will find the tomb of the illustrious Conde de Carvalhal (*see* p.145).

Rua Dr Fernão Ornelas is one of Funchal's busiest shopping streets. Workaday supermarkets and furniture stores rub shoulders with quaint apothecaries and grocery shops – still with 19th-century wooden interiors, personal service and the odd staff member who looks as if he has been there from day one. Poke about here and you could come away with a metre-high plastic madonna, bottles of sticky-sweet island liqueurs, or one of the terracotta doves that decorate the roofs of houses on the island. On the street corners farmers sit behind conical baskets of fruit, and peasant women sell bunches of obscure herbs and berries. One old man has a large box of *barretes de lã* (Madeiran woolly hats). At lunchtime he simply turns the cardboard price tag face down, and heads off to a local café.

At its lower end, the street crosses the **Ribeira de João Gomes**. Like most of Funchal's rivers this is little more than a malodorous trickle. It seems odd that the town council should have built walls 12m high to contain it, but sudden storms in the interior can turn the river into a raging torrent of chocolate-coloured water that brings huge boulders crashing down to the sea. From time to time Funchal is ravaged by floods. In October 1993 the water rose so high that it swept over the bridges. In 1803, in one of the biggest deluges ever, 400 people lost their lives and the home of the English Tatlock family (who were having a dinner party at the time) was washed out to sea in its entirety, where, every window ablaze with light, it went down like a large ocean liner.

Across the river is the **Mercado dos Lavradores**, the Farmers' Market. Designed in the late 1930s by Edmundo Tavares, one of Portugal's leading modern architects, the market has strong Art Deco lines together with local touches, such as an echo of a *torre-mirante*. Two storeys of arcades run around a central courtyard. The court is crammed with stalls selling grapes and guavas, passion fruit, oranges and mounds of bananas, familiar fruits such as apples and pears, and strangely shaped, luridly coloured exotica. A heady mix of fragrances wafts across from the flower stalls.

Sturdy young lads hump conical baskets piled high with produce from the lorries outside, old men vend lottery tickets pinned to opened umbrellas, bakers' assistants wheel baskets of bread, emitting puffs of flour-smoke as they walk. In the covered shops around the edge you can buy wicker, wine, handmade boots, embroidered bags and any amount of tourist tat. There is more fruit and veg upstairs, and it is a little cheaper. In one corner there is a stall laden with fresh and dried herbs, where the stallholder gives advice on cures as well as cooking. Doors lead from the far end of the market to the **fish market**, where fishmongers wielding machetes chop huge tuna fish into manageable steaks. Long, black, evil-looking *espada* lie draped over the stone slabs alongside clusters of bright-eyed orange, silver and metallic blue fish, just a few hours out of the sea.

Rua da Boa Viagem leads down behind the market towards the sea. On the way you pass the tiny **Capela de Nossa Senhora da Redenção**, built in 1683, but now derelict. Its most recent incarnation was as a grocery store. As you get to Rua Dom Carlos I, you find an **open-air market** where you can buy anything from fruit to *fado* tapes or enormous pairs of bloomers.

A few yards further on, at No.14, is the headquarters of **Clube Sport Marítimo**, one of the island's oldest and most successful football teams. In the museum (*open Mon–Fri 10–12.30 and 2.30–5; adm free*) there is case upon case of glittering trophies, from a thimble to a 2m-high creation in chrome, including elephant tusks and some expertly crafted silverware from the first part of the 20th century.

Across the way is the **Electricity Museum** (*open Tues–Fri 10–12.30 and 2–6; adm €2*), which with its rows of antique street lamps and ancient, working generators is far more interesting than one might expect.

Cobbles and Cafés

To the east of the market, the Old Town proper starts. Isabella de França complained that the *Zona Velha* was 'a perfect rookery', and the stretch of seedy bars along the first part of **Rua Dom Carlos I** would seem to bear her out. Hard times in the fishing industry have left large numbers of middle-aged men disconsolate and unemployed, and alcoholism is a severe problem on the island. Unshaven, bleary-eyed men tumble out of narrow doorways and the occasional bored streetwalker leans up against a wall – but there is no danger to the passer-by, and soon the bars give way to more upmarket cafés and restaurants; the tastiest food in Funchal is to be had in the Old Town. Since the late 1990s this part of the Old Town has been undergoing extensive renovation, emerging from crumbling neglect with a new smart mantle. A large hotel has appeared on what was a derelict patch of land on the seashore, its *faux* traditional architecture and modest four-storey height just about excusing its presence.

More controversially, the Old Town is the site of a new **cable car** (*between Rua Dom Carlos I and Avenida do Mar; operating daily 10–6, last boarding 5.45, upward trip €8, round trip €13*) that takes you up to Monte (*see* p.142). It offers magnificent views as you swing up over the rooftops, then the treetops, and Funchal's traffic noise gives way to clean, cool air, silence and the odd bird twitter. But the people who live along the route, whose once private apartments and garden terraces can now be peered into by tourists passing just feet away in plastic bubbles, are not at all happy with the innovation.

Back down in the Old Town, a little way along Rua Dom Carlos I, motor traffic stops and you find yourself walking on sharp cobbles. This is where the 15th-century settlers first built their village, and some of the houses here are very old indeed. The most ancient – tiny, single-storey dwellings with red (rather than grey) basalt around the windows – probably date back to this first settlement. Many of them are being taken over as workshops and studios. In one, an artist churns out saints and madonnas for local churches; in another, a cabinet-maker planes and polishes, restoring heavy, antique island furniture. At Barros & Abreu (No.20–22) a cobbler makes solid, traditional *botas*. But the Old Town is by no means twee. It is one of the poorest parts of Funchal. Whole families live crammed into some of the cute one-roomed houses, and the larger 18th- and 19th-century buildings may be home to dozens. At night you can see through the open shutters into small front rooms, almost entirely taken up by a big TV.

Soon after you start treading the cobbles you come to the **Capela do Corpo Santo**. A simple 16th-century church with a Manueline doorway, it was built by local fishermen in honour of their patron saint, São Pedro Gonçalves. Bulging from the first floor of the wall of the house next door like a giant pair of brick buttocks are two of the wood-burning ovens that were built into the kitchens of many Madeiran 18th- and 19th-century homes.

Beyond the church, through an obstacle course of Madeiran dogs (brindle mutts with sickle-shaped tails, who spend most of their lives sleeping, then wake up to snap at your ankles), you reach the **Fortaleza de São Tiago** (*open Mon–Fri 10–12.30 and 2–5.30; adm to fort free, to exhibitions €2*). Begun in 1614, the fortress was extended in the 18th century. This is the one fort in Funchal that you can roam about freely, climbing up narrow stairs and wandering along arched passages, standing on windy ramparts and staring out to sea through the narrow windows of sentinels' towers. The fortress houses a contemporary art museum, with a small, but in parts surprisingly good, display of Portuguese art since the 1960s.

The narrow **Travessa do Forte** winds up the side of the fort. At times no wider than a doorway, it is strung with washing and lined with pot plants. Canaries in cages hang out of upstairs windows, and ancient wizened women sit gossiping on their front steps. If wandering up narrow alleys in strange towns doesn't appeal to you, then take the wider **Rampe do Forte**. Both deposit you on **Rua de Santa Maria** where, a short walk to the right, you'll find the **Socorro Church**, a stately Baroque church that was built on the site of a chapel put up to commemorate victims of the 1523 plague.

Opposite the church is the **Barreirinha** municipal swimming complex. A lift takes you down through the equivalent of five storeys to the swimming jetty at the foot of the cliff (*see* 'Sports and Activities', p.98). From the upper terraces you can see the wreck of the *Zarco*, a cargo ship that was washed up on to the rocks during a storm in the late 1980s.

Rua de Santa Maria, the oldest street in Funchal, will lead you back towards the market. On the way poke your head in at the wine lodge at No.273. There is no fancy labelling or hype here; this is an old family business that makes the sort of wine that fills the bottles in souvenir shops and the barrels from which some restaurants dispense complimentary glasses to customers. If they're not too busy, they will let you have a look around, taste some wine and buy a bottle or two. A little further down, at No.237, is the **Madeiran Hat Factory**, a shop-cum-workshop where you can watch someone weaving straw boaters, sewing the odd spiky blue skull-caps of the traditional costume, or embroidering designs on handbags. On **Rua dos Barreiros**, which crosses Rua de Santa Maria a little way further on, there is a rare, if somewhat decrepit, example of a domestic Manueline doorway (at No.31).

As Rua de Santa Maria nears the market, it gets narrow and a bit pongy, so you might prefer to duck down one of the side-streets and make your way back into town along the esplanade.

Tourist Town

The western part of Funchal is so thick with hotels that it is called the *Zona Hoteleira* ('Hotel Town'). Thundering through the middle of them, the **Avenida do Infante** becomes the **Estrada Monumental**, one of the busiest, noisest and most polluted roads on the island. First along the route is the gargantuan **Carlton Park** hotel, a casino, hotel and conference complex designed in the 1970s by Oscar Niemeyer, the Brazilian architect who is also to blame for the city of Brasília (*see* 'Where to Stay', p.100). One of the most sumptuous *quintas* on the island and acres of beautiful gardens bit the dust to make way for this concrete monstrosity.

Behind the hotel, **Rua Imperatriz D. Amélia** preserves some older buildings and gives you a faint taste of what this end of the city was like before developers got hold of it. Down the narrow **Rua Penha** you come to the little **Capela da Penha de França**, built in 1622 and revamped in 1712. The chapel belonged to the nearby Quinta da Penha de França, at one time the summer residence of the Bishop of Funchal. Roman Catholic services in English are held here on Sunday mornings (*see* p.89).

Beyond the Carlton Park the Estrada Monumental crosses a ravine, lush with flowering trees and plants. On the other side, set in five acres of garden on a promontory 50m above the sea, is **Reid's Hotel** (*see* p.99). Reid's is a classic, set in that constellation of hotels that includes Raffles in Singapore, the Savoy in London and Shepheard's in Cairo. It was built by William Reid, a Scot who had come to Madeira in 1836 to seek his fortune. He was 14 when he arrived and he had £5 in his pocket. After a spell as a baker's boy he ventured into the wine trade, did well for himself and started to manage and let *quintas* to visitors. Later he expanded into the hotel trade and began to dream of a truly luxurious island hotel. He had his eye on a promontory to the west of Funchal, but there was already a *quinta* there belonging to Dr Michael Grabham (*see* p.163). In 1887 Reid bought the *quinta* and set to work. Sadly, he died before the hotel was completed, and it was his sons, Willy and Alfred, who stood at the door to shake the hands of the first guests in 1891. In 1937 the hotel was bought by the Blandy family, who recently sold it to Orient Express.

Tarnished Gold

Reid's most distinguished guests sign their names in the hotel's *Golden Book*. Slipped in between the princes, prime ministers and philosophers are a few names whose eligibility for the list is undeniable, but whose qualifications may seem a little dubious. Ian Smith, Prime Minister of Rhodesia after the unilateral declaration of independence, is there, as is his neighbour Pik Botha, erstwhile South African Minister of Foreign Affairs. General Batista fled here after the Cuban revolution. He was not the first deposed ruler to come to Reid's. In 1921 the exiled Emperor Karl I of Austria sought refuge in Madeira. Reid's hotel bills proved too steep, and he moved out with his family to a *quinta* in the hills. He died there a few months later at the age of 35 and is buried in the church at Monte (*see* p.142).

In 1891 one of Karl's predecessors, the beautiful, tragic 'Sisi', Empress Elizabeth of Austria, made her second visit to Madeira and stayed at Reid's. Sisi was a sort of 19th-century Princess Diana. Married to her cousin, Emperor Franz Josef of Austria, her life at court was made hell by her mother-in-law, the domineering Duchess Sophie. Publicly, Sisi was wildly popular. Privately she began to put herself through punishing fasts. Soon the 1.72m-high empress weighed just 50kg and had a waist measurement of 50cm. She developed fevers and coughs which disappeared the moment she was away from Vienna, her husband and her mother-in-law. It was on one of these rest cures that she first came to Madeira in 1861. She locked herself up in Quinta Vigia and spent most of the time crying and complaining about how dull the island was. In 1886 another cousin, and her closest friend, King Ludwig II of Bavaria ('Mad King Ludwig') drowned in mysterious circumstances, and three years later her son and his mistress were found naked and dead in an apparent joint suicide. From then on Sisi

The hotel breathes wealth and (with every bit of meaning with which the British can endow the word) class. Winston Churchill has stayed here, and George Bernard Shaw; also Sacheverell Sitwell, Lloyd George and members of most of the royal families of Europe. Afternoon tea, English-style, is an institution. Part of the dining room is reserved, by tacit understanding, for British peers of the realm. Stalwarts winter here year after year, staying in the same room and eating at the same table. Changes in décor can put regulars in a proprietorial huff. But great changes are afoot. At one time it seemed as if the Reid's guest list was drawn up on the principle that if you weren't British, you had to be royal. After some years of dwindling occupancy the hotel is now looking to a wider Europe and a younger market. It remains to be seen whether this will change its style. ('Too many bloody Bosch about,' harrumphed one pink colonel beside the pool; others complain of the behaviour of Russian *nouveaux-riches*.)

Inland from Reid's, up Rua do Dr Pita, is the **Quinta Magnolia**. Formerly the British Country Club, this too has been opened to the masses (*see* p.99).

Continuing along the Estrada Monumental after Reid's, you come to the **Barbeito Wine Lodge** (*open 9–1 and 2–5.30*) where you can see women bottling wine in wicker-covered flagons. There is also a small tasting room. The Estrada leads on through the heart of the *Zona Hoteleira* to the municipal **Lido** and some less-frequented natural **rock pools** (*see* p.99).

wore only black, and it was a melancholy figure who made an appearance each morning on her veranda at Reid's to acknowledge a royal salute. On 10 September 1898, while she was taking an evening walk, heavily veiled, she was fatally stabbed by an Italian anarchist who had mistaken her for somebody else.

Ex-King Umberto of Italy visited the hotel in 1965. Also a guest at the time was an American woman who had married into the Grimaldi family and was desperate to meet the ex-king. The hotel staff decided that her social standing did not warrant an introduction and discreetly foiled her every attempt. She had her revenge. The night before she left the hotel, she crept around gathering all the shoes that had been left out in the corridors for cleaning, and left them in a pile on the lawn.

Another titled lady much known for her errant ways was the thrice-married Lady Docker, wife of the industrialist Sir Bernard Docker and easily identifiable in London by her gold-plated Daimler with zebra-patterned seats. Her behaviour had resulted in the couple being banned from Monaco (and consequently the French Riviera). An irritating little contretemps with a customs officer had made Italy a no-go area as well, so the couple began to frequent Madeira, anchoring their yacht offshore and dining at Reid's.

Not in the *Golden Book*, but even more fêted in the press than Lady Docker, was Dr John Adams. His *Times* obituary styled him 'the classic enigma of the history of mass killing'. Over 130 old ladies to whom the doctor had prescribed morphine and heroin had left him money in their wills and died soon afterwards. Dr Adams was arrested in 1956 after one such death, but the judge refused to admit evidence about his other patients and he was acquitted. His holiday at Reid's was part of the post-trial celebration.

One of the more admirable features of the building boom that has shaken Funchal over the past few years is the laying out of a seaside **promenade** running all the way from the Lido to Praia Formosa in the east. Previously, the only way for pedestrians to get about was along the noisy, fuggy Estrada Monumental, but now it is possible to take a leisurely stroll on a walkway atop the rocks along the shore, far from traffic. At its far end the promenade plunges down a stairway, past fishermen's huts and disappears into a tunnel – built in 1939 as part of the island's defences, and now with piped classical music to compete with the thundering sea – to emerge on the rocky **Praia Formosa** beach (*see* p.99).

As an interesting alternative route back into town, walk past the Quinta Magnolia and take the path down the side of its grounds, past the small **British School**. After a steep descent into the ravine you pass through a small banana plantation, then up cobbled steps and across the Avenida Luís Camões to **Rua dos Ilhéus**, where through garden gates and over the tops of walls you can glimpse some grand old Funchal *quintas*. From the end of the street you get an excellent view of **Fortaleza do Pico**, the massive stone fortress that seems to grow out of a rock above the city. Built by the Spanish when Portugal was part of their empire, it was finished in 1632. Today it is a military transmitting station and is not open to the public.

Around Funchal

Just a few minutes' car or bus ride from the centre you'll find Funchal's most beautiful gardens. A little further inland you come to some of the most dramatic scenery on the island.

Monte

Cable car, see p.137, bus 20, 21 or 84 to Monte, or bus 22 to Capela da Conceiçâo.

In the cool, clean air 600 metres above sea level, some 6km from the centre of Funchal, is the suburb of Monte (). The twin towers of the **Nossa Senhora do Monte** are visible from all over town. The 18th-century church is built on the site of a 15th-century chapel, put up by the first person born on Madeira (who was appropriately called Adam). Each year on 15 August faithful penitents climb the 74 steps up to the church on their knees. The object of this somewhat painful pilgrimage is a diminutive doll, swathed in fine cloth. The story goes that in the 15th century a young shepherd girl claimed that a mysterious friend came to play with her on the mountainside at nearby Terreiro da Luta. Her sceptical father decided to spy on her. He didn't see the imaginary friend, but he did find a small sculpture of the Virgin. It is this small image, said to have miraculous powers, that is the object of such veneration. Today it has pride of place on the high altar. Covered in flags and trinkets in a side chapel is the tomb of the ex-Emperor Karl I of Austria, who died at a *quinta* in Monte soon after his exile to Madeira in 1921.

To one side of the church is a large shady **square**, complete with 19th-century bandstand. Monte has long been a fashionable destination for jaunts out of Funchal. From 1894 a rack-and-pinion railway brought picnic-parties up from the city, but it was closed down after an accident in 1939 (*see* box, over). You can still see the station on one side of the square, and the remains of a railway bridge arch delicately over the gardens below. One old mode of transport that still does exist is the **toboggans** (*see* over). These leave from the foot of the church stairs and (guided by able drivers) slide down over the cobbles to Livramento in the upper reaches of Funchal (*€10 per person*).

The Monte church is surrounded by beautiful gardens. Below the square is the **Parque do Monte** (*unlimited access*). A cobbled path zigzags under the arches of the old railway bridge through terraces of flowers and tree ferns down to a stream.

The magnificent **Monte Palace Tropical Garden** (*entrance around the corner from the toboggans; open daily 9–6; adm €7.50*) stretches for 7 hectares around the old Monte Palace Hotel. When he returned to Madeira, Joe Berado (*see* pp.134–5) bought the old hotel as a home and has filled the garden with indigenous flowers, orchids, proteas, ferns and heathers. He has collected together more cycads (a rare prehistorical tree fern from southern Africa) than can be found in one spot anywhere on the globe. Dotted around the gardens you'll see giant crystals, classical statues, walls with *azulejos* and arches from old gardens and homes. There is also an Oriental Garden and a Koi carp pond.

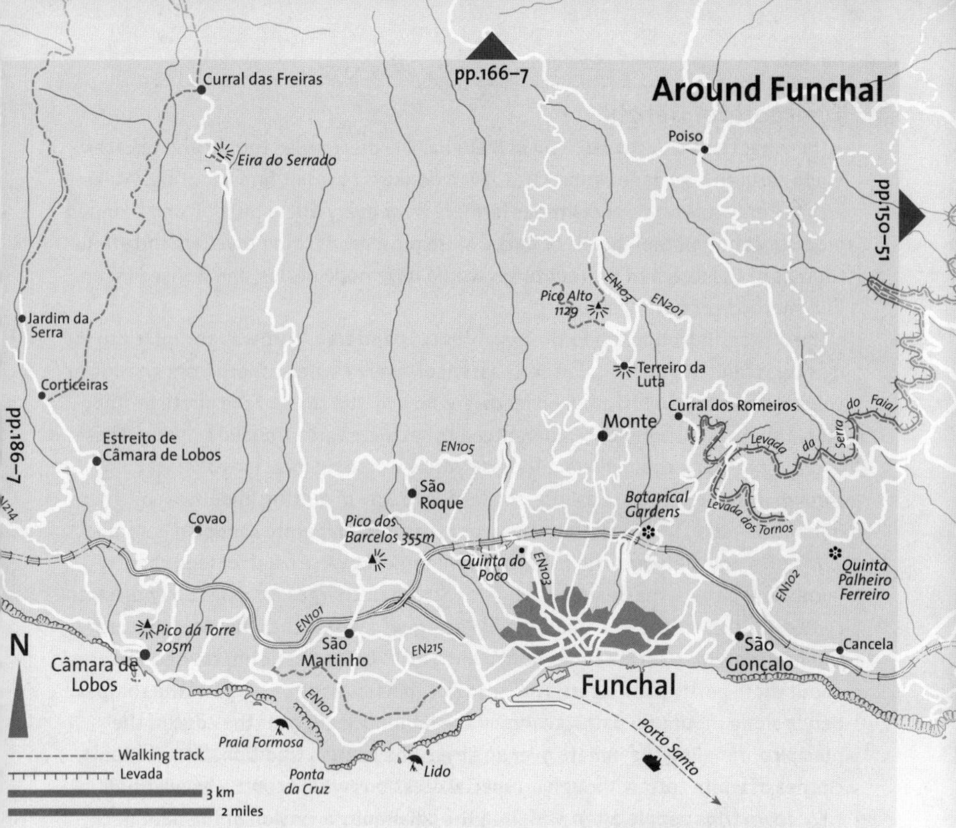

A little way past the entrance to these gardens, on a square of its own, is the 18th-century **Capela da Conceição** which has an altar panel of inlaid coloured ivory taken from the old Franciscan convent in Funchal.

Halfway between Funchal and Monte, the **Quinta do Poço** is, in fact, a municipal nursery. It has a terrace with a fine view over the town and a café-kiosk.

More Gardens

The **Botanical Gardens** (*open daily 9–6; adm €1.50*) were created in the 1960s in the grounds of the Quinta do Bom Sucesso, overlooking the town. (*It's a steep and exhausting walk, but bus 29, 30 or 31 will get you there in around 10 minutes.*) Most of the plants are indigenous or come from the Azores, the Canaries or the Cape Verde Islands, with an exceptionally good collection of cacti. There is ample shade along the paths that climb up through the garden terraces, and many a spectacular view of Funchal. The *quinta* itself is now a **Natural History Museum** (*open Mon–Sat 9–12.30 and 2–5.30; adm included in garden ticket*) where you can see a thick, twisted trunk of tree heather that was covered in burning lava over 10 million years ago. The rest of the museum contains a (literally) colourless collection of dried plants, stuffed birds and bottled crustaceans and spiders.

Transports of Delight

The wheel was slow to catch on in Madeira. The precipitous terrain and terraces made carts and carriages impractical. Even donkeys couldn't find a footing. Walking was the only solution. For centuries farmers went everywhere on foot, and humped produce about on their heads or backs. More prosperous town-dwellers and effete tourists of the 18th and 19th centuries would have none of this, and devised ingenious methods of getting about.

The visitors' introduction to the novelties of island transport was abrupt. Until the quay was built at Funchal, alarmed passengers were carried ashore from arriving ships by 'swarthy and half-naked fellows' who had 'the cross of the pirate or smuggler in them' – an experience guaranteed to set Victorian adrenalin running. Those awaiting carriage could distract themselves by watching local lads dive for coins thrown into the sea. Once ashore, the favourite way of getting about was by **hammock** (*rede*). Two local stalwarts would carry an elaborate canopied hammock slung on a pole between their shoulders. Hammocks were used for long country jaunts and picnics, the bearers having to carry their charges for miles on end. A 19th-century British visitor who understood Portuguese writes that the men 'cheered themselves with a sort of rude chant' which included sarcastic improvised verses about more portly passengers. They also got their revenge on some of the sharper bends along mountain paths, swinging the hammock out over the edge of the precipice, dangling the inmate over an abyss. The bearers traditionally wore cool clothes of white cotton, though on special occasions would sport a heavier twill.

For town trips people often preferred the **palanquin**, a version of the hammock with a metal frame. The transport was not always sedate. A visitor in 1825 witnessed sailors on shore-leave racing in hammocks and overtaking one another on corners.

In 1848 one Major Buckley was faced with a problem. He had a somewhat sturdy wife, and her long-suffering hammock men were threatening mutiny. So he invented the **bullock cart** (*carro de bois*), a sled with a canopy and basket chairs, pulled by strong young oxen. The sled runners went more easily over Funchal's sharp cobbles than did wheels. A boy walked ahead, guiding the animal by means of a cord tied to its horns. Others yelled and goaded the animal on, prodding it with sticks, while still more trotted alongside, slipping squishy cactus under the cart to keep it sliding easily. Bullock carts were finally banned in the 1980s because they held up the traffic.

One odd form of transport still in use is the **toboggan** (*carro de cesto*). Two-seater toboggans, deftly controlled by a pair of toboggan men who run alongside, hit downhill speeds of 10kph. Since 1860 these toboggans have been making the journey from Monte down to Funchal. They are still popular with tourists and not nearly as frightening as the same journey in a city bus. At one time you could also travel from Monte on a **rack-and-pinion railway**. The railway opened in 1893 and was tremendously popular, but the drop-off in tourism to the island during the First World War resulted in a massive hike in prices, and in 1919 a boiler exploded, killing four. The rail company went bankrupt and the rolling stock was sold as scrap. The tracks were dismantled in 1943, when they were shipped back to England to be made into weapons.

Just below the Botanical Gardens, the **Jardim dos Loiros** (*open daily 9–6; adm €1.50*) contains not plants but gaudy tropical birds. There is an exceptionally good array of lories, parrots, parakeets and macaws to dazzle the eyes. Have a look for the Scheepmaker's Pigeon, almost the size of a peacock, with a showy feathery crest.

Signposts lead on to the **Jardim Orquídea** (Rua Pita da Silva 37; *open daily 9–6; adm €3.25*), about 15 minutes' walk further down the hill. Wild orchids and hybrids are grown under laboratory conditions, then transferred out to the small terraces and greenhouses. There are rare varieties from China, bright Madeiran blooms, simple, delicate flowers and strange breeds that look more like exotic insects than plants. At the end of your visit you can buy an orchid growing in a bottle to take home.

There are more orchids to be found at **Quinta Boa Vista** (Rua Luís Figueiroa de Albuquerque; *open Mon–Sat 9–6, adm €1.50; bus 39 or 34*), the home, with four acres of garden, of the ex-British consul Sir Cecil Garton and his wife Betty, who is an orchid breeder of international repute. Terrace upon terrace of orchids and other tropical plants make the gardens worth the climb, even if you're not a botanical expert.

A little further out of town is the **Quinta Palheiro Ferreiro** (*open Mon–Fri 10–12.30; adm €4.50; bus 36*). Built at the end of the 18th century as a country home for the Conde de Carvalhal, the *quinta* was bought by the Blandy family in 1885 and has arguably the most magnificent garden on the island. The Conde had to flee to England during the Miguelite revolution and when he returned he bought a wilder, more English idea of landscaping to his formal grounds. A century later Mildred Blandy, an avid and creative gardener, added protea and other plants from her native South Africa. Today oaks and chestnuts grow alongside flowering trees and semi-tropical plants. From November to April the camellia trees (some over 10m high) come out in bloom, while in one corner of the garden the Ribeiro do Inferno, a dank hollow full of giant ferns, has an eerie prehistoric atmosphere. Many of the plants are extremely rare; others might be familiar to you from front rooms and conservatories – only here they are ten times the size.

Before you leave, have a look at the **chapel**, a Baroque building with a stucco ceiling. It is said that it was positioned so that the Conde could watch the priest performing Mass from the comfort of his veranda. An inveterate gambler, the count used to creep away to an octagonal hideaway in the forest to play cards well into the night (it is still there, though now it forms part of the Palheiro Golf Course).

Curral das Freiras

The ravine of Curral das Freiras is an easy excursion from Funchal (*bus 81, or 15km/45mins' drive northwest along the 203*). HN Coleridge, nephew of the poet and a seasoned explorer, enthuses that the Curral is 'perhaps one of the great sights of the world', and a 19th-century guidebook frankly admits that 'though often a theme for the traveller's pen, its grandeur remains untold'. If you make no other trip from Funchal, try at least to see the Great Curral.

Walks

These are suggestions for walks you can follow, not a detailed guide to the routes. It essential to go properly equipped and to take a good map with you (*see* pp.57–9).

Levada dos Tornos

Easy. 1½ hours.

Over 100km (60 miles) long, the Levada dos Tornos (built 1966) is not only one of Madeira's most important *levadas*, but also one of its most popular walks. The main reason for this is that it is within quick reach of Funchal, and parts of it are flat and very easy going. This walk is really a quiet stroll – but the extension mentioned below can make it more challenging.

Join the *levada* outside the village of Curral dos Romeiros (city bus 29), and turn to the right. Just amble along the *levada*. You pass through forests and get good views over Funchal. After about half an hour you come to the Quinta do Pomar, which has a little chapel in the trees with a terrace lined with *azulejos*. At one point, towards the end of the walk, you need to cross the main road, and shortly afterwards a sign points down to the Jasmine Tea House (*see* 'Eating Out', p.109), where you can sit back and enjoy lunch or afternoon tea. The gardens of Palheiro Ferreiro (*see* p.145) are another ten minutes down the hill, but they close at 12.30, so if you want to include them in the outing you'll have to leave early or do the walk in reverse.

Bus 36, 37 or 47 take you back into town.

Monte–Levada dos Tornos–Jasmine Tea House

Difficult. 2hrs. Optional tunnel (add 1hr).

This will spice up the Levada dos Tornos walk considerably. Take city bus 22 to Monte, and get out at the terminus, Largo das Babosas. A stone path leads down into the ravine. A short way down, a sand path branches left to join the Levada dos Tornos at the entrance to one of its many tunnels. (You could pop through the tunnel – allow at least 20mins each way. At the end is a lush cauldron of green, a little waterfall and an old stone bridge.) Alternatively, turn right on to the *levada*. For much of the way it

The valley gets its name (which translates literally as 'The Nun's Corral') because it was to here that the sisters of the Santa Clara convent fled in 1566, to escape the ferocity of the repeated pirate raids on Funchal. Today there is a hamlet at the spot where they settled, a smudge in a hollow between almost perpendicular mountains. These curved, precipitous cliffs led geologists to believe for many years that the Curral das Freiras was an extinct volcanic crater, though now the theory is that the gigantic cauldron was caused by erosion. For centuries these high walls made a natural fortress that kept out not only pirates, but nearly everyone else. It was only in 1959 that a road was built to the village. Even today, as you sit at the café on the square, locals eye you with a faint surprise tinged with mistrust – rather as if you had just fallen from the heavens.

hugs the wall of the ravine. There are no railings and you've only the narrow *levada* wall to walk along. There is a dizzy drop on one side, and a cliff on the other – over which small waterfalls cascade on to your head. You reach Curral dos Romeiros after half an hour. Here the *levada* disappears for a while, but you can pick it up again on the other side of the village. Then follow the 'Levada dos Tornos' walk above.

Corticeiras–Curral das Freiras

Difficult. 3½hrs.

This is one of Madeira's musts. Doing the walk this way round is not only easier, but – as you are descending rather than climbing – gives you more leisure to appreciate the view. Walking in the other direction, from Curral das Freiras to Corticeiras, is for the stalwart and exceptionally fit only. The climbs are so steep that your whole body will be (quite literally) steaming by the time you reach the thin, cool air at the top of the ravine. But you are compensated for all these travails if your first view of the Curral has been the shocking, sudden vista that opens before you as you emerge from the road tunnel (*see* above). If you do tackle the walk in reverse, allow at least another hour.

Bus 96 takes you past Câmara de Lobos to the tiny village of Corticeiras. Take the road below the school on the outskirts of the village and bear left past the Quinta Mis Muchachos.

Follow the sign to Curral das Freiras, up a steep slope through eucalyptus forests to a clearing where a boulder with a red arrow points you on to the left. Soon you begin the steep, sometimes slippery, descent into the Curral. On the way you pass through glades of chestnut trees, encounter lonely houses covered with climbing roses and bougainvillaea and learn just what efficient shock-absorbers thighs can be. Roadworks and some building development rather chop up the last stretch of the walk, but if you keep aiming at the stone bridge over the river in the valley below, you won't get lost. Once at the bridge it's a stiff climb (much of it on a concrete stairway) up through the terraces to Curral das Freiras. For the faint-hearted, or those who balk at being skipped past by four-year-olds who could be tripping along a Dutch dyke for all the energy they seem to be spending, there is an occasional bus up to the village.

If at all possible you should try to walk for at least one leg of the journey (*see* 'Walks', above). As a tiny human speck passing through this huge valley, all you can hear is birdsong and the sound of bubbling water. Scents of eucalyptus and honeysuckle waft around you, ferns, mosses and wildflowers spread out beside the path, and you are confronted with awesome views along the way.

If you arrive by road, you come upon the Curral suddenly, after winding up through pine forests and passing through a tunnel that looks like part of an opera set. Often you enter the tunnel in mist, but come out in the green, sunny valley, where the only clouds are small ones that scud below the tops of the surrounding peaks. **Eira do Serrado**, a *miradouro* just beyond the tunnel, gives you the full sweep of the valley. The air is so clear, and the ground plummets so sharply, that it can quite bewilder your senses. Here Isabella de França thought she saw a brown butterfly, but then realized it was a large hawk, flying way below her. HN Coleridge was sent reeling: 'I absolutely started with terror...so unexpected was the scene that it was a minute or two before I could steadily look at it.' A traveller in the 1950s – long before the road was built – was certain that he could see a car driving back and forth in the village below. This turned out not to be an illusion. A villager who had made his money abroad had returned with a brand new motor, and, not deterred by the fact that there was just a winding goat track to his family home, dismantled the vehicle, carried it down piece by piece, and successfully put it back together again.

Pico dos Barcelos

The road leading up out of Funchal to Curral das Freiras passes Pico dos Barcelos (*city bus 12 or .9*). Here, from the top of one of the hills that forms the Funchal basin, you can get a superb view over the city. There's a restaurant and snack bar and a series of broad terraces that make this a favourite spot for viewing the New Year's fireworks.

The Eastern Spur

At its easternmost tip Madeira peters out in a spindle of arid rocks. Condensed into the few square kilometres between Funchal and this windswept promontory is a drop or two of nearly everything Madeira has to offer. Along the coast you'll find ancient churches, forgotten fishing villages, coves of crystal-clear water, and the oldest inhabited spot on the island. Doubling back inland, you cross misty plateaux and travel up lush valleys full of orchids and trout. On the way you'll pass through the villages of Santo da Serra (a sort of semi-tropical Surrey) and Camacha, home of the island's best wicker-weavers.

The Eastern Spur

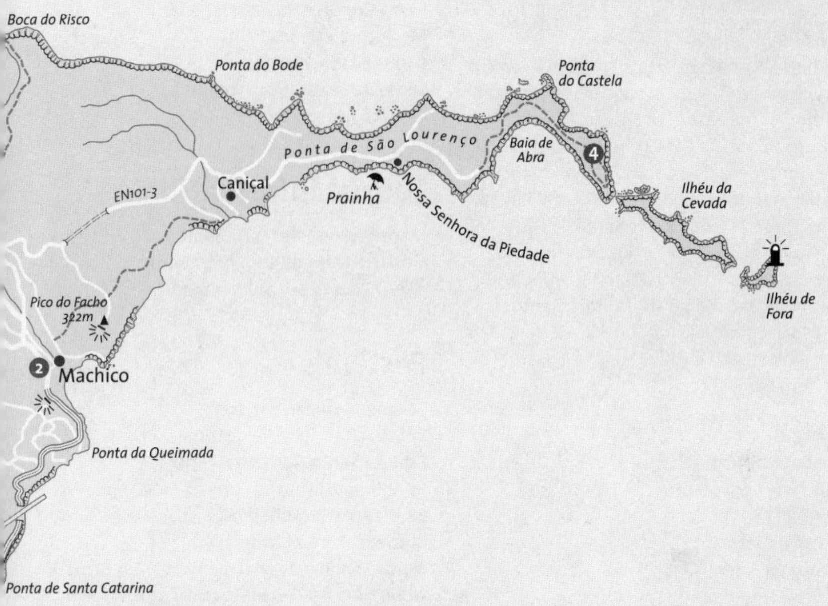

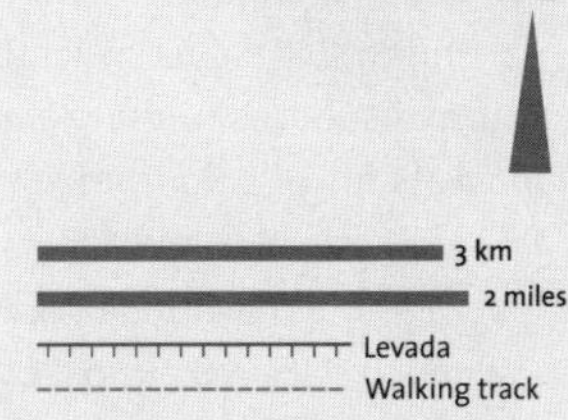

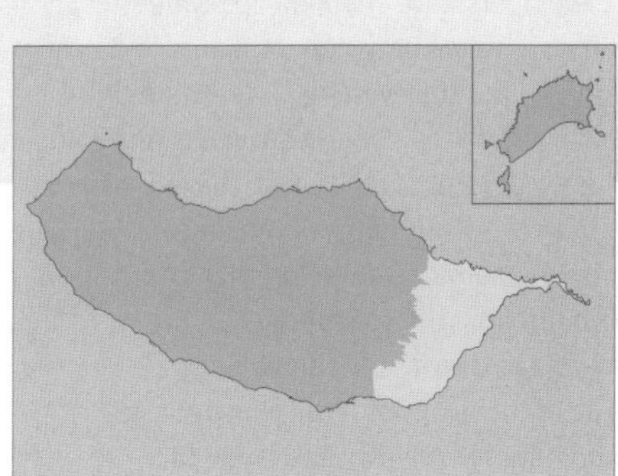

Highlights

1 Gracious old *quintas* at Santo da Serra
2 Igreja da Nossa Senhora da Conceição in Machico, for its outstanding Gothic portal
3 Swimming in deep water, beneath the otherworldly cliffs at Garajau
4 A bracing hike across to the end of the jagged São Lourenço peninsula

Getting Around

By Bus

The S.A.M. bus company (bus station on Rua Dr João Brito Câmara in Funchal) is the main carrier for the east of the island.

Bus 109 goes to Caniço; **bus 113** goes all the way up the coast to Caniçal and on to the end of the road at Ponta de São Lourenço; **bus 77** goes through Camacha to Santo da Serra; and **buses 103** and **138** take in Ribeiro Frio on its way to the north coast. Many S.A.M. buses (including **113** and **77**) stop at Larguinho de São João before leaving Funchal – a more convenient stop if you're staying in central or eastern parts of town.

By Taxi

Santa Cruz: **t** 291 524 430.
Machico: **t** 291 962 480.
Caniçal: **t** 291 961 989.
Santo da Serra: **t** 291 552 100.
Camacha: **t** 291 922 185.

Distances (from Funchal)

Santa Cruz: 20km/20mins.
Machico: 26.5km/30mins.
Caniçal: 33km/40mins.
Santo da Serra: 26km/40mins.
Camacha: 12km/25mins.

Tourist Information

Machico: Forte de Nossa Senhora do Amparo, on the seafront, **t** 291 962 289; *open Mon–Fri 9–12.30 and 2–5, Sat 9–12.30.*

Festivals

St Amaro: Santa Cruz, Jan.
St Sebastian: Câmara de Lobos, Jan.
Espirito Santo: Camacha, April.
St Anthony: Santo da Serra, 13 June.
Santissimo Sacramento: Caniço, 21 Aug.
St Lawrence: Camacha, 21 Aug.
Nossa Senhora do Livramento: Caniço, Sept.
N. Senhora da Piedade: Caniçal, 3rd Sun Sept.

East from Funchal: The Coast to Caniçal

Garajau and Caniço

Funchal is edging eastwards. Once Garajau and Caniço were sleepy fishing and farming villages just beyond town, but soon they will be at the sleeker end of a spectrum of suburbs running along the coast. Already, Madeirans returning with their pockets full of gold from jobs abroad are building large villas on the cliffs overlooking the sea – often in spectacular bad taste. Developers have snapped up prime sites for package-holiday hotels. A long stretch of the shoreline between Garajau and Caniço is owned and visited almost entirely by Germans, and the evening air resonates with the sound of Bavarian beerfest parties. But, if you rootle about a bit, you can still find lonely coves, unspoiled nooks and down-to-earth local eateries. Take the old road out of town (Estrada Conde Carvalhal) rather than the straight new highway, and you'll be rewarded with sudden, splendid panoramas – first in one direction then the other – as you wind through the tortuous bends that follow the coastline. (Your driver, though, will probably end up a frazzled martyr to the others' enjoyment.)

Garajau, named by the original settlers after the flocks of terns (Portuguese: *garajau*) they found here, is little more than a sprawl of villas. But if you take the right-hand fork of the road that passes through the village, you'll end up on a high bluff alongside a towering **statue of Christ**, modelled on (though somewhat smaller than) the one at Rio de Janeiro. The local *morgado* (landowner) and his wife put it up in 1927 in fulfilment of a private vow. Nowadays it is both an object of veneration (layers of candle wax cover the base) and a night-time trysting place for courting couples. As you crunch about on volcanic gravel between prickly clumps of aloes you get views back to Funchal and across to the Desertas that outshine even those from Cabo Girão (*see* p.192). Down a sheer drop, some 200 metres below you, the ocean is deep and blue. It was off this point that the bodies of dead Protestants were thrown into the sea (until 1767, when they were finally allowed to be buried in island soil).

A stony track winds down to a rocky beach beneath the cliffs. A narrow concrete causeway hugs the base of the cliff, working its way around the bluff. The water that laps against it is fathoms deep. At one point it flows into a fissure in the rock, just a metre or so wide but seeming to reach to the bowels of the earth. There is an eerie, prehistoric atmosphere, and you wouldn't bat an eyelid if a pterodactyl came flapping out of the darkness. The path ends in a deserted bay. Like nearly everywhere else in Madeira, the beach is made up of volcanic boulders, but you can dive straight into the water off the causeway, and there is plenty of space to sit about. It's a spectacular

Shopping

At Caniçal and in car parks along Ponta de São Lourenço out-of-work whalers sell **scrimshaw** – decorated shells and delicate boats carved out of whalebone (or, these days, any bone they can get their hands on).

Sports and Activities

Swimming

Garajau: Solitude, good snorkelling and a strange, otherworldly atmosphere await you around the bluff, though there is not much of a beach for sunbathing. To get there, take the narrow track that leads down from the car park at the statue of Christ.

Santa Cruz: Praia das Palmeiras, *open 7–6; adm free*. Recently restored municipal complex near the town library. There are paddling pools, a larger swimming pool, swimming jetties and a café. Floating platforms are anchored out at sea.

Where to Stay

Hotels at Garajau and Caniço de Baixo (the coastal resort below Caniço) are aimed at the package holiday market and are fairly self-contained. Both villages are served by buses, but unless you hire a car you could feel that you have ended up in the middle of nowhere.

Garajau and Caniço

Quinta Splendida, Sítio da Vargem, 9125 Caniço, **t** 291 930 400, **f** 291 930 401, *www.a-zqualityhotels.com, quintasplendida@mail.telepac.it* (*expensive; €105*). Relentlessly pink complex in the grounds of an 18th-century *quinta* up in Caniço village. The gardens are indeed splendid, and the rooms modern and well appointed, but a U-shaped design means that terraces and balconies are not very private. There's a health centre with a sauna and jacuzzi, a medium-sized pool and a good restaurant in the old house.

Inn & Art, Rua Baden Powell 61, 9125-036 Caniço de Baixo, **t** 291 938 200, **f** 291 938 219, *www.innart.com, innart@mail.telepac.pt* (*expensive; around €135 per night, including car hire, for a minimum two-night stay*). An art gallery cum hotel, attractively spread through five modest buildings in a cliff-top garden, with fine views out to sea. Rooms are tastefully and imaginatively decorated, and there's a good restaurant (*see* below). Prices include car hire, and drop for longer stays and bookings made more than three months in advance.

Oasis Atlantic, Caniço de Baixo, 9125 Caniço, **t** 291 930 100, **f** 291 930 109, *oasisatlantic@mail.telepac.pt* (*expensive–moderate; from €80*). Large hotel at the end of the promenade. Comfortable and well-equipped – though it can seem a bit impersonal. The pool features a swim-up bar.

spot for a dawn picnic: perch on the rocks as the sun comes up behind the Desertas, throwing them into silhouette against a sky soaked with colour.

Caniço, another ten minutes' drive along the main road, was the original boundary between the eastern and western halves of the island. The west, governed by Zarco, had its capital at Funchal; the east, centred on the settlement at Machico, was ruled by Vaz (*see* **History**, p.36). The first sugar mill on the island was built just a little inland from Caniço, but all that remains of it today is the name it left behind for a village – Moinhos.

Caniço itself has a large, shady village square, complete with fountain and aviary. All is very much in the shadow of a big 18th-century **church** with a tower that boasts two belfries, a balcony, an elaborate weather-vane and a clock. Despite the large tourist encampments on its doorstep, Caniço has kept its village atmosphere.

Just beyond the village (in Mãe de Deus, to the right of the main road, past the Camacha turn-off) is the **Capela da Madre de Deus**, built in 1536. Its doors and arches have some of the most delicate examples of Manueline carving on the island.

Dom Pedro Garajau, Garajau, 9125 Caniço, **t** 291 930 800, **f** 291 930 801, *www.dompedro.com, dp.garajau@dompedro-hotels.com* (*moderate; from €72*). Chain hotel set among suburban villas. The rooms are not over-large, but they all have balconies. Most look out over a small garden and the sea. Go for the rooms on the upper floors of Buildings 1 and 2.

Royal Orchid Hotel, PO Box 38, 9125 Caniço, **t** 291 934 600, **f** 291 934 700, *www.hotelroyalorchid.com, director.royal@rocomar.pt* (*moderate; from €60*). The most upmarket of the seaside hotels at Caniço de Baixo. A sparkling newcomer with sumptuous apartments, each with fully equipped kitchen and most with a private balcony and sea view. There's a good gym and a sauna and Turkish bath. The pool is heated, but small.

Residencial A Lareira, just off the village square, 9125-038 Caniço, **t/f** 291 934 284 (*inexpensive; from €38*). Large rooms with balconies overlook a rather gaudy graveyard and there is a sun terrace on the roof.

Santa Cruz

A Quinta, Casais Próximos–Santo da Serra, 9100 Santa Cruz, **t** 291 550 030, **f** 291 550 049 (*moderate; €60*). Smart hotel, built in the style of an old *quinta*. Rooms have all mod cons, and some have views over the surrounding countryside.

Residencial Santo António, Rua Cónego César de Oliveira, 9100 Santa Cruz, **t** 291 524 198, **f** 291 524 264, *residencial.santoantonio@oninet.pt* (*moderate; from €41*). Quiet *pension* with friendly owners in the centre of Santa Cruz.

Machico

Amparo, Rua da Amargura, 9200 Machico, **t** 291 968 120, **f** 291 966 050 (*moderate; from €40*). Small, prettily decorated hotel in a converted old townhouse in the heart of Machico.

Residencial Machico, Praceta 25 Abril, 9200 Machico, **t** 291 965 575, **f** 291 965 210, *npo28957@mail.telepac.pt* (*inexpensive; €35*). The pick of Machico's cheaper accommodation, overlooking a busy square near the sea. All rooms have private bathrooms and TV and there is a restaurant/snack bar.

Parisienne, Praceta 25 de Abril, 9200 Machico, **t** 291 965 330, **f** 291 965 563 (*inexpensive; from €35*). Pleasant family-run hotel on Machico's leafy promenade. Some rooms have sea views.

The Machico tourist office (**t** 291 962 289) can recommend **private rooms** in town for around €25 B&B for two.

Caniçal

Quinta do Lorde, Sítio da Piedade, 9206 Caniçal, **t** 291 960 200, **f** 291 960 202 (*expensive; from €100*). Quiet, lonely hotel

Santa Cruz

One of the versions of the legend of Madeira's discovery by Robert Machin tells that Santa Cruz is where his mistress Anne d'Arfet is buried, and that it was given its name by a heartbroken Machin as he placed a cross over her grave (*see* **History**, pp.34–5). Today, people speed past on their way to the airport, barely giving the dumpy tower of the parish church a second glance. But if you leave the main road for a while you'll find an alluring village with some remarkable architecture and a lively seaside promenade. The **esplanade** is dotted with palm trees, and has recently been elongated and given a makeover. Midway, there is a café that serves tasty cakes and excellent mega-*pregos*; across the way a bustling fish and vegetable market. Beyond the market, the road takes you past Praia das Palmeiras (an attractive lido – *see* 'Sports and Activities', p.153), and on to the **municipal library** which often has work by local artists exhibited in its gallery. Behind the library a small **open-air theatre** has the ocean as a backdrop; in front is an elegant terrace, where you can relax, breathe in the bracing sea air,

on the Ponta de São Lourenço, with swimming pool and sun terraces on the rocks beside the sea and new marina alongside.

Eating Out

Garajau

California, Garajau (opposite Dom Pedro hotel), **t** 291 933 935 (*moderate; €20*). Busy restaurant with friendly staff, serving generous salads and well-prepared meals. There's a good range of wine, too, including some from California.

Giuseppe Verdi, **t** 291 934 663 (*inexpensive; €13–18*). Local favourite for good pasta, whether it's with simple oregano, garlic and tomato or more extravagant seafood. On the road between Garajau and Caniço de Baixo.

Caniço

Cliff Restaurant, Inn & Art hotel, Rua Baden Powell 61, Caniço de Baixo, **t** 291 938 200 (*moderate; €18–22*). Imaginatively prepared food such as duck breast with cherry chutney and Chinese cabbage, or intriguing touches to Madeiran standards (chicken *espetada* with oregano) in an attractive clifftop setting.

Isidiro, **t** 291 934 342 (*inexpensive; €11–15*). Tucked behind a snack bar next to the church and responsible for delicious aromas that waft across the square. So popular with the villagers at lunchtime that it gets to be quite a squeeze. Try the mouthwatering tuna *espetada*.

Machico

Escondidinho, **t** 291 965 442 (*moderate; €22*). Big restaurant with a jolly atmosphere and good *espetada*. On the road out of Machico, towards Caniçal, and a cut above the restaurants in town.

O Galã, Rua General António Teixeira de Aguiar, 1–7, **t** 291 965 720 (*inexpensive; €17.50*). Glintingly clean with blue floor tiles, blue and white wall tiles, blue and white checked tablecloths and blue chairs. Salads are multi-coloured and tasty, and it's a good spot for a simple meal.

São Cristovão, Caramanchão, **t** 291 962 444 (*inexpensive; €17*). One of the few places on the island that really taps into the variety of local cuisine. A mile or so from Machico, towards Santo da Serra, it looks inland for culinary inspiration. There is tender rabbit stew, sucking pig and even goat on the menu – though you'll also find good fresh fish. The home-made desserts are a must. Park outside the church in the village of Caramanchão, and walk down the steps. The restaurant is on the left.

O Túnel, **t** 291 962 459 (*inexpensive; €14*). On the main road, before the Caniçal tunnel. Meat and fish grilled on a wood fire and served with salad and potatoes. Good value.

Dragon Trees

Dragon Trees are bizarre natives of Madeira, the Canaries and the Cape Verde Islands. The pithy, cylindrical trunk travels straight upwards, then branches out suddenly into lots of different stems, giving the impression that the tree has been planted upside down, with its roots in the air. The bunches of spiky, greyish, sword-shaped leaves, and the fronds of orangy, date-like fruit that adorn the tops of these branches make Dragon Trees look like slightly surrealistic palms. Cut into the fleshy trunk, and the tree 'bleeds' a vivid red sap. Long ago this gum was collected, dried and ground up for 'Dragon's Blood', a pricey red dye that was supposed also to have magical healing properties. Unfortunately, early settlers bled the trees dry, and *Dracaena draco* has all but died out in the wild. But they do still adorn gardens all over Madeira, and those in Santa Cruz are fine specimens.

admire the Dragon Trees...and watch aeroplanes come past almost at eye level. Doubling back from the library along Rua da Ponta Nova, parallel to the beachfront, you come to the 19th-century **law court**, reached through a garden of flowering trees. Wooden verandas run the length of its façade on each of the three floors, and a grand stone stairway sweeps you up to the main entrance, one storey above ground level.

A little further on you come to the main village square and the parish church. The **Igreja de Santa Maria de Santa Cruz**, one of the few churches on Madeira with three parts to its nave, grew up in fits and starts between 1479 and 1533. Pedro Anes and Gil Eanes, the builders responsible for the cathedral in Funchal, also had a strong hand here. The stocky tower, small windows and graceful Gothic arches echo those in the larger church, and there is some fine stone-carving inside, including the arches over the side chapels, a Manueline vestry door and a tomb that dates from 1516. Across the way is the **town hall**. A traveller passing through in the early 19th century noted that it 'until recently bore the date 1513, but the authorities, seemingly ashamed of its advanced age, have removed the figures, and have made other attempts to give the building a juvenile air'. Similar ham-fisted attempts were made in the 1960s and 1970s, so today all that remains of the original building is part of the façade. From the square, alleys lined with old houses will take you back to the esplanade.

About five minutes' drive past Santa Cruz is Funchal **airport**, built across the tip of a peninsula and out on stilts across land reclaimed from the sea. Beyond the airport the landscape begins to look more barren, a hint of the desert Madeira could be if not for the *levadas*. Five kilometres later you round a corner and see the bay of Machico.

Machico

'Machico is the oldest and most miserable place in Madeira,' writes a crestfallen young Edward Watkinson Wells in his diary in 1837. 'I did not see a decent house in it.' Machico is the spot where humans first set foot on the island. History records that these first feet were those of the great Captain Zarco, but legend has it that he came across the graves of two castaways, Robert Machin and his mistress, and named the settlement he founded in their memory (*see* pp.34–5). Machico has, however, cheered up a bit since it so disappointed Edward Wells. The odd lick of paint to its three historic churches, a facelift for the old market and some judicious patching up of the 18th-century fort have made the town eminently more visitable.

Occasionally, the little brook that trickles between high walls on the eastern side of the town turns into a raging torrent that deposits mud and all sorts of unmentionable things into the bay. Even when this hasn't happened, the water here is murky, and swimming in the bay is not a very delectable prospect. People do it, though, and many tourists see Machico as a quieter alternative to Funchal as a base for a holiday.

Around the Largo do Município

The chief occupation on the town square, the Largo do Município, is to sit under the shade of the massive oak trees waiting for buses. Walkers who wander in from the hills to find that they have an hour or so before the next bus join locals who hang about for ages before theirs is even scheduled. Conversations echo about the square as if it were a giant, leafy hall. From time to time someone wanders over to the bootblack to have their shoes shone in the comfort of his elaborate canopied chair. One of the uninitiated might bang away at the drinks vending machine. The eventual arrival of a bus creates a slight flurry and a momentary depletion of numbers.

Across the northern side of the square is Machico's large parish church, the **Igreja da Nossa Senhora da Conceição**. It was built in the 15th century at the instigation of Branca Teixeira, wife of Tristão Vaz, one of the original governors of Madeira. She must have had quite some influence at court back home in Portugal – King Manuel himself donated the statue of Our Lady for the high altar, the organ, liturgical silver, a polychrome carving of the *Virgin and Child* (now in the Museum of Sacred Arts in Funchal) and three marble pillars for the south portal. These pillars support two lancet arches in what is the most outstanding Gothic portal on the island. Highlights inside include the Capela de São João Baptista, with a Manueline arch that incorporates the Teixeira coat of arms, and the Chapel of the Blessed Sacrament, with a fine vaulted ceiling.

Past the 1920s **town hall** and across a hump-shaped **bridge** to the east of the Largo do Município, you come to a smaller square, shaded by Indian fig trees that are over a century old. Somewhere near here Robert Machin and Anne d'Arfet are supposedly buried. In one corner of the square is the tiny **Capela dos Milagres** (Chapel of the Miracles), the focus of one of Madeira's most fervently celebrated festivals. The original church at this site, the Capela do Cristo, built by Vaz and Zarco in 1420, was one of the first on the island. Flood and fire took more than their usual toll of chapels on the spot. A new one was built after a conflagration in the 16th century, and in 1803 the entire church was washed into the Atlantic. When an American galley found the crucifix from the high altar floating far out at sea, the people of Machico thought that they had been granted a miracle, and named the new chapel they built accordingly. On 8 October 1815 the crucifix (which had been stored in Funchal for safekeeping while the new chapel was being built) was returned at the head of a procession. Since then, on 8 October every year the cross is taken in procession around town, and 9 October is a local holiday. The chapel was twice more rebuilt after floods, once in 1883 and again in 1957, but the crucifix stayed put. In the 1980s five centuries' worth of paint was carefully stripped off the Christ figure to reveal the sensitive Gothic carving.

The Seafront

Rua General António Teixeira de Aguiar leads from the Largo do Município towards the sea. At the end of the street, the old **market** with its jacaranda trees and marble fountain has recently been restored, and is due for conversion into a restaurant and café. Across the way is the **Forte de Nossa Senhora do Amparo**, a quaint triangular fortress built in 1706. It was one of three forts in the bay built as a defence against pirates. Another, **Forte São João Baptista**, near the quay, is now a private residence. The third, which was on the western edge of the bay, has not survived. All three forts were fiercely fought over during the 1828 Miguelite Rebellion (*see* **History**, p.40), and Fort Amparo was the last to fall. Today it houses the Machico tourist office.

To the east of the fort is Machico's busy **fish market**, built mainly in the 19th century. To the west is the **football stadium**. Machico's team is one of the best on the island. The stadium has something of the run-down charm of an old bullring; on match days it is bright with bunting and echoes with rousing brass band music.

Towards the end of the bluff that forms the western arm of the bay is the **Capela de São Roque**, built in 1739 on the site of a 15th-century chapel. São Roque was protector against the plague and patron saint of dogs; walkers on Madeira might be forgiven for wishing that he didn't exercise this latter calling quite so diligently on the island. The chapel contains some superb 18th-century *azulejos* depicting scenes from his life.

East from Machico: Pico do Facho

After Machico the main road splits in two. The right-hand fork winds up through the terraces to Pico do Facho (literally 'Peak of the Torch').

In the days when pirates ravaged the shores, lookouts posted on Porto Santo, Ponta de São Lourenço and Pico do Facho would alert the islanders by lighting huge bonfires. The guard on Porto Santo would usually be the first to spot a Jolly Roger, and the alarm would shoot along this relay of torches to warn the people in Machico, giving them a good few hours' notice of an attack. (Another fire at Garajau passed on the warning to Funchal.) The townsfolk would head for the hills – inaccessible to all save goats and hardy landlubbers – leaving soldiers in the forts to fight off the invaders. Pico do Facho (322m high) offers a commanding coast view, but the road to the top is appalling. You could park on the main road and leg it (1km), or visit the peak as part of a longer walk along the old coastal path between Machico and Caniçal.

Just beyond the turn-off to the Pico the main road plunges into a **tunnel** 740m long. You leave green terraces and emerge a few minutes later into a dry landscape of scrubby grass and palms. A couple of kilometres further on is Caniçal, which, before 1956 when the tunnel was built, could only have been reached by boat.

Caniçal

Caniçal seems locked in a permanent Sunday-afternoon atmosphere. Once it was a busy whaling port, but in the 1980s an international ban on whaling scuppered the local economy. The Free Trade Zone which the Madeiran government opened just outside the village has so far failed to attract much foreign interest, and Caniçal remains something of a ghost town. Old fishermen in flat caps sit on upturned crates playing cards, a few boys mess about in the water and there is a half-hearted attempt at a fish market in the deserted whaling station.

The whalers in Madeira were among the last in the world still to hunt their prey in open boats, rowing up to the whale and plunging in the harpoon by hand rather than firing it off from the safety of a distant deck. Men would sit atop Pico do Facho, scouring the ocean for telltale spouts. As soon as they saw one, the call would go out and half the village would head for the boats. Battles with whales were long and bloody. The harpoon did not in fact kill the whale, but helped the hunters keep a hold on the animal so that they could stab it in the heart with their spears. The pain from the first jab of the harpoon frightened the whale into diving. On the surface the men fed out the rope, and waited for the whale to come up for breath – then they lunged in for the kill, sometimes climbing on to its back, seldom reaching the heart in one go.

Sometimes the hunters themselves were killed. A full-grown bull can stay underwater for up to an hour, and when it surfaces it does so with a force that could easily capsize a boat. One thrash of its tail could shatter small craft into splinters. Caniçal's cemetery is full of the graves of young men.

When John Huston was filming *Moby Dick*, Herman Melville's classic tale of a man obsessed with a huge white whale, he came to Madeira to shoot authentic opening sequences. Gregory Peck played Captain Ahab, Melville's 19th-century protagonist, and the part of Moby Dick was played by a 27m-long latex-covered model. Early versions of the great white whale kept sinking (at a cost of £15,000 apiece), and when the designers finally came up with one that worked, the weather was too bad for filming. The tow rope snapped and Moby floated out to sea. An ocean liner reported it as a danger to shipping, and it eventually turned up on a beach in Holland. Meanwhile the film crew had given up on Madeira and had gone to London to finish filming in a 360,000-litre water tank at Shepperton Studios.

While they were in Madeira, Huston and Gregory Peck were taken out on a whale hunt. In a single day their party killed 20 whales, and the director returned grinning with excitement. Marine biologist Pietra Diemer was less enthusiastic after her first trip with Madeiran whalers. She was so sickened by what she saw that when she got home to Germany she set up the Society for the Protection of Marine Mammals, the organization that was instrumental in having commercial trade in whale products abolished worldwide in 1981. Today the waters for 200,000 sq km around Madeira have been declared a **Marine Mammal Sanctuary**. The numbers of seals, whales and dolphins are gradually beginning to increase, but it is still rare to see a whale. Some ex-whalers bring in a little extra money carving scrimshaw – the decorated shells and pieces of whalebone that they used to whittle away at while waiting for the whales to arrive. The old office of the whaling company has been turned into a **whaling museum** (*open Tues–Sun, 10–12 and 1–5; adm €1.50*). Here you can compare a life-size model of a sperm whale with one of the tiny boats that were used to hunt them. There is a vicious-looking selection of hooks and harpoons, some gory photographs of dead whales and pictures of the different varieties found in local waters. You can also watch a short video (in English) on the history of whaling here.

Ponta de São Lourenço

As you leave Caniçal you pass the high fences and concrete shells of the **Free Trade Zone**. A deep-sea port, 100 acres of industrial park (with another 197 acres to come) and a promise of tax exemption until 2011 are all designed to lure masses of foreign investment. The people of Caniçal look on sceptically.

Beyond Caniçal the island narrows sharply and the landscape becomes so dry that it looks almost lunar. Clumps of brown grass give way to volcanic grit, shale patterned with fossils, cacti and the odd bright dots of desert flowers. A serrated line of cliffs tapers off into a few jagged, rocky islets. There is an enveloping silence, broken only by the hollow whoosh-whoosh from a row of electricity-generating windmills. This is Ponta de São Lourenço, named by Zarco after the boat that carried him ashore, and dismissed in one 19th-century guidebook as a 'peninsula of rude and utterly bare rocks with an outline of strange unevenness'. Perhaps the writer would have been more impressed if he had visited in spring when, for a few weeks, the land bursts out in flowers. At other times Ponta de São Lourenço has a stark, desolate beauty.

The road goes almost to the end of the point. Along the way a track to the left takes you to a ***miradouro*** and picnic spot with views up the north coast – more rugged and dramatic than the south of the island. Opposite the turn-off, on a large round hill (which is affectionately known as *Gordo* – 'Fatty'), is the **Capela de Nossa Senhora da Piedade**. Every year on the third Sunday in September an image of the Virgin is carried from the parish church at Caniçal down to the beach, where a fleet of decorated boats is waiting to escort her on the 4km journey to the chapel on the hill. At the foot of the hill is **Prainha**, the only real stretch of sandy beach on the main island.

From the car park at the end of the road it is possible (and exhilarating) to walk to the end of the peninsula, where a 167m-wide channel separates the island from the tiny **Ilhéu de Fora** with its lighthouse. After that there is little alternative but to go back the way you came, as far as Machico.

Sports and Activities

Swimming

Prainha: 100 metres or so of soft brown sand in a cove below the Capela de Nossa Senhora da Piedade. It is the only real beach on the island and packs out on hot days. There is a bar/restaurant.

Cais do Sardinha: Swimming jetty with a ruggedly beautiful backdrop about 20mins' walk from the car park at the end of the road. It was built in 1905 by a Funchal family who had a house here, and makes a cooling stop-off if you're on a walk. You'll need to take a picnic, though there is a clear natural fountain nearby.

Inland

Santo da Serra

The second fork of the main road outside Machico runs up the valley, then climbs steeply to Santo da Serra, on a plateau 700m above the sea. The cool air at Santo da Serra made it the traditional retreat of the local British population in the hotter months. The *quintas* and villas that they built, and the gardens they planted, give the village something of the air of a leafy, rather prosperous southeast England suburb – though the large, flat village square could quite easily be from a deserted Mexican town in a spaghetti western.

At the northern end of the square is a simple 19th-century **church** dedicated to Santo António da Serra, patron saint of the parish. The name proved a bit of a mouthful for the British, who are responsible for the shortened version by which the village is known today. In the 1930s a passing motorist got stuck in the mud just outside the village. The parish priest popped into the church to get some boards to help him out. Back on dry land, the driver noticed that the boards had figures painted on them. He took them to Lisbon, where they were cleaned up and found to be part of a triptych attributed to the 16th-century Flemish painter Gerard David. This

Shopping

The main buy in the area is **wickerwork**, which you can find in abundance at the wicker supermarket in Camacha. On the outskirts of Camacha village is a busy **shopping mall** where you'll find more wicker on sale, a supermarket, cinemas and a bowling alley.

Sports and Activities

Golf

Campo de Golfe da Madeira: Golf course with driving range, bar, pro shop and panoramic views – worth a visit even if it's just for a coffee on the terrace. Clubs, trolleys and buggies for hire. Green fees €48.50 (9 holes) and €70 (18 holes).

Where to Stay

Camacha

Estalagem Relógio, Achada, 9135-053 Camacha, **t** 291 922 777, **f** 291 922 415 (*moderate; €40*). A new hotel with enthusiastic, friendly management. Rooms have terracotta floors and are decorated with bright fabrics. Views across the valley and out to sea are breathtaking.

Eating Out

Santo da Serra

A Nossa Aldeia, Sítio dos Casais Próximos, **t** 291 552 142 (*inexpensive; €18*). Wine bladders, gnarled logs and other rustic bits and bobs for décor, locals for customers and food from garlic soup to burgers and *espetada*.

Camacha

Café Relógio, **t** 291 922 114 (*moderate; €20*). Café and restaurant on the town square, in the same building as the wicker supermarket. Standard tourist issue, but with spectacular views.

O Boléu, **t** 291 922 128 (*inexpensive; €14*). Tiny restaurant beside the church with good solid helpings of mountain food, such as tripe and onions or bean stew. Excellent home cooking and friendly service.

sparked off a search through old village churches, and a number of valuable Flemish paintings were unearthed. They had been used in payment for sugar during the boom, had ended up in churches and had long been forgotten. Today most of the paintings are in the Museum for Sacred Art in Funchal.

Behind the church is a small **market**, where you'll find stalls selling Madeiran fruit, island liqueurs, and chicken grilled on wood-fires, served up with home-made bread.

A large pair of wrought-iron gates at the southern end of the square leads to **Quinta da Serra** (*open until sunset; adm free*). The pink *quinta* now houses government offices and the grounds are a public park complete with avenues of camellias and azaleas, formal gardens, shrubberies, tennis courts, a small zoo and a playground. The gardens get wilder as you walk further in, and eventually blend into the surrounding forest. In the easternmost corner is a belvedere from which, when the weather is right, you can see Porto Santo. The narrow lane that runs past the *quinta* winds through forests and past lusciously laden farm terraces back on to the Machico road. It is by far the most beautiful route up to Santo da Serra, but can be hair-raising if you meet any traffic.

South of the village square you can glimpse a few of the more impressive *quintas* through the trees. On the outskirts of town is the **Campo de Golfe da Madeira**, one of two island golf courses (*see* p.90 and p.153). Beyond it the land drops sharply to the coast. As you tee off, you feel that you could drive the ball far out to sea. But come for a game early in the morning, when the mists are still hanging in the valleys, and you could find yourself playing above the clouds – standing under a brilliant blue sky and hitting the ball along a fairway that dips into picture-book fluffy cotton wool.

Camacha

The road south of Santo da Serra runs through forests to Camacha, some 12km away. As you near Camacha you begin to notice bundles of long canes propped up against the houses. This is basket country, and wicker working is still very much a cottage industry (*see* pp.49–50).

Camacha's village square is, in fact, a circle – an odd flattened mountaintop with a magnificent view over the coast. Local Brits used to come up here to play cricket, and islanders say that this is where Madeira's first ever game of football took place, in 1875. (Another version of the story says that it happened in the Hinton *quinta* nearby.) Along the southern side of the square, the **Relógio**, an odd white building with a small clock tower, blocks out the view to all but those who visit its restaurant and café. The Relógio (literally 'Clock') gets its name from yet another public clock donated by the timepiece fanatic Dr Michael Grabham. This particular *relógio* was bought from a church in Liverpool in 1896. Inside the building, besides the restaurant and café, is a **wicker supermarket**, packed to the ceiling with bags, baskets, laundry chests, cane chairs and curious souvenirs. In the basement you can see people at work creating some of the extraordinarily elaborate wicker furniture that is on sale. Despite the fact that there is an almost endless stream of day-trippers past the tills, prices are

The Grand Old Man of Madeira

When Dr Michael Grabham died in 1938, at the age of 98, his obituary in *The Times* stated succinctly: 'Dr. Grabham **was** Madeira'. A medical doctor who did enormous good work on the island, a naturalist who supplied the Regent's Park Zoo with much of its tropical fish collection, an expert on – *inter alia* – earthquakes and meteoric dust, and (with his brother-in-law Lord Kelvin) a pioneer of research into electronics, Dr Grabham was also an accomplished organist and collector of clocks. He cast his own bells and owned over 200 timepieces – one with a five-metre-long pendulum. When in London he was often invited to play the organ at St Paul's Cathedral. On Madeira he gave frequent organ recitals in the English Church. But Dr Grabham was no boring worthy. His love for Madeira and his ebullient good nature endeared him to British and Portuguese Madeirans alike. The quality of the wines in his cellar was legendary, and he was generous with his hospitality. In 1933, on his 93rd birthday, he served guests some of the original 1792 Napoleon madeira (*see* p.53), remarking that it had been made in the year that his father was born, and bottled by his in-laws in 1840 – the year in which he was born. The 'Grand Old Man' was also renowned for his wicked sense of humour. Once, irritated by petty squabbles between factions of the British expats on the island, he secretly engineered a dogfight in the Letters columns of the press – writing both sides of the incensed debate himself, then revealing the sham to the embarrassment of those who had scuttled to take sides. When his great-nephew Noël Cossart asked the old man how he managed so knowledgeably to hold forth on Madeira's flora and fauna, and on so many other scientific subjects, Grabham answered – probably with some truth – 'What I don't know, I invent.'

In 1929 Punch came up with a limerick to mark the Grand Old Man's 89th birthday:

There was an old man in Madeira
Whose stories got queera and queera
The guests gathered round
Said the vinum was sound
But his veritas was rather too vera.

reasonable and the quality of work generally high. Do consider, though, how you would get your purchase home on the plane.

On the other side of the square is a flashy new **Casa do Povo** (village hall), home to what is reputedly Madeira's best folk music and dancing group, the *Grupa Folclórico da Camacha* – though you are more likely to catch sight of them at one of their frequent gigs around the island. They have even been known to venture as far as community halls in south London and social clubs around the United States. Occasionally, though, you might find an exhibition of musical instruments or photographs of various festive events displayed inside.

Tourists tend to stick pretty close to the Relógio; townies climb the hill behind the Casa do Povo, past the Quinta da Camacha to a smaller square outside the **parish church**. There are one or two good restaurants along the way, and this part of town has a friendly, village atmosphere. The church dates back mainly to the 18th century, and has been more sensitively restored than most Baroque churches on the island. Curious features inside include a carved wooden chandelier in the shape of a trumpeting angel, and a Baroque chapel to the Virgin decorated completely in white.

Of the various routes back to Funchal from Camacha, the one via Palheiro Ferreiro is the most attractive, passing through fragrant wattle plantations before knotting itself back into the chaos of Funchal's traffic.

Walks

These are suggestions for walks you can follow, not a detailed guide to the routes. It essential to go properly equipped and to take a good map (*see* pp.57–9).

The Levada da Serra is one of the most well-walked *levadas* on the island.

Camacha–Levada da Serra–Levada dos Tornos

Easy. 3hrs.

Follow the road up the hill out of Camacha, past the parish church. A signpost directs you to the Levada da Serra. Turn left and follow the *levada* through the Vale Paraiso to Romeiros (follow signposts to 'Choupana' – but be careful, there is another Choupana to the north!). Here you join the Levada dos Tornos, and can walk on to Monte or the Jasmine Tea House (*see* p.109). Or you could take city bus 29 to Funchal.

Camacha–Levada da Serra–Santo da Serra/Portela

Easy. 5–6½hrs.

Join the Levada da Serra, but this time turn right. For much of the first part of this walk the *levada* is under a road, so you might prefer to join it a little further on, at Águas Mansas (where road 206 joins road 102; bus 77). When the *levada* crosses the Poiso/Santo da Serra road you can either follow the road into Santo da Serra, or walk on to the Levada Nova. Here a right turn will take you to Santo da Serra and a left to the Levada da Portela. Head east along the *levada* to get to Portela (*see* p.174).

Caniçal Tunnel–Boca do Risco–Porto da Cruz

Difficult. 4–4½hrs. Check weather and landslide conditions before leaving.

Join the Levada do Caniçal near the west side of the Caniçal tunnel (bus 113) and head northwest. After about 45 minutes a path leads uphill to Boca do Risco ('Dangerous Pass') on the north coast. From here you head west along an exhilarating clifftop path to Porto da Cruz, where you can catch bus 53 to Machico/Funchal.

Ponta de São Lourenço

Difficult/moderate. Up to 3hrs.

A path leads from the car park at the end of road 101 towards the tip of the island. A half-hour walk will take you to some of the more spectacular viewpoints, but further on the going can get pretty hair-raising. Red paint on the rocks marks the way.

Inland and the North

11

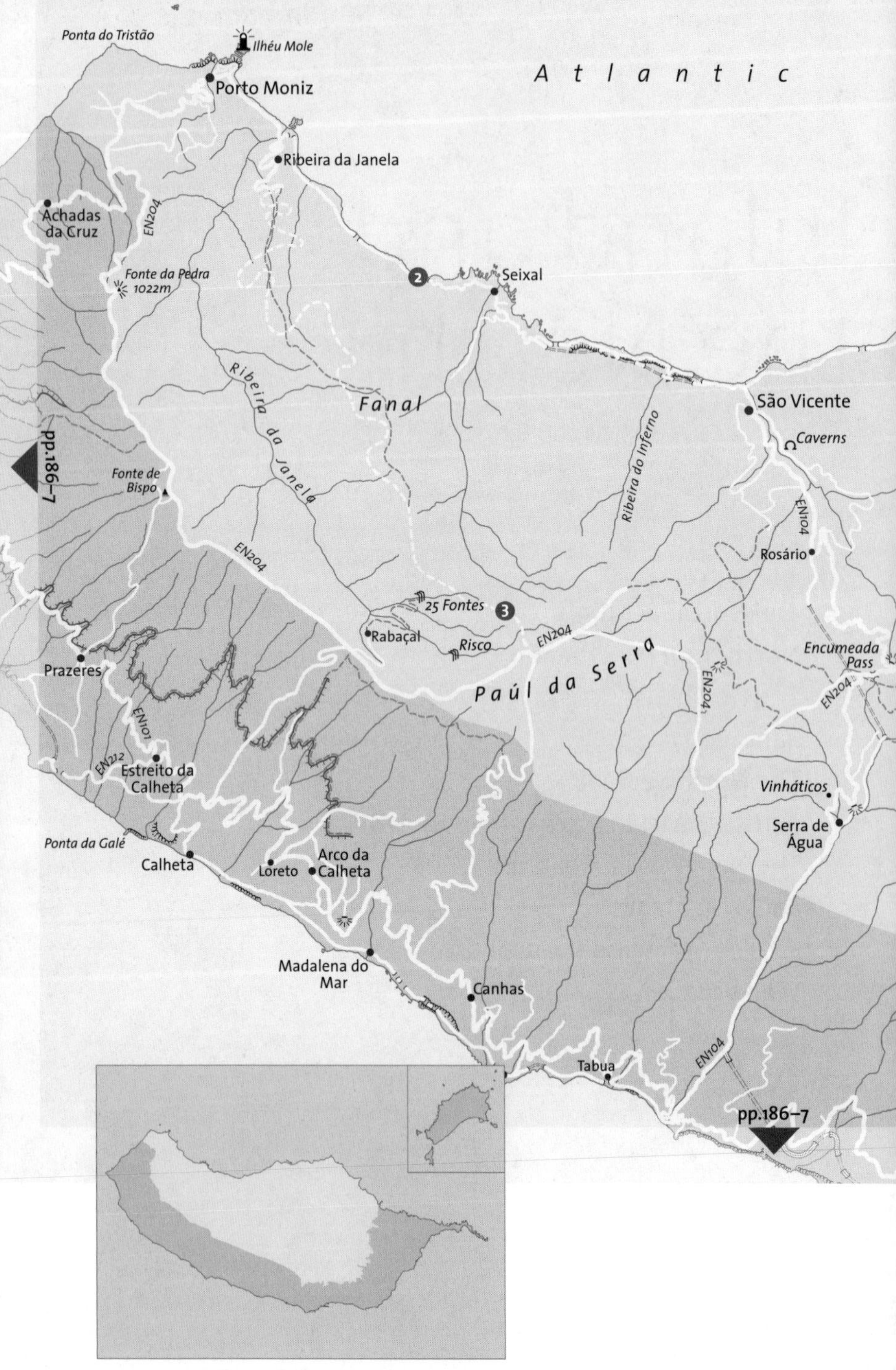

Ponta do Tristão
Ilhéu Mole
Atlantic
Porto Moniz
Ribeira da Janela
Achadas da Cruz
EN204
Fonte da Pedra 1022m
Seixal
Ribeira da Janela
Fanal
São Vicente
Caverns
Ribeira do Inferno
pp.186–7
Fonte de Bispo
EN204
EN104
Rosário
25 Fontes
Rabaçal
Risco
EN204
Paúl da Serra
Encumeada Pass
Prazeres
EN204
EN204
EN101
Estreito da Calheta
EN212
Vinháticos
Serra de Água
Ponta da Galé
Calheta
Loreto
Arco da Calheta
Madalena do Mar
Canhas
Tabua
EN104
pp.186–7

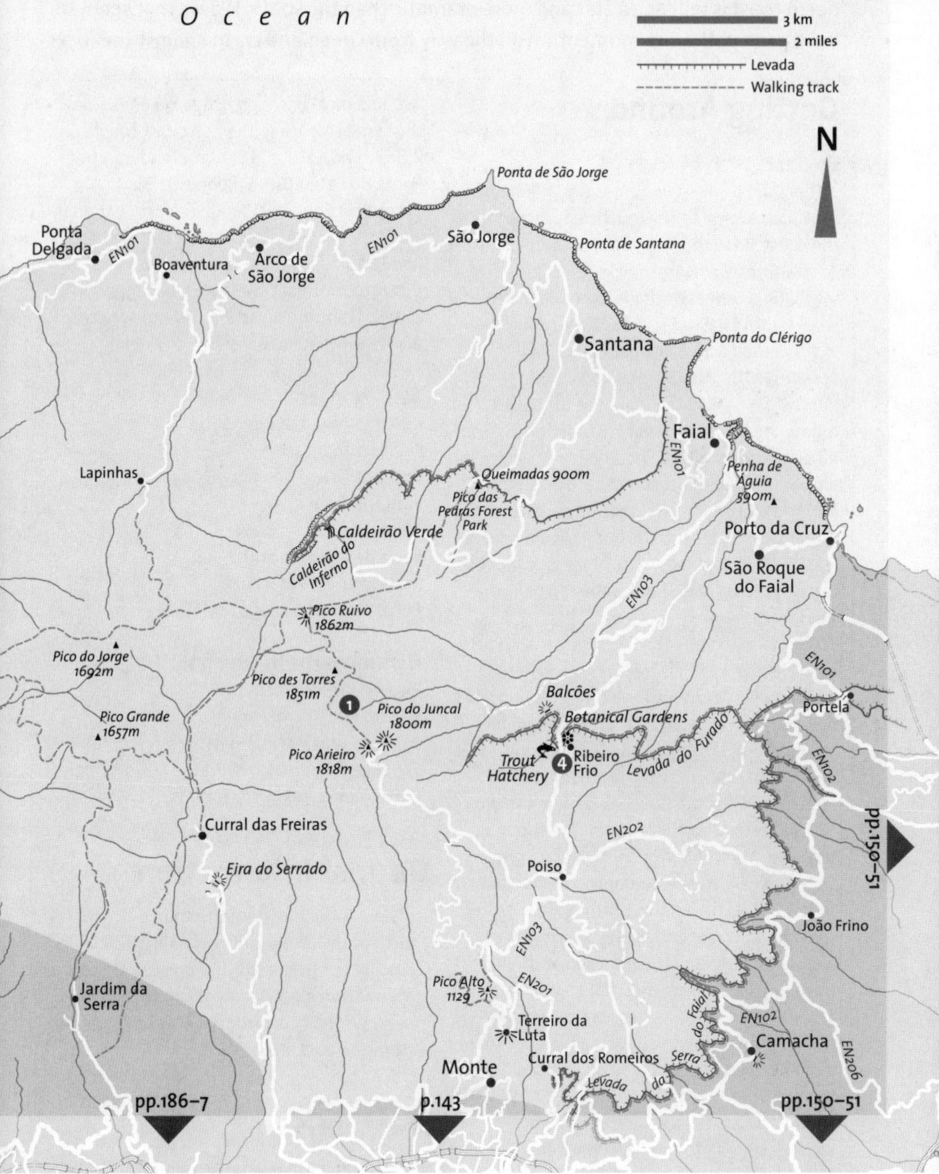

pp.186–7
p.143
pp.150–51
pp.150–51

Highlights

1 Walking across the top of the world, between Pico Arieiro and Pico Ruivo
2 The narrow, cliff-hugging Old North Coast Road
3 The windswept, exhilarating solitude of Paúl da Serra
4 Icy streams full of trout at Ribeiro Frio

Whipped by winds from across the Atlantic and pounded by breakers, Madeira's north coast is wilder, wetter and more dramatic than the south. Waves that seem to have been gathering momentum all the way from Greenland crash against the rocks

Getting Around

By Car

There are three main routes north. **Road 103** runs past Monte to the northeastern part of the coast. **Road 104**, an extension of the south-coast motorway, is the quickest route, involving a tunnel through the middle of the island from Ribeira Brava to São Vicente. There is also a **road across the plateau** of Paúl da Serra to Porto Moniz in the northwest.

It is still possible, avoiding the tunnel, to follow the far more beautiful route north from Ribeira Brava over the Encumeada Pass, but, as always on Madeira, distances are deceptive. A round trip on the old roads might measure out at well under 200km, but it would take at least 6–8hrs to drive it. The highest point you can drive to on the island is the top of Pico Arieiro (1,810m).

The old road between São Vicente and Porto Moniz is the one that features on postcards – a narrow ledge cut into the cliff. Today this has been largely replaced by a straighter, wider road passing through tunnels, though it is still possible to follow the old route for some stretches. These are now one-way, in the direction of Porto Moniz. It is a sobering thought that well into the 1990s these ledges, often barely a vehicle wide, not only bore two-way traffic, but as the only road along the northern coast had to cope with buses and trucks as well. Faint bulges in the road allowed vehicles travelling in opposite directions to pass each other, and progress was sporadic, involving frequent reversing to allow the big boys space to go by. Even the new road disappears from time to time into the old tunnels (dimly lit and hewn through the rock, not bright and concrete-lined like the new ones), and is generously sprayed by waterfalls from above.

By Bus

Bus 103 runs up the northeast road, then along the coast as far as Boaventura (departure point in Funchal at the eastern end of the Avenida do Mar, *see* p.77). **Bus 138** goes from the same stop up to the northeast coast via Ribeiro Frio, Faial and Santana, ending up at Ponta do Pargo. **Bus 6** (Rodoeste Bus Company) goes west to Ribeira Brava, then up via São Vicente to Boaventura. **Bus 139** (also Rodoeste) follows the same route to São Vicente, but then travels west as far as Porto Moniz. There are no scheduled bus services across the plateau or up to Pico Arieiro.

By Taxi

Ribeira Brava: t 291 951 800.
Faial: t 291 572 416.
Porto da Cruz: t 291 562 411.
Santana: t 291 572 540.
São Jorge: t 291 576 222.
Serra de Água: t 291 952 012.
São Vicente: t 291 842 238.
Porto Moniz: t 291 852 243.

Distances (from Funchal)

Pico Arieiro: 20km/1hr.
Ribeiro Frio: 18km/20mins.
Santana: 35km/1hr 10mins.
São Vicente (via Ribiera Brava): 55km/50mins.
Porto Moniz: 70km/1hr 10mins.

Tourist Information

There is no tourist information office in the north of the island, but the main office in Funchal can help with your queries. There is an **information kiosk, t** 291 951 675, in the old tower on the beachfront at Ribeira Brava, but opening hours are sporadic.

Festivals

Santa Maria Madalena: Porto Moniz, 22 July.
Festival of Our Lord: Porto da Cruz, last Sun Aug.
Nossa Senhora do Rosário: São Vicente, 1st Sun Oct.
Bom Jesus: Ponta Delgada, 1st Sun Sept.

and spray many metres into the air. Large chunks of land break off and crumble into the sea. Streams that chortle through the uplands oblivious to their fate plunge to a sudden death over the cliffs. A ridge of sharp peaks weathers the Atlantic storms, protecting the southern side of the island. Looking up at the jagged, conical mountains, attended by wisps of cloud, you feel you could be in China or the Himalayas.

In some years up to 200cm (80ins) of rain fall along the north coast. But there is plenty of sun too, and the combination covers the slopes in lush greenery. On tiny terraces chiselled out of the mountainside, farmers grow banquets of fruit and vegetables, squeezed in between the stalks of banana trees and vines. Higher up, though, where the climate is too harsh for much to grow, gorse and brush break through the rocks and the wind twists the trunks of tree heather into fantastical shapes. To the west, the mountains flatten out into a wide shaly plateau from where you can see both sides of the island at once, or, on some days, look down on to the tops of the clouds.

The Northeast

North from Funchal

The 103 road north of Funchal winds up, through forests and over a mountain, to the northeast coast.

Terreiro da Luta and Pico Arieiro

Two kilometres above Monte, just beyond the tang of the eucalyptus forests, you come to **Terreiro da Luta**. (Alternatively, you can get there on the 201 road via Palheiro Ferreiro, winding through woods filled with birdsong and past banks of bracken and flowers.) This is the spot where Our Lady of Monte appeared to a young shepherdess in the 15th century (*see* p.142), so becoming Madeira's patron saint. It was also the end point of the rack-and-pinion railway that ran up from Funchal until 1939.

Today you will find an enormous **statue of the Virgin**, over 5m high, weighing in at 20 tonnes and laden with a rosary of rocks and chains. She was put up in 1927 in thanksgiving after a narrow shave with the Germans during the First World War. In 1916 a U-Boat had sunk three ships in Funchal bay and shelled the town. When another submarine began to pepper the seafront in 1917, people fled to Monte to pray for salvation. The local priest vowed that he would build a monument to Our Lady of Monte if they were spared. Ten years later the promise was fulfilled, and 20,000 people came to see the statue blessed. It took some 300 of the faithful most of the day to carry up sea-rounded rocks for the rosary, which is made from the anchor chain of one of the sunken battleships.

Across the way is the building that was once the **railway station café**, now restored to its former glory as a fashionable restaurant. You can wander around the small formal garden, gaze out at the views, and have a look at a **statue of Zarco** made in

Shopping

Perched alone on the cliffs between São Jorge and Arco de São Jorge, the **Cabanas** motel complex has the potential for being a tourist rip-off – but the souvenir shop here is not only large and well-stocked, its prices are low too. This is the place to buy hand-made boots, *bolos de mel*, woodcarving, traditional hats and other curios – though you'll get a better deal on wines in Funchal, and a wider selection of wicker at Camacha.

Sports and Activities

Swimming

São Roque do Faial: There's fresh-water swimming to be had in seemingly bottomless rock pools in the river below the village. Follow the path signposted to Água d'Alto, and scramble down one of the overgrown racks that lead down the hill.

Porto da Cruz: A large tidal pool has been built into the rocks on one end of the promenade, with a waterside café nearby.

Santana: About 6km west of Santana a '*Praia*' sign sends you down a dirt track to a quiet (but rocky) beach at the foot of the cliffs. In the summer a small *venda* near the beach sells drinks and provisions.

Ponta Delgada: A tidal pool built out from the rocks near the parish church is a great favourite with children when waves come splashing over the sea wall. A poolside snack bar supplies the ice-cream, colas and other ingredients necessary for kiddie-nirvana.

Where to Stay

Tour companies will pack you off to Porto Moniz, there is a cluster of hotels at São Vicente, and there are some gems at Boaventura and São Roque do Faial.

Pico Arieiro

Pousada do Pico Arieiro, central reservations, **t** 291 230 110, **f** 291 228 611 (*expensive–moderate; €90*). The government *pousada* at the very summit of Pico Arieiro wouldn't win any design prizes, but the views are so captivating that you hardly notice. All the rooms are centrally heated (most necessary at this height), have balconies and look out across the valleys. There's a games room, and a cosy restaurant with an open log fire.

São Roque do Faial

Hotel Sanroque, São Roque do Faial, 9230 Santana, **t** 291 575 249, **f** 291 575 534, *www.angelfire.com/ma/deira* (*inexpensive; from €27.50*). Family-run hotel discreetly slipped into a peaceful village. The upstairs rooms in the old wing look out over the deep Ametade valley, or down on to Penha da Águia and the sea. Rooms in a new annexe look up towards the peaks. The **restaurant** (*moderate*) is superb (soups made from vegetables out of the garden; meat and fish grilled on a wood fire, as well as a log fire and fine views), and in harvest time the neighbours crush their grapes in the ancient wine-press downstairs. Excellent value.

Porto da Cruz

Penedo, Casas Próximas, 9225 Porto da Cruz, **t** 291 563 011, **f** 291 563 012 (*moderate; €50*). Simple hotel with the waves breaking below its windows. Rooms are featureless, so make sure you get one with a balcony and a sea view. 'Mountain view' is a euphemism for 'back alley with rocks'.

Quinta da Capela, Sitio do Folhadal, 9225 Porto da Cruz, **t** 291 562 491 (*moderate; €65*). An 18th-century *quinta* on the cliffs outside Porto da Cruz, still owned by the original family and now run as a guest house. Rooms are large; some furnished with heavy wardrobes and four-poster beds. The surrounding village is entirely residential, so you'll need a car to get anywhere for dinner.

Santana

O Curtado, 9230-088 Santana, **t** 291 572 240, **f** 291 574 538 (*moderate–inexpensive; €50 new building, €30 old building*). Clean and simple roadside inn a kilometre or two east of Santana. A *levada* flows behind, and the hills roll out in front. A new wing on the mountainside behind the original building offers panoramic views up and down the coast. The restaurant serves good home cooking, and the staff are refreshingly friendly to customers.

O Escondidinho das Canas, Pico António Fernandes, 9230 Santana, **t** 291 572 319 (*inexpensive; €30*). Spend a night in a traditional A-shaped Santana cottage. There's room for two downstairs, and two more up in the loft.

Quinta do Furão, Achada do Gramacho, 9230-082 Santana, **t** 291 570 100, **f** 291 573 560, *www.quintadofurao.com*, *quintadofurao@mail.telepac.pt* (*expensive; €100*). The luxury option in the north, attached to the Blandy wine lodge and surrounded by vineyards. A clifftop location ensures magnificent views, especially from rooms on the north-east corner of the hotel.

Boaventura

Solar de Boaventura, Serrão Boaventura, 9240-046 São Vicente, **t** 291 860 888, **f** 291 863 877 (*moderate; from €59*). An 18th-century farmhouse that once served as a school, now converted into a choice guesthouse. While away the hours in a basket chair on the veranda, potter about in the pretty garden or snuggle up with a good book in an armchair in the old kitchen. Rooms are tastefully furnished, and there is a new extension, complete with a glass-walled breakfast room.

Ponta Delgada

Corte do Norte, Sítio do Lugar, 9240-121 Ponta Delgada, **t** 291 862 070, **f** 291 862 072 (*moderate; €48*). Comfortable, family-run hotel that would make a good base in the north. There are great views out to sea from the northernmost upstairs room, and the restaurant downstairs offers large portions of well-prepared Madeiran cuisine.

Casa da Capelinha, Terreiro, 9240-121 Ponta Delgada, **t/f** 291 862 127, mobile 966 124 017, *www.apartment-on-madeira.com*, *casadacapelinha@hotmail.com* (*moderate; €40–55*). A gem for self-caterers. Four apartments in a converted house adjoining a 16th-century chapel, in a quiet part of the village just a short walk from the tidal pool. Kitchens are really well equipped, and there's a small garden complete with sun-loungers and barbecue. The downstairs apartments are a little subterranean, but upstairs ones have a fine view up the coast. Apartments can sleep up to four.

Eating Out

Pico Arieiro

Pousada do Pico do Arieiro Restaurants, **t** 291 230 110 (*expensive; €35*). The **restaurant** in the *pousada* building itself is classy, cosy and has good views. The menu is imaginative, and the food is good. Try the seafood pancake, or rabbit simmered in wine. At the **snack bar** beside the car park (*moderate–inexpensive*) you can have cakes, toasted sandwiches and a range of soups.

Poiso

Abrigo do Pastor, Estrada das Carreiras, **t** 291 922 060 (*moderate; €20*). Large hunting-lodge-style restaurant on the road between Poiso and Camacha. Tuck into such tummy-warmers as Brazilian *feijoada* (black bean stew), goat stew or rabbit 'hunter's style', with mushrooms.

Ribeiro Frio

Victor's Bar, **t** 291 575 898 (*moderate–inexpensive; €15–20*). Woody cabin with a log fire and view over a trout-inhabited stream. Trout – smoked, grilled and boiled – find their way on to the menu, and there is a deliciously thick trout soup.

Portela

Miradouro de Portela, **t** 291 966 169 (*inexpensive; €12*). Bustling crossroads bar and restaurant serving simple Madeiran fare with loads of vegetables and salad to accompany the meat or fish, with good home-made cider to wash it all down.

Santana

Grutas do Faial, **t** 291 572 541 (*moderate–inexpensive; €15–20*). Restaurant in a cave (once the garage for the local bus) beside the road between Ribeiro Frio and Santana. Good *pratos do dia*, though the fish can be a little tired.

Quinta do Furão, **t** 291 572 130 (*expensive–moderate; €20–40*). Newly created *quinta*, established by the Madeira Wine Company, and very much for tourists. The kitchen churns out the usual grills and *espada* with banana, but the food is well prepared, and the views pleasing.

1919 by Francisco Franco, Madeira's most respected artist, in celebration of the fifth centenary of the discovery of the island.

At Terreiro da Luta, the eucalyptus forest comes to an abrupt end and laurel and pine trees take over. Poking out of the tops of the trees is **Pico Alto**, a *miradouro* and picnic area that offers a vista over the ocean. **Montado do Pereiro**, a few kilometres further along the 103, is a shadier picnic spot (and it boasts a toilet), but the views are not as impressive. A while later you come to the crossroads at Poiso, where you'll find a (somewhat touristy) restaurant.

The road to the left takes you up to **Pico Arieiro**, which at 1,810m is Madeira's third highest mountain. As suddenly as the pine forest began, it gives way to bracken, heather and stunted conifers. You climb higher and higher to the rocky, windswept peak, your ears popping from the change in altitude. Heaved up by volcanic turbulence, then eroded by wind and water, the surrounding mountains look as if they have edges of jagged steel. Crevices and valleys seem hacked into the earth's surface, as if they had been torn out by the slash of a giant claw. At first it looks as if barely anything at all grows on the gaunt rocks, but sit for a moment, take your eyes away from the vast panorama, and within touching distance you'll find another world. Poking through the stones are diminutive versions of plants that grow lower down the slopes, together with tough little herbs and heathers that can hold their own at this height. In spring and early summer especially, the ground is speckled with tiny flowers. You might even be lucky enough to find a delicate mauve rock orchid.

It is cold up here, and often misty – though you may find that you break out into the sunlight above the cloudline. On clear days the view is breathtaking, taking in most of the island. Sunrises that infuse the mist with pink, and sunsets that splash orange and purple over the peaks and plateaux, are well worth a drive in the dark. There is a café/restaurant where you can warm yourself up with tasty soup, a *pousada* where you can spend the night and a stone path that leads to the island's highest peak (*see* p.175).

Ribeiro Frio

After **Poiso**, road 103 winds down through natural forests to Ribeiro Frio ('Cold River'). Hydrangeas and agapanthus line the way for most of the year, pink belladonna lilies bloom from September to November, and the thick blue brushes of Pride of Madeira push their way through the foliage between February and May. Stop off for a short wander in the woods, and you'll find other indigenous plants – bushes of Madeiran yellow foxgloves, or lupin-like *piornos*. Along the streams and *levadas* are fine examples of the Madeira orchid, with its curious inch-long purple flower.

Ribeiro Frio consists of a handful of buildings in a quiet glade, but will probably detain you for a good hour or two. First comes the **Trout Hatchery** (*free access*), where the stream is dammed and channelled into terraces of troughs and pools. Trout the size of a pinkie flit about in some of the ponds; in others swim big, fat, pan-ready fish, following each other nose-to-tail in an endless circle. Around the hatchery, and continuing across the road, is a small **Botanical Garden** where, helpfully labelled, you can see examples of Madeira's indigenous plants, as well as other species common on the island. Next door, beside the stream, is a cosy chalet-style restaurant with an open log fire. In the kitchens, trout from the hatchery meet their fate. Walkers warm themselves around the fire, sipping coffee and soup – for although it looks as if you are at the bottom of a valley, Ribeiro Frio is a good 800 metres above sea level, and is often quite nippy.

There is a small chapel beside the restaurant, and a wooden bridge over the stream. Farmers pass by, leaning on thick sticks and carrying conical baskets laden with apples, rich black soil, bracken – or whatever the season demands. The air is clear and bracingly fresh, and despite an increasing popularity with tourists Ribeiro Frio manages to keep its peaceful ambience. (The calm was momentarily shattered in 1994 when a severed leg, complete with climbing boot, came floating down the brook. A solitary walker had disappeared a month or two before in the hills nearby, but the leg turned out not to be his. Both mysteries remain unsolved.)

Just past the restaurant, on the left, a path leads off the road to the **Balcões**, wooden balconies built on a ledge overlooking a magnificent, craggy valley. It is an easy walk (*20 minutes each way*) past apple orchards, oaks and chestnuts and through a mossy mini-ravine, rather like one of the grottoes built by 'mad' King Ludwig of Bavaria (*see* 'Walks', p.183).

Road 103 heads on from Ribeiro Frio past forests, farms and fruit trees, down to the coast. After about 5km the road forks. The main part plunges down into the valley and on to Faial; a smaller road off to the right leads to São Roque do Faial and Porto da Cruz.

The Northeast Coast

São Roque do Faial and Faial

São Roque do Faial is a charming, rural hamlet tucked away from the tourist throngs. São Roque offers a close-up view of Madeiran farming life, and there is an excellent small hotel which puts the village near the top of the list as a base in the northern part of the island. On the way into the village a sign to Levada do Baixo/ Água d'Alto points you on to a path that winds through farmland and up into the surrounding hills. Steps lead down a precipitous slope to a series of **waterfalls** and limpid **rock pools**, so deep, villagers say, that nobody has ever touched the bottom. A generation ago these were favourite local swimming holes, but the São Roque youth headed off to less remote spots that had bars and sunbeds, and the paths to the pools became overgrown. The parish council has recently promised to clear the brambles and renovate the path, but until they do the way down remains difficult.

Just past the hotel, a *miradouro* sign (marked 'Veredão do Chão do Cedro Gordo') leads you off the road into a little cluster of farmhouses. In harvest season you'll have to pick your way around blankets covered with beans and maize, laid out in the sun to dry. Odd smells and noises emanate from small huts along the way. There is so little flat grazing land in Madeira, and the slopes are so treacherous, that cows, pigs and goats are kept permanently in custom-built shelters. Most families have only one or two animals and tend them lovingly, bringing piles of bracken, grass and even arum lilies for bedding and fodder. Cows have names – ranging from the Portuguese equivalents of 'Daisy' and 'Bluebell' to those of soap opera stars – and on Sundays you might catch a rare glimpse of a Princesa or Rita on the end of a rope, joining the family for a walk. The birth of a calf, or the slaughter of a pig, is a great event involving neighbours, relatives and many glasses of wine and *aguardente*.

The village church is a fairly modern one, built in 1925, but has a terrace with a view over a wide valley and back up into the mountains. All you hear is birdsong, the odd rooster crowing, occasional volleys of dog barks, and the water running over the rocks way below. There is another *miradouro* on the road to Porto da Cruz. Here you share a hilltop with a graveyard, and get a view in all directions.

São Roque do Faial overlooks **Penha da Águia** (Eagle Cliff), a massive block of rock rising almost vertically on all sides to a height of some 600m. On one side of the rock is the village of Faial, on the other is Porto da Cruz.

Faial gets its name from the Azorean wax myrtle (Portuguese: *faia*), the waxy-leafed tree which produces candleberries and which was once prolific in the area. The village seems to come in for more than its fair share of elemental battering. During a storm in 1993 a whole chunk of the coast here was washed out to sea, and the Ribeira do Faial, normally almost dry, can turn into a raging, destructive torrent. (In the 1980s it completely destroyed the main road bridge.) Today Faial is a fairly nondescript village, and its only past claim to fame was that it was once presided over by a scandalously eccentric *morgado* (landowner). He used to ride his horse into church and trained it to kneel at the elevation of the Host. Because he was the *morgado* he was given a decent burial but, when a flood washed his tomb out to sea, locals considered it an act of divine retribution.

Porto da Cruz and Portela

Porto da Cruz is one of the oldest towns on the coast and it is famed among the Madeirense for producing the best local plonk, called *vinho americano*. Descendants of Tristão Vaz began growing sugar cane here in the early 16th century. For many years Porto da Cruz thrived as a centre of the island's sugar industry, and it is one of the few places still to have a working mill and *aguardente* distillery. But, in the shadow (as one 19th-century guidebook put it) of the 'black and dismal precipice' of Penha da Águia, Porto da Cruz has a lost and desolate air. EU grants, however, have helped rebuild the seaside promenade and construct a big tidal swimming pool between the rocks, making Porto da Cruz a pleasant place to stop off for a quiet day or two beside the sea.

From Porto da Cruz a road climbs steeply inland, through a series of extraordinary bends, to **Portela**, 669m above sea-level. Positioned at the junction of roads to Machico, Santo da Serra and the north coast, as well as being the meeting point of a number of footpaths and a *levada*, Portela has long been a travellers' rest spot. There is still a restaurant here (*see* p.171), and when the weather is fine the view up the coast is hard to beat.

Santana, Queimadas and Pico Ruivo

Next stop along the coast road from Faial is **Santana**, named after Santa Ana, the mother of the Virgin. The 16th-century chronicler Dr Gaspar Fructuoso enthused that the fertile soils of Santana brought forth 'an abundance of chestnuts, nuts and fruit of every sort'. Little has changed, except that experiments by the Regional Government have recently added kiwi fruit to the cornucopia.

Santana is the birthplace of Baltazar Diaz, a 16th-century poet and playwright known mainly for his dramas on the lives of saints. But those not *au fait* with the recondite corners of Portuguese literature link the village more readily with the **triangular thatched huts** that feature in Madeiran tourist literature. These eye-catching cottages have become something of an island icon, but are really only to be found in the area around Santana (*see* **Architecture, Arts and Crafts**, p.47). The village itself has little to warrant more than a fleeting visit, but it is the setting-off point for two of the most awesomely beautiful parts of the island.

Just east of the town centre a road leads to a small cable car that takes you sideways down the cliff face, past a waterfall, terraces and pendant greenery to the rocky shore below.

From the southeastern side of town a road leads right up to the **Pico das Pedras National Park** (*free access*), from where you can reach Pico Ruivo, which at 1,861m is the highest peak on the island. After an uninspiring stretch of villas and motor scrapyards you enter thickets of laurel, then climb steeply beyond the treeline to bare rocks, scrubby vegetation and mountain goats, and on upwards into mountain scenery of overwhelming grandeur. On the way you pass the striking **Homem em Pé** ('Standing Man'), towering shafts of basalt thrust up from the turf. (There are a couple of snack bars along the first part of the road, and picnic spots with dramatic, commanding views in the park itself.)

From the car park at the end of the road it is a relatively easy 40-minute walk to the summit of **Pico Ruivo** – often high above the clouds, with a view across the whole island. The air is sharp and clean. There is no sound of a distant motorway, no passing jet, no reminder of the 21st century at all – just birds, wind, running water and the hollow tink-tink of goatbells.

> *The utter silence and absence of all habitations or cultivation gives one the sensation in these mountain solitudes of being a thousand leagues away from the haunts of men.'*
>
> 19th-century traveller Ellen Taylor, in a letter home in 1881

Her words hold just as true today. There is something primitive about the landscape – a powerful, elemental quality that makes you feel that the gods are very close at hand. In bad weather, the swirling mists, strange shadows and glowering skies are awesome. More than one writer has remarked on how you might expect Wotan to make a sudden appearance, and there is something curiously Olympian about being so high up on such a small piece of land, looking out across the ocean.

The walk onwards to **Pico Arieiro** is one of the most spectacular the island has to offer (*see* p.182).

A short way beyond the turn-off to Pico das Pedras is a narrow track leading to the **Queimadas**. You can (if your nerves and suspension can take it) drive the 6km to a government rest house, after which cars are forbidden. The rest house is surrounded by tranquil gardens with ponds and fountains, and around that is one of the thickest and most luscious of all Madeira's natural forests. Ironwood, laurel, til and Madeiran mahogany trees cover the slopes; ferns, flowers and creepers crowd in between them. Soft mosses and lichens fill the gaps. Birdsong filters through the leaves, and with every breath you seem to catch a different fragrance. Queimadas is untouched. It will make you very careful about giving the label 'Eden' or 'paradise' to anywhere else, ever again.

From the rest house at Queimadas you can walk to **Caldeirão Verde** (the 'Green Cauldron'), a 300m-high waterfall that plunges into a deep pool, and on via some rather flimsy bridges and through tunnels to the bottom of **Caldeirão Inferno** ('Hell's Cauldron'), a dramatic volcanic chasm that local shepherds once refused to go into. 'Souls that enter must stay for eternity,' was the dire warning. (The walk takes over two hours each way; *see* pp.182–3.)

Santana to São Jorge: Quinta do Furào

On the western outskirts of Santana is the **Quinta do Furão** (*see* 'Eating Out', p.171), a new enterprise of the Madeira Wine Company, aimed squarely at the tourist market. At harvest time you can see local lads stripped to the waist, crushing grapes by foot, and can even join in if you like. If this is not really your idea of fun, or if you arrive at the wrong time of year, you can sit in the restaurant and gaze out to sea over the cliffs – though the best view is to be had for free by taking a walk through the vineyard behind the *quinta* complex. From here you can see waterfalls plunging over the precipice into the sea.

After Quinta do Furão the road hugs the edges of the mountains, winding through jungly growth and past terraces of vines, which splash the hillsides with red, orange and brown in October when the leaves begin to die. If you're driving and have time for a short diversion, take the Ilha turn-off. After about two kilometres another smaller road (marked 'Achada do Marquês') takes you through a tunnel to a wild, wooded valley. Just after the Ilha turn-off a dirt track leads through the vineyards to a quiet beach at the foot of the cliffs (*see* 'Sports and Activities', p.170).

São Jorge and Arco de São Jorge

Next stop along the main road is **São Jorge**, which has an 18th-century church with a curious façade. Set into the wall inside is a pulpit decorated with carved drapes and surmounted by a trumpeting angel. After a short drive along the clifftops you descend to **Arco de São Jorge** (St George Arch), a flat semicircular basin where the crumbling stone terraces and the square farmhouses with their green shutters and peeling pink or cream walls give the village an Italian air. Good soil, abundant *levada* water and the mountain shield against cold winds make this the most fertile spot on the island. The climate must be good for brains too, for people from Arco de São Jorge have a reputation for being the island eggheads – and, in fact, in the first part of this century illiteracy rates were much lower here than elsewhere on Madeira. The brightest light in the village firmament was the eccentric 19th-century troubadour Manuel Gonçalves, most known for his ballad 'The Wizard of the North'.

A tunnel takes you out of the Arco de São Jorge basin into a **valley** surrounded by hills that sweep up into delicate sharp peaks, like cake icing. A road marked 'Falça de Baixo' takes you into the heart of the valley. For the moment the road stops after a few kilometres, but one day it will plough through the island to Curral das Freiras, destroying some of Madeira's most unspoiled scenery en route. Until then, this is fine walking territory (*see* pp.182–3).

Boaventura

The main road winds on, past a couple of little waterfalls, to Boaventura, a busy farming village perched on top of the cliffs. Prime spot on a promontory is taken by the parish graveyard, but the authorities have tucked in a picnic table alongside so that you can share the view.

At grape harvest time there are baskets of the fruit everywhere, black mush left over from pressing is piled on street corners, and the air is filled with the musty smell of new wine. But Boaventura's most lucrative crop is the cane used by the wicker-workers of Camacha. The damp climate is just right for the reeds, which grow to great heights. In January and February, farmers' lorries outrageously overladen with teetering bundles of reeds career about the mountain passes.

Ponta Delgada

Ponta Delgada, a few kilometres further on, appears from the main road to be little more than a spread of modern villas, but a flagstoned street leading down to the sea takes you through an older, more attractive part of the town. (The pink house on the corner of this street was the home, until his death in the 1980s, of the writer Dr Horácio Bento de Gouveia, lauded for his sketches of rural island life.)

At the end of the street, built out over the rocks on the beach, is the church of **Senhor do Bom Jesus**. While the first chapel on this site was being built in the 16th century, a crucifix washed up on shore. Parishioners saw this as a particularly auspicious miracle, and the cross became the focal point of what is now one of Madeira's biggest religious festivals. The original church burnt down on 12 July 1908, but the Christ-figure was saved – though badly charred. Today it is kept in a glass box in the right-hand corner of the nave. Near the church is a popular tidal **swimming pool** (*see* 'Sports and Activities', p.170).

After Ponta Delgada the road tightly follows the coastline – often hemmed in by cliffs and occasionally splashed from above by waterfalls – to São Vicente.

The Northwest

Across the Island to São Vicente

Road 104 cuts straight through the middle of the island, from the town of Ribeira Brava ('Wild River') on the southwest coast to São Vicente in the north. At first it follows the riverbed (despite its name Ribeira Brava is usually no more than a trickle), past boulders and willows through a steep-sided valley where the mountains have pointy peaks – as if they'd been drawn in by children. Then it disappears into a tunnel that cuts under the mountainous interior and emerges on the northern coast.

Alternatively, you can follow the old road that climbs suddenly from near the entrance to the tunnel, twisting through the lines of narrow terraces that are combed into the lower slopes, to the balder heights of **Serra de Água**, and on to the top of the **Encumeada Pass** (just over 1,000m high). There are picnic spots along the way, and a couple of restaurants where you can stop and soak in the view.

As you go over the pass the prospect suddenly changes. The stark, rocky mountains get covered in the bracken, ferns, creepers and trees that flourish in the damper climate of the north. The road winds down through the forest, past the odd sprinklings of houses, to São Vicente. (Just before you get there, at the hamlet of **Rosário**, a country road leads off to the right. It makes an attractive alternative route, travelling through farmland and vineyards, and ending up in the village itself.)

São Vicente

An attractive spot at the junction of two main roads, and with a number of walks nearby, São Vicente makes a good base for exploring the northern part of the island. The village straggles uneventfully for some distance along the main road, but eventually comes to a focus around the parish church. Much of the centre is closed to motor traffic and has been sprucely renovated. Cobbled streets lined with tubs of flowers run between high-walled gardens and sparkling white Baroque houses. Old men sit under the palm trees on the village square, looking a bit bemused that their cosy *venda* bar has sprouted decorative canopies and plastic terrace furniture. Enthusiastic restorers have also had a go at the church, painting and gilding the Baroque interior to pristine brightness. On a knoll overlooking the village is the **Clocktower of Our Lady of Fátima**, put up in the 1940s. It is inaccessible unless you feel like beating your way through bracken, scrambling over rocks and scratching your way through brambles. The view that you'll get is (quite literally) not worth the sweat.

The main part of São Vicente is set a little inland, in the valley of the **Ribeira do São Vicente**. Road 104 carries on along the riverbank for the few hundred metres to the coast, where it joins the North Coast Road (101). Here a solitary chunk of rock pokes up out of the dry riverbed. Carved into it is a tiny **chapel**, built at the end of the 17th century. On asking his Funchalese guide about the origin of the *capelinha*, Edward Wells, a young American who passed by in 1837, got the reply: 'People tell sea came up around this rock, Governo said Build a Chapel when chapel built sea come up no more, I don't know perhaps people tell lies.' Today a few tons of concrete help keep the waters at bay, and a few hotels and restaurants line up along the shore.

Just inland from the village are the **São Vicente Caverns** (*open daily, tours approx every 15mins 10–6.30, tours last around 20mins; adm adults €4, children free*). Unlike so

Sports and Activities

Swimming

Seixal: A road labelled '*Praia*' just outside the village leads to a large natural rock pool surrounded by concrete terraces (a recent addition that has not improved the site). The water is limpid, you're protected from heavy waves and strong currents, and there's good snorkelling – all in all, the best spot for a swim on the coast, and not nearly as busy as the pools at Porto Moniz.

Porto Moniz: Natural rock pools here are popular all year round, and get very crowded in the summer. You can dive into the open sea from concrete jetties. Bars, cafés and restaurants are all close at hand.

Where to Stay

Serra de Água

Pousada dos Vinháticos, Serra de Água, 9350-306 Ribeira Brava, **t** 291 952 344, **f** 291 952 540 (*moderate; from €80*). Lonely stone building alongside the mountain pass, with a view down a wild and craggy valley. A good base for walkers; the rooms in the main building are cramped, though there are spacious log cabins alongside.

Encumeada

Residencial Encumeada, Serra de Água, 9350 Ribeira Brava, **t** 291 951 282, **f** 291 951 281, *www.residencialencumeada.com*, *recepcao@residencialencumeada.com* (*moderate; from €80*). On a prime spot towards the top of the Encumeada pass. The best views are from rooms facing back down the valley towards Ribeira Brava.

São Vicente

Estalagem Praia Mar, Calhau, 9240 São Vicente, **t** 291 842 383, **f** 291 842 749 (*moderate; €40*). Right on the seafront and good value. The rooms are comfortable, and have double-glazing in case you find that the sound of waves doesn't have the lullaby effect described in romantic novels. Rooms 10 and 20 have large balconies overlooking the sea.

Estalagem do Mar, Juncos-Fajã da Areia, 9240 São Vicente, **t** 291 840 010, **f** 291 840 019 (*moderate; €55*). Swishest and priciest of the São Vicente hotels, though perhaps in need of a little renovation. Complete with tennis court, jacuzzi and panorama bar. All rooms have a balcony and sea view.

Casa da Camélia, Sítio do Poiso, 9240-031 São Vicente, **t** 291 842 206, **f** 291 842 208, *www.svicente.pt* (*moderate; €35*). A nicely converted house, which for generations belonged to a family of carpenters, in the upper part of the village. Madeiran antiques abound, and the heavy-beamed lounge has the atmosphere of an ancient inn. Communal kitchen.

Casa da Piedade, Laranjal, 9240-031 São Vicente, **t** 291 846 042, **f** 291 846 044, (*moderate; €50*). *Quinta*-style house in a beautiful garden in the upper reaches of São Vicente village. Rooms are comfortable and there's a communal kitchen for the use of visitors.

Solar da Bica, Sítio dos Lameiros, 9240-211 São Vicente, **t** 291 842 018, **f** 291 842 023 (*moderate; from €35*). Rural B&B-style accommodation for a real sense of peace, in a delightful spot at the foot of hills, with vineyards coming up to the back door, just outside São Vicente.

Seixal

Estalagem Brisamar, Cais, 9270 Seixal, **t** 291 854 476, **f** 291 854 477 (*moderate; €40*). Small, quiet, modern, family-run inn on the quay. Rooms 2, 3 and 5 have balconies with attractive views of the bay.

Porto Moniz

Prices in this favoured spot for tour operators may rise in summer months.

many other experiences billed as 'a journey to the bowels of the earth', a visit to these caves is not accompanied by lurid lights and piped organ music. Instead, you are taken on a fascinating walk through the tubular underground hollows made deep within the mountains by volcanic magma.

Residencial Calhau, 9270-095 Porto Moniz, **t** 291 853 104, **f** 291 853 443, *www.residencialcalhau.web.pt*, *calhau@residencialcalhau.web.pt* (*moderate–inexpensive; €35–40*). Simply furnished rooms, many of them built dramatically right on top of the rocks, with waves crashing almost at your bedroom wall.

Gaivota, 9270-095 Porto Moniz, **t** 291 850 030, **f** 291 850 041, *aptgaivota@net.sapo.pt* (*moderate–inexpensive; €35–40*). Spacious new holiday apartments overlooking the village at Porto Moniz.

Rodrigues, 9270-095 Porto Moniz, **t** 291 852 233 (*inexpensive; €25*). Beachfront guesthouse. Downstairs, the landlady's washing flaps on the line, as if in a soap-powder advert. In the bedrooms upstairs there are frilly counterpanes and big wardrobes. Two rooms have a sea view.

O Salguerio, 9270-095 Porto Moniz, **t** 291 850 080, **f** 291 850 089, *hotelsalgueiro@hotmail.com* (*inexpensive; from €35*). Cheap and cheerful rooms near the sea.

Euro Moniz, Vila do Porto Moniz, **t** 291 850 050, **f** 291 853 933, *www.euromoniz.com*, *reservas@euromoniz.com* (*moderate; from €50*). Modern hotel near the sea, complete with pools, sauna, mini-gym. Front rooms have balconies and sea views.

Paúl da Serra

Pico da Urze, Sítio dos Palheiros, 9370 Calheta, **t** 291 820 150, **f** 291 820 159, *picodaurze@picodaurze.com* (*moderate; €43*). Windswept and splendidly isolated inn, standing all alone in the middle of the open Paúl da Serra plateau.

Eating Out

Encumeada

Snack Bar Restaurante Encumeada, **t** 291 952 319 (*inexpensive; €11–15*). Small restaurant and barrel-lined bar perched at the top of the Encumeada pass. You can get char-grilled chicken, a good bean stew, and lighter meals. There's also a potentially head-thumping selection of home-made liqueurs.

São Vicente

Ferro Velho, **t** 291 842 384 (*inexpensive; €7*). Friendly bar and restaurant near the church in the village centre. Jostle with the locals for a table at lunchtime, and enjoy a tasty *prego* or light meal.

O Virgílio, **t** 291 842 467 (*moderate; €18*). Virgilio da Silva Pereira's bar on the beachfront has gradually expanded to take a restaurant and small shop under its wing, with a veranda that spans all three. This is the place where things happen in São Vicente. Locals and visitors alike crowd in for drinks, snacks and good home-cooked food (which includes *espetada* cooked as it should be done – on a laurel stick over a log fire).

Caravela, **t** 291 842 814 (*inexpensive; €18*). Cheerful fish restaurant on the seafront, popular with Madeiran families over weekends. Also hamburgers and lighter meals.

Restaurante Many, Fajã da Areia, just outside São Vicente on the Porto Moniz road, **t** 291 842 243 (*moderate–inexpensive; €14–22*). Current hot tip among locals, and hugely popular for Sunday lunch. Seafood is the speciality of the house, though you'll also get hearty stews and other traditional Madeiran dishes.

Paúl da Serra

Jungle Rain, Estalagem Pico da Urze, **t** 291 820 150 (*inexpensive; €12–18*). Bizarrely named – and even more bizarrely decorated, given its location on an arid mountain plateau. Tuck in to healthy wholewheat pasta and vegetable bake or curried chicken with fruit, while sitting in a cavern hung rather alarmingly with plastic jungle creepers that follow the theme.

The North Coast Road

Most of us preferred walking to being carried along this 'ledge', which is really quite six feet wide, but has no parapet. It is cut in the cliff several hundred feet above the sea. The scenery is most splendid, with very beautiful waterfalls descending from a great height... The path is tunnelled wherever a waterfall interposes.

Ellen Taylor on the experience of a hammock journey to Seixal, 1881

With the addition of a low parapet, but with very little increase in width, Ellen Taylor's 'ledge' was, until the late 1990s, the North Coast Road, a hot contender for the title of the most beautiful corniche in the world. Waterfalls tumbled over tunnel entrances, giving you, or your car, a good dousing. It is still possible to follow this road (now one-way in the direction of Porto Moniz) instead of going through the new tunnels; waves crash against the cliffs below, vines cling to minute, precarious terraces, and the views are breathtaking.

Seixal is a small fishing port, ignored by most tourists who head on to the more commercial Porto Moniz. A few brightly painted fishing boats lie upside down at the end of a crumbling jetty (from where you get a good view of the waterfalls up the coast). The beach is cleaner here than at São Vicente, and there are rock pools for the children. Some of the best **swimming** on the whole north coast is to be had just beyond the village (*see* 'Sports and Activities', p.179).

Porto Moniz

Eight kilometres past Seixal is Porto Moniz, the most touristy of the north coast towns. The main attraction is the series of large **natural pools** in the volcanic rock on the seashore. Tourists and islanders alike flock here to swim and lie in the sun. A cluster of hotels and restaurants has grown up beside the pools and Porto Moniz has become a popular stop-off for coach parties of day-trippers. Originally, the village was called Ponta do Tristão, but this led to confusion as the same name was given to a neighbouring promontory (the point from which a diagonal line across to Ponta da Oliveira, near Caniço, divided Madeira into the east and west *capitanias* ruled over by Vaz and Zarco respectively, *see* p.36). In 1577 the port was given its new name – after Francisco Moniz, an Algarve nobleman who was married to Filipa da Câmara, one of Zarco's granddaughters. Little of old Porto Moniz remains, but up on the steep slopes, away from the pools, there is a quiet village square and a small 17th-century church, much renovated over the years, but with some decorative original stonework.

Just before you drive into Porto Moniz, a road leads up to **Fanal**, one of the eeriest and most ancient parts of the island. A ridge along the mountaintops, over 1,000m high, Fanal is often shrouded in thick mist. Stunted, twisted trees cast strange shadows through the fog and a deadening silence hangs over all. The road through Fanal is all but impassable to anything but four-wheel-drive vehicles, but it does go on to connect with the road across Paúl da Serra. The heart of Fanal is a good two hours' walk from either of the main roads, and isn't somewhere that you should venture alone. Mists descend suddenly, it can get very cold, and it is possible to get quickly and horribly lost.

Walks

These are suggestions for walks you can follow, not a detailed guide to the routes. It essential to go properly equipped and to take a good map (*see* 'Walking', pp.57–9).

Pico Arieiro–Pico das Torres–Pico Ruivo

Moderate–difficult. 3–3½ hours. Tunnels.

A strenuous but exhilarating walk between Madeira's three highest peaks. Much of it is fairly easy going, along a path, but there are hundreds of stone steps to tackle and many sudden drops, unprotected by rails. It is essential to check the weather report before setting out. Landslides may block the path from time to time. There is no road to Pico Ruivo, so once there you either have to return the way you came, or make a longer walk of it.

Pico Arieiro–Pico Ruivo–Homem em Pé–Queimadas–Santana

Moderate–difficult. 7 hours. Tunnels.

Follow the above walk to Pico Ruivo, then follow the eastward path to the car park above the Pico das Pedras National Park. A further path leads from the rest house, past the towering rocks of the Homem em Pé and on to the road. The path continues a little further down the road towards the Queimadas rest-house, where you can follow the stony track into Santana.

Santana–Queimadas–Caldeirão Verde–Caldeirão do Inferno–Queimadas–Santana

Moderate–difficult. 6–6½ hours.

The track to Queimadas is signposted from the outskirts of Santana. If you take a car as far as the Queimadas rest house you'll knock around 2½ hours off the total

Paúl da Serra and Rabaçal

Beyond Porto Moniz the road turns and heads back south. After 5km a road to the left sweeps you within minutes up to **Paúl da Serra**, a vast, flat moor, quite unlike anywhere else on the island. The plateau – 17km long, up to 6km wide and over 1,500m above sea-level – was probably once a smooth lava stream flowing from a volcano in the distant mountain range. Scrubby grass pokes up through the shale, and gets well cropped by the cows that roam around freely (it's the only place on Madeira where they can). Mists swirl across the flats, then cascade down to the coast, leaving you in warm sun above the clouds. On clear days you get expansive views over valleys and shores on both sides. No buses pass this way, few cars either, and Paúl da Serra is completely uninhabited. It has a wild, lonely romance.

About 15km along the road you come to a turn-off to **Rabaçal**. A narrow track – quite literally just one car wide – twists downhill. 'The descent is perfectly frightful,' journey-time. Follow the *levada* from the rest house (signposted to Caldeirão Verde) across ravines and through tunnels. You come to Caldeirão Verde after the fourth tunnel. Caldeirão do Inferno is reached by following the *levada* for another half-hour, then taking the steps up to a second *levada* (the Levada do Pico Ruivo). After another half-hour, and a few more tunnels, you're there. Then you will have to return the way you came.

Ribeiro Frio–Portela

Moderate. 3 hours.

A sign just below Victor's Bar leads you on to the Levada do Furado. After about 2½ hours you come to a waterhouse, and a few metres later a path leads down on to a smaller *levada*, from which a track leads on to Portela. (For onward walks, *see* p.164.)

Ribeiro Frio–Balcões–Ribeiro Frio

Easy. 30–40 minutes.

Follow the signpost left off the road, just past Victor's Bar. A covered *levada* winds through forests and fruit trees to the viewing balconies. Rather than return, you could follow the *levada* further, past some vertiginous drops. After about half an hour a path hives off right to the forests of Fajã da Nogueira, but the going gets much tougher.

Encumeada–Pico Grande–Curral das Freiras

Moderate–difficult. 6 hours.

From below the snack bar at Encumeada (*see* p.178) a track leads towards Relva (Pico Grande). A signposted path leads off to Curral das Freiras, via Fajã Escura and Casas Próximas.

exclaimed Isabella de França after being carried to Rabaçal in a *rede* (hammock), 'the road so narrow, that every time the *rede* passes one of the many turnings, you hang over the precipice without seeing a particle of the road itself, and are litterally [sic] suspended over the abyss beneath, while the rede is turned!' What you find at the end of the road, however, rewards all your travails. A government rest house nestles in a lush glade. Great swathes of lichen drape over the branches of chestnut trees, brooks cascade over mossy rocks and pour over ledges like miniature waterfalls, making tiny rainbows. The surrounding forest is like the enchanted wood from a fairytale illustration, the trees curling and twisting into such lithe shapes that it would seem perfectly natural for one to start moving, its branches forming a claw-like hand that could pluck you off the path. A 15-minute walk along a *levada* (signposted) brings you to the **Risco Waterfall**. 'I looked up,' wrote Isabella de França after her visit, 'and felt as I can never feel again!... A tall, tall, semicircular concave rock, covered with a profusion of the most exquisite foliage...ferns and mosses and hanging wreaths, bright scarlet moss cups, white flowering plants, orange-coloured fungi...and over this exquisite tapestry of leaves, and moss, more than a hundred sparkling jets of liquid silver, dashing from the top of the rock, and falling over into the basin of the river beneath.' A tunnel takes you beneath the falls (take something waterproof with you – you have to duck through a shower of water to get in). Most people ignore the 'Danger' ('*Perigo*') sign at the entrance and walk as far as a platform under a rocky ledge from where you get a view all the way down the ravine – but it is unwise to go any further as the ground is treacherously slippery, and it is a very long drop.

A fork off the Risco path leads, after another 40 minutes, to the **25 Fontes** where a few smaller waterfalls (though not quite 25) tumble into a pool that feeds a number of *levadas*. There are places where you can picnic along the way, and, although only civil servants can stay overnight in the rest house at Rabaçal, there are tables under the surrounding trees where you are quite welcome to spread out your lunch.

The main road across Paúl da Serra forks a few kilometres past Rabaçal. The right-hand branch descends quickly to the coast. The left-hand road develops into a dramatic mountain pass that joins the 104 at Encumeada. From March to July the gaunt rocks are carpeted in the bright yellow flowers of broom, but for much of the rest of the year the bare peaks look like the setting for one of the more ominous scenes of a Wagner opera. Landslides occur frequently, especially after heavy rains. A few years ago a large boulder reduced the concrete table at a roadside picnic site to rubble. Rather discouragingly, rock and ruined table remained where they were for some months.

One or two smaller roads go up on to the Serra from the west coast. The most attractive of these is one from **Lombo de Salão**, on the outskirts of **Calheta** (*see* pp.195–6). After an almost vertical (and very narrow) ascent past old pink, green and yellow houses, crumbling stone walls with wrought-iron gates, and groups of curious old women who sit on their front steps and peer in through your car window as you edge past, you wind up, via forests, on the plain.

The Western Coast

12

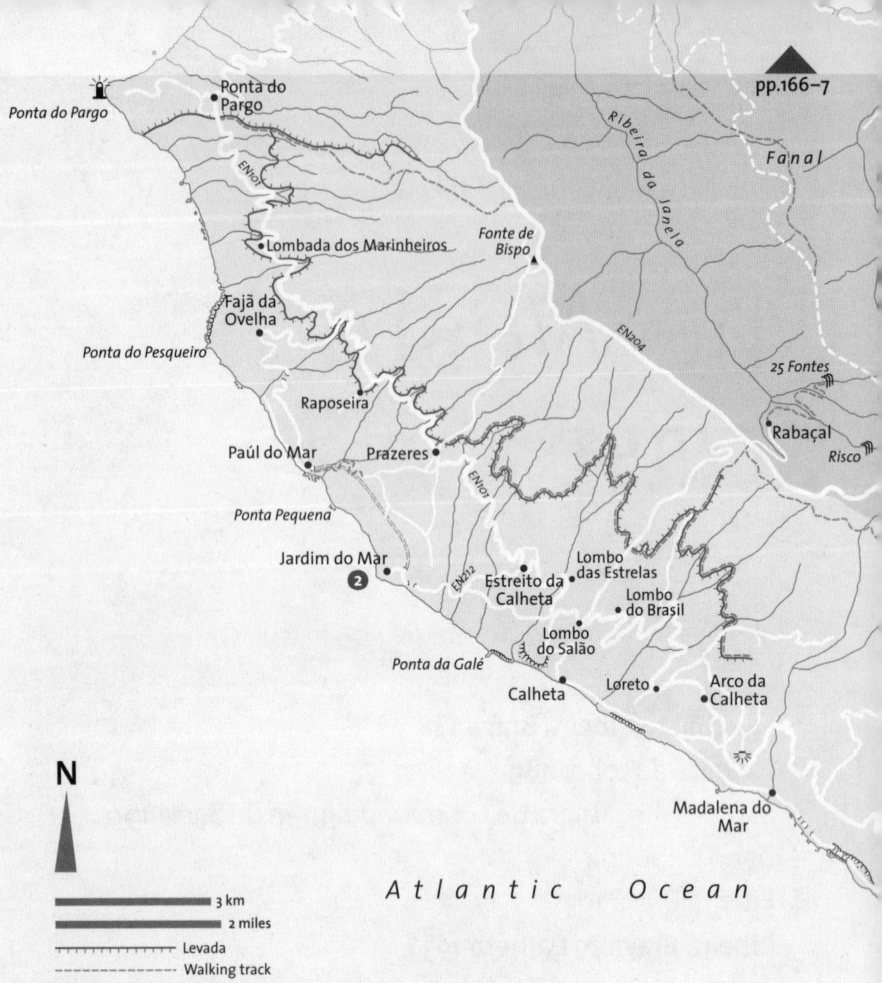

pp.166–7

Ponta do Pargo
Ponta do Pargo
Ribeira da Janela
Fanal
EN101
Lombada dos Marinheiros
Fonte de Bispo
Fajã da Ovelha
Ponta do Pesqueiro
EN204
25 Fontes
Raposeira
Rabaçal
Risco
Paúl do Mar
Prazeres
EN101
Ponta Pequena
Jardim do Mar
2
EN212
Estreito da Calheta
Lombo das Estrelas
Lombo do Brasil
Lombo do Salão
Ponta da Galé
Calheta
Loreto
Arco da Calheta
Madalena do Mar
Atlantic Ocean
N
3 km
2 miles
Levada
Walking track

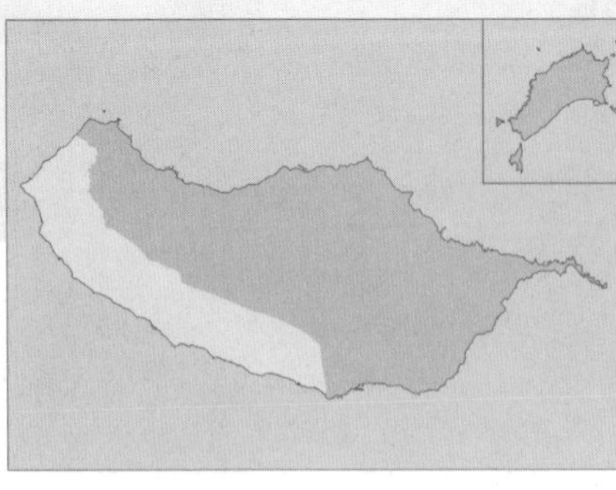

Highlights

1 Cabo Girão, one of the highest sea-cliffs in the world
2 Jardim do Mar, for its cobbled stairways, and flowers bursting from garden walls
3 The Cherry Festival at Jardim da Serra
4 Wooden boats built to an age-old design at Câmara de Lobos

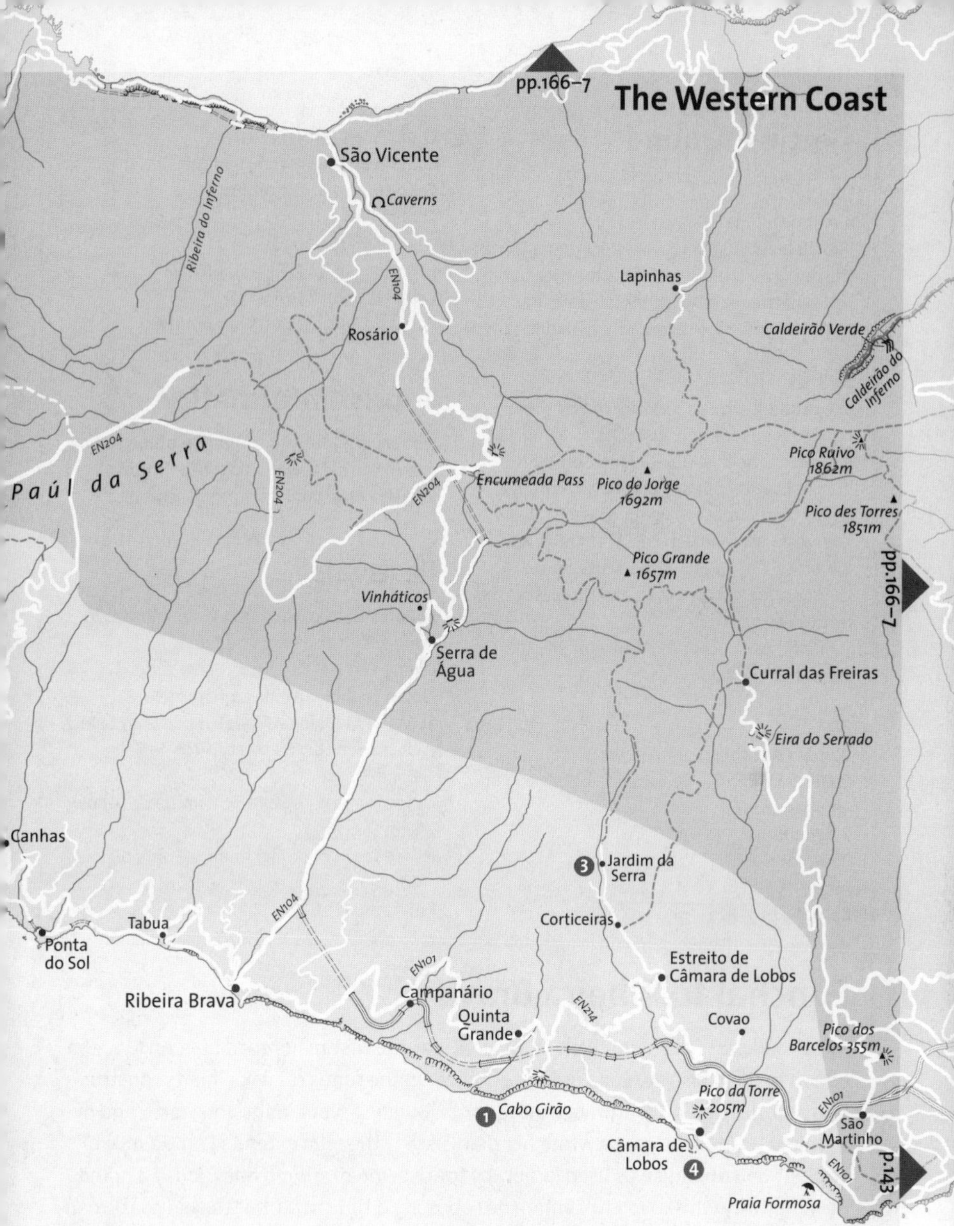

Tour coaches thunder westwards out of Funchal to Câmara de Lobos, where Winston Churchill sat and painted the harbour, then on to Cabo Girão, the second highest promontory in the world. Then, at the coastal resort of Ribeira Brava, passengers tumble out for tea. Groups going north cut across the island from Ribeira Brava. Others make a U-turn and head for home. Very few continue west. Yet along this rather forgotten coast you'll find some of Madeira's quaintest villages, good spots for swimming and a cluster of churches that are the architectural pearls of the island.

Getting Around

By Car

A new double highway runs between Funchal and Ribeira Brava. After Ribeira Brava the going on the old road gets twistier, but a series of tunnels now connects seaside towns that were once accessible only with difficulty.

By Bus

Most buses to the west are run by the Rodoeste bus company, which has a bus station on the Rua Ribeira João Gomes in Funchal, *see* p.77. **Buses 142** and **107** run the length of the coast to Ponta do Pargo. **Bus 4** goes as far as Madalena do Mar, and **bus 6** travels to Ribeira Brava, then cuts across the island to the north coast. Cabo Girão is served by **bus 154**.

All of these buses (and a handful of others) stop at Câmara de Lobos.

By Taxi

Câmara de Lobos: **t** 291 942 144.
Estreito de Câmara de Lobos: **t** 291 945 229 or **t** 291 948 316.
Ribeira Brava: **t** 291 951 800.
Ponta do Sol: **t** 291 972 110.
Arco da Calheta: **t** 291 822 423.
Calheta: **t** 291 822 129.

Distances (from Funchal)

Câmara de Lobos: 9km/15mins.
Cabo Girão: 20km/20mins.
Ribeira Brava: 17km/25mins (new road), 31km/1hr (old road).
Ponta do Sol: 38km/35mins (coast road).
Calheta: 47km/45mins.
Ponta do Pargo: 70km/1hr 20mins.

Tourist Information

There is a tourist information office, **t** 291 951 675, in the old tower on the beachfront at Ribeira Brava, but its hours are sporadic.

Festivals

St Peter: Câmara de Lobos, Ribeira Brava, 29 June; Ponta do Pargo, 24 June.
Cherry Festival: Jardim da Serra, June.
Nossa Senhor: Arco de Calheta, 17 July.
St Maria Madalena: Madalena do Mar, 22 July; Nossa Senhora do Loreto, Arco de Calheta, 7 and 8 Sept .
Grape Harvest: Estreito de Câmara de Lobos, Sept.
Nossa Senhora do Livramento: Ponta do Sol, Oct.
Philharmonic Bands: Ribeira Brava, Oct.

Funchal to Ribeira Brava

The road past Reid's Hotel out of Funchal was the first major road built on Madeira. Begun in 1815, the New Road quickly gobbled up the funds set aside for its construction and suffered hiccoughs in consequence. Building went in fits and starts, and by the time Isabella de França wrote her diary in 1853 the road extended only a mile or two out of town and was used largely by tourists for afternoon rides. Today a brand new highway whisks you to Câmara de Lobos in no time at all, but the old coast road (which was finally finished towards the end of the 19th century) makes a more attractive alternative if you have the time to dawdle.

First stop, after a winding journey past terraces of banana trees, is **Praia Formosa**, a beach covered in smooth, loose rocks that might be called pebbles if they didn't measure ten inches by eight (25cm by 20cm). This is where the dreaded Bertrand de Montluc landed with his 1,000 pirates in 1566, before swooping on Funchal (*see* p.37). Today the Funchalese sweep in the other direction and come here to swim (*see* **Funchal**, 'Sports and Activities', p.99).

Câmara de Lobos

A few kilometres past Praia Formosa you come to the fishing village of Câmara de Lobos. When Zarco discovered the bay, seals were cavorting in the water, so he named it 'Chamber of Wolves' (a sea lion in Portuguese is called a 'sea-wolf') and the name stuck. The '*capitano*' made his first settlement here and built a chapel – though it was not long before he and most of his settlers had moved along the coast to the bay at Funchal. Today Câmara de Lobos is known for the power of its *ponche*, as the spot Winston Churchill loved to paint, and for the size of its *espada* catch. It is also the scapegoat for most of the island's ills. Even the most cultured Madeirense will tell you, without a trace of irony, that the people of Câmara de Lobos are beggars and thieves and breed like flies. What is evident, even in the most fleeting of visits, is that beneath

Where to Stay

There are not many hotels along the western coast. People are beginning to use Ribeira Brava as a base for walks, but it is not an especially attractive village, and São Vicente (*see* p.179) makes a better alternative.

São Martinho

Orca Praia, Prainha do Arieiro, São Martinho, 9000-236 Funchal, **t** 291 763 322, **f** 291 763 311, *h.orcapraia@mail.telepac.pt* (*moderate; from €55*). A rather desolate hotel that tumbles in layers down a cliff face to a black-sanded cave. Acres of marble, walls of glass, a good-sized pool and even a little sand on the beach. All rooms have a sea view, and most have balconies.

Câmara de Lobos

Quinta do Estreito, Rua José Joaquim da Costa, Estreito da Câmara de Lobos, 9325-034 Câmara de Lobos, **t** 291 910 530, **f** 291 910 549, *www.charminghotelsmadeira.com*, *quintaestreito@charminghotelsmadeira.com* (*very expensive; from €185*). Luxurious, tastefully converted *quinta* set in a walled garden in a village high above Câmara de Lobos, with a pool terrace and a good restaurant.

Ribeira Brava

Residencial São Bento, 9350 Ribeira Brava, **t** 291 951 506, **f** 291 951 505 (*moderate; from €30*). By far your best bet here. Liberally done up with solid Madeiran wooden furniture, marble and *azulejos*. Rooms at the western end of the building have better views.

Vale Mar, 9350 Ribeira Brava, **t** 291 952 563, **f** 291 951 166 (*moderate; from €70*). Apartment hotel tucked away in the back streets of Ribeira Brava. Large rooms and a well-regimented sun terrace.

Eating Out

Câmara de Lobos

Ribamar, **t** 291 942 113 (*inexpensive; €15–18*). Fish restaurant that looks out to sea from the square on the west side of the village. Start with octopus in tomato and onion, then choose from an impressive selection of fresh fish or (if you don't mind a 45min wait) gorge yourself on the house speciality – *caldeirada* cooked to an old family recipe.

Churchill's Place, **t** 291 944 336 (*moderate, unless you feel like the lobster; €20*). Restaurant with a view – as near as you'll get to the one Churchill painted. Sit on the terrace and partake of elaborate salads, sticky desserts and main dishes that range from grilled pork to smoked lobster with fruity mango.

Estreito de Câmara de Lobos

São António, **t** 291 910 360 (*moderate–inexpensive; €18–22*). From the outside it looks like a warehouse. Inside it's all neon light, checked tablecloths and blaring televison – but you can have *espetada* that beats any other fish dish on the island. There are other grills too, all done over a wood fire, and good helpings of potato, salad and crispy *milhos frites*.

the crust of romantically crumbling fishermen's cottages there is naked poverty of a degree more reminiscent of a Third World country than of anywhere in the EU.

The Western Village

A bulbous hill splits Câmara de Lobos into two halves. The main road, and the bus, will deposit you in the western part of the village where there is a quiet, cobbled square, complete with a turn-of-the-last-century bandstand and a rocky, rather dirty beach. Just off the square is the 16th-century church of **São Sebastião** which, despite alterations over the centuries, preserves its original, simple shape intact. Inside, St Sebastian braves his arrows in a riotously gilded wall-niche and there are some good Baroque *azulejos*.

A narrow road leads east off the square, along the side of the cliff to the other half of the village. A row of houses, crammed with young families, squashes up against the rock face. One tap, out in the street, brings them water. Plastic basins of dirty dishes line up on the sea wall and washing, strung up along the façades, flaps against the crumbling plaster. Toilets and showers are in a separate building at the end of the row. Beyond this lies the bay.

The Bay

Most of the western side of the bay is taken up by a concrete walkway and an ugly commercial fish market that remains shut up for much of the day. The walkway frays into a tangle of alleys that twist between old whitewashed houses. Halfway through the arc of the bay is a fishermen's chapel, dedicated to **Nossa Senhora da Conceição** and the focus of a lively festival in June. This was the second chapel to be built on the island, after the one put up over the grave of Anne d'Arfet in Machico (*see* pp.34–5). It is a sombre little church with a badly restored Baroque altar. Among the paintings that line the nave is one of an apostle landing an *espada* on the shores of Galilee.

After the chapel the prospect begins to improve. Scores of brightly painted fishing boats lie upturned on the shingle – small *canoas* for coastal fishing and larger *embarcações* for the deep sea. Under the palms on the far side of the bay workmen chop, saw and carve, making boats to a plan that has changed little in the past 500 years. The skeletons of unfinished hulls look like illustrations from a 'how-to' book, and the air is tangy with the smells of tar and freshly cut wood. Behind the boatyard a steep stairway leads up to the terrace on which, according to the plaque, Winston Churchill used to sit and paint. The terrace still affords the best view there is to be had of Câmara de Lobos, but you would have to half-close your eyes and use some imagination to come up with the view the old Bulldog had.

Estreito de Câmara de Lobos and Jardim da Serra

From Câmara de Lobos the main road turns sharply inland, through banana plantations that suddenly give way to vineyards, and up to **Estreito de Câmara de Lobos**, a mountainside village overlooking the bay. Islanders say that the tastiest *espetada* on the island is to be had here (*see* p.189). The big 19th-century church has a spacious terrace from which you can admire the view. Lovers of religious kitsch will find the surrounding shops temptingly stocked with plastic Virgins and saints that light up at night – but there is little else to detain you.

Rather than continuing along the main road, duck off through the village and travel inland – the road forks twice, and you should take the left option each time. Soon the vineyards give way to cherry trees (bright with blossom in the early spring). The road narrows and becomes steeper, twisting through hairpin bends to the hamlet of **Jardim da Serra**. Here there are just a handful of buildings – a house or two, a shop selling farmers' conical baskets and agricultural equipment of biblical design, and an *espetada* bar. But in June, at harvest-time, Jardim da Serra erupts with a cherry festival. The villagers build roadside bars from laurel branches, put up clay ovens, stages and stalls. You can buy whole chickens, flattened out and spiced up for the barbecue, cubes of succulent beef and green laurel sticks, so that you can make your own *espetada* in one of the clay ovens; and *tis*, a light, locally made wine that you sip between nibbling on greasy, garlicky pork knuckles and dried fish. And of course there

Henry Veitch

Henry Veitch was born in Selkirk, Scotland, in 1782, and came to Madeira early in the 19th century. A philanderer, epicure and consummate wheeler and dealer, he soon amassed a vast fortune. A contemporary visitor to Madeira noted that Veitch was 'a most active scheming merchant, and most of the undertakings here owe their origin to him'. At one time he supplied the entire Portuguese navy with madeira, and somehow managed to wangle a £3 levy from every ship that entered Funchal Bay. Showing some flair as an amateur architect, he designed the English Church in Funchal (*see* p.127) as well as a number of houses for himself – including the building that is now the headquarters of the Madeiran Wine Institute (*see* p.122) and the Quinta do Jardim da Serra. He quite openly and cheerfully installed at least one mistress in each of his houses, and his descendants on the island are legion.

Of all his houses the *quinta* at Jardim da Serra was his favourite. He surrounded it with a magnificent garden, importing plants from all over the world. He entertained lavishly. 'Henry Veitch's cellar and madeira parties were famous,' writes Noël Cossart, 'and it is a source of wonder where the cavalcade of gentlemen who rode up to the *quinta* were accommodated. It is known some of them slept on or under the dining table.' Feasting was rounded off with a sumptuous choice of desserts, including 'Royal Eggs' (spun out like vermicelli), sticky cakes called 'Friars' kisses', pastries in the form of icicles and sculpted sugar sweetmeats. At a 'Horticultural Breakfast' the next morning, guests would find tea, coffee, butter, a variety of breads and fruit and flowers – all island produce. This opulence didn't seem to run to furnishings, however. Katherine Perry notes in her diary after visiting Quinta do Jardim da Serra in 1844 that, 'The only furniture in the drawing room besides the chairs and the table were a clock and a piano, or rather the skeleton of each, for neither had any go in them.'

In 1809 King George III appointed Veitch British consul on Madeira, but Lord Palmerston recalled him to London in disgrace in 1828. The ship carrying Napoleon

are cherries – fresh by the kilo, distilled into liqueurs or baked into sticky cakes. Folk dancers and local bands liven up the atmosphere – and hardly a tourist in sight.

Jardim da Serra's other attraction is the ruined, pink **Quinta do Jardim da Serra**, once the home of Consul Henry Veitch. The garden that was famed throughout the island is now luscious and wild. Huge fuchsias drip down on to giant ferns. Bright flowers push out through knotted creepers. The elegant terrace and the fountains lined with *azulejos* crumble and grow moss. The old house is shuttered and silent.

At the far end of the garden a path leads up to Veitch's grave, which is marked by a simple tablet.

Cabo Girão

After Jardim da Serra, the road peters out among farm terraces, so it is best to double back to the main road. About 10km farther along the coast you come to Cabo Girão. With a 589m sheer drop to the sea, Cabo Girão is the second highest sea cliff in the world (after one in Norway). This is the point, when he was first exploring the

to exile in the island of St Helena had stopped off at Madeira. Veitch had gone on board with books, wine and fruit and had insisted on addressing the deposed emperor, whom he greatly admired, as 'Your Majesty' (*see* p.53). This did not go down well at the Foreign Office, but such was Veitch's popularity that his dismissal caused an even bigger rumpus on the island. Overwhelmed by requests from British and Portuguese merchants alike, Palmerston relented and reinstated Veitch as British consul in 1831.

But by 1836 he was in trouble again. His sybaritic lifestyle had scandalized the Portuguese and sent shudders of disapproval through the British community. The intrigues he wove and his high-handed, dictatorial manner had begun to antagonize local merchants. Letters were fired off to Palmerston complaining of the consul's immorality and accusing him of being 'an intriguing disturber and vexatious oppressor of all that is useful and beneficial among us'. A group of religious enthusiasts were certain that the society Veitch had founded for the promotion of dancing was a pernicious instrument of Satan. They held a meeting to discuss what should be done. One wag managed to convince them that dancing in itself was not sinful, if done with religious feeling – whereupon he proposed dancing a quadrille 'to the glory of God'. Word got back to Palmerston that Veitch had actually allowed a quadrille to be named 'To the Glory of God'. Wearying of this salvo of correspondence, Palmerston sent a letter dismissing Veitch on 7 December 1836. A rival merchant, George Stoddard, became the new consul.

Veitch retired to Quinta do Jardim da Serra with one of his illegitimate daughters, shunning British residents on the island and (Katherine Perry notes in her diary) nursing his hatred for 'Mr Stoddard and all other merchants besides, as well as the Duke of Wellington, Dom Miguel and all the Tories'. He died in 1857 and was buried in his favourite spot in the garden – the small hill behind the house where he would sit for hours looking down the valley.

coast, that Zarco decided to turn his boats around (hence 'Girão') and head back to settle at Câmara de Lobos. Today there is a snack bar and viewing platform on the bluff. You can lean over the railings to inspect the dizzying drop, or take in views up and down the coast. Way below the viewing terrace, lapped by the waves, are a few small vineyards and vegetable patches that can only be reached by boat – for Madeiran farmers every bit of land counts.

Ribeira Brava

Ribeira Brava is a seaside resort at the mouth of a steep-sided valley. Once the town was at the heart of a choice sugar-growing area, and the parish church, **São Bento**, still shows signs of this prosperity. It was built in the second half of the 15th century, and, though much renovated since, still contains many of the original features, including a massive baptismal font donated by Dom Manuel I and a carved stone pulpit. There is also a 16th-century altar statue of the Virgin of the Rosary, carved in Portugal but much influenced by Flemish work of the time.

Behind the church is a recently restored 18th-century **town hall**, with a budding botanical garden outside. Lumps of machinery from an old sugar mill are scattered among the lilies and daisies. There is a good specimen of a kapok, the thorny tree whose pods burst with silky puffs of cotton wool that are used to stuff pillows. A little to the north of the town hall is the **Madeira Ethnographic Museum** (*open Tues–Sun 10–12.30 and 2–6; adm €2*), which contains interesting displays on island life – from fishing boats and hand-operated mills to a live weaver. It is sobering to see how, on the tiny island terraces and poorer farms, methods have hardly changed in centuries.

The road past the front of the town hall takes you past a small **market** to the beach. A tunnel at the eastern end of the esplanade leads off to a quiet **fishing harbour**. The seafront itself clatters with the sound of small change and teacups as passing coach parties pile out to buy souvenirs. Halfway along the promenade is the stump of the tower of a **fortress** (now a tourist office) built at the beginning of the 18th century.

Ribeira Brava's most talked-about military moment didn't happen in her fortress at all. The **Cherry Campaign**, so the story goes, took place just before the cherry harvest in 1820. Mainland Liberals had just passed a new constitution (*see* **History**, p.40), but local peasants would have none of it. They beat up officials who came to try to organize elections and the governor was forced to send in the army. Anxious to avoid further violence, he ordered the soldiers to go into the orchards and eat up the cherries, which they did happily. Dispirited, the locals soon gave up on their rebellion.

Ribeira Brava to Calheta

The Coast Road

A new road runs along the foot of the cliffs between Ribeira Brava and Paúl do Mar. It travels in as straight a line as Madeira can manage, over the beach and through any bluffs that get in its way. After 4km it gets to **Ponta do Sol**, named for the beautiful sunsets that seem to aim themselves directly at the village promenade. Like Ribeira Brava, Ponta do Sol was also once home to prosperous sugar merchants. The village church has an ancient green ceramic baptismal font to rival that of Ribeira Brava, and some superb 17th-century *azulejos*.

Ponta do Sol's solid Baroque and 19th-century homes are pushed up against the mountainside, separated from each other by steep flights of steps and narrow cobbled paths. Perhaps it is these narrow thoroughfares that have saved the village from modern development. Cars can't get far beyond the main road, and Ponta do Sol is silent and clean, with a gently fading elegance.

The American writer John dos Passos comes from good Ponta do Sol stock; his grandparents left the village for Chicago in the mid 1800s. A small plaque on their old house in Rua Príncipe D. Luís I commemorates a visit the writer made to the village in 1960. Islanders are more likely to remember the village as the birthplace of Dr António Pita, the professor of the Funchal School of Medicine who did much to improve health standards and fight cholera on the island during the 19th century.

Sports and Activities

Swimming

Ponta do Sol: Small, clean beach with a covered veranda bar. Swim, then sip a drink while you watch the sun set.

Where to Stay

Ponta do Sol

Baía do Sol, Rua Dr João Augusto Teixeira, 9360-215 Ponta do Sol, **t** 291 970 140, **f** 291 970 149, *www.enotel.com*, *info@enotel.com*, (*moderate; €60*). One of the best of the new generation of Madeira hotels, with top marks for design. The hotel has been constructed behind the renovated façades of what was once a run-down beachfront. Inside, it's a world of style magazine interiors, with rooms that are minimalist but still warm and alluring. Nearly all the rooms have a view of the Porto do Sol sunset (the main reason for staying over in the village), and there's a good restaurant, large pool and mini-gym. An absolute bargain; excellent value for the price.

Estalagem da Ponta do Sol, Quinta da Rochina, 9360 Ponta do Sol, **t** 291 970 200, **f** 291 970 209, *www.pontadosol.com*, *info@pontadosol.com* (*expensive; €100*). Chic designer hotel high on the cliff above Ponto do Sol. The rooms, decorated entirely in pristine white, may be a little stark for some tastes, but the hotel is well equipped with two pools, sauna, gym and jacuzzi. Some rooms have sunset views, others look out over the sea to the morning sun, others face inland.

Quinta do Alto de São João, Lombo de São João, 9360 Ponta do Sol, **t** 291 974 188, **f** 291 974 187, *www.qasj.cjb.net*, *qasj@qasj.cjb.net*, (*expensive; from €90*). Country-house-style hotel converted from a *quinta* in a village high above Ponto do Sol. The public rooms are furnished in old Madeiran style, but the bedrooms are more modern. There are also apartments and a detached annexe.

Eating Out

Ponta do Sol

Poente Golí, Cais da Ponta do Sol, **t** 291 973 579 (*inexpensive; €4–6*). Bar/snack-bar with a balcony hanging over the breakers and offering superb views of the sunset.

Baía do Sol, Rua Dr João Augusto Teixeira, **t** 291 970 140 (*expensive; €30–35*). Stylish hotel restaurant serving up such delights as warm duck-breast salad, and chicken supreme stuffed with mango. A designer environment that makes a relaxing place to retire to after watching the sunset.

The Unsolved Mystery of Henry the German

In the 15th century the land around Madalena do Mar belonged to one Henrique Alemão (Henry the German), who got his nickname because locals found the language he spoke incomprehensible. Historians think that Henrique was probably Ladislau III, King of Poland and Hungary. Ashamed at having disastrously lost a battle against the Ottomans at Varna in 1414, he had fled and gone on a pilgrimage to the Holy Land in penance. On Mount Sinai he was made a Knight of St Catherine, but he then disappeared. The belief is that he eventually made it to Portugal where Dom João I offered him refuge on the newly discovered island of Madeira. Henrique came to the island, married a local woman, built a chapel and became a prosperous farmer here. We know that he got his supplies not only from Funchal, like everyone else, but also directly from the court at Lisbon.

He would frequently sail to Funchal to chat with Zarco (there was no road to Madalena for over four centuries). On one of these visits he was recognized by two Polish friars who, some people think, had been sent there to fetch him. Henrique denounced them as mad and sent them packing, but a short while later he was called to Funchal to be told that the Portuguese king had summoned him to Lisbon. On his way back from this meeting his boat ran into rocks at Cabo Girão and he was drowned. His son, Segismundo, decided to travel to the mainland to find out who his father really was – but his ship sank in a storm before he could bring back the news.

Henrique's body was found and is buried in the chapel at Madalena. In the Museum of Sacred Art in Funchal you can see a painting of *St Joachim meeting St Anna*, commissioned by Henrique for his chapel and thought to portray him and his wife.

A few kilometres farther along the road you come to **Madalena do Mar**, a run-down village that straggles along between the cliffs and the shore.

After Madalena do Mar the road carries on along the coast to Calheta, Jardim do Mar and Paúl do Mar.

The Old Road

You can also follow the old main road to Calheta – a tortuously twisting extension of the road to Ribeira Brava. This will add at least another 45 minutes to your overall journey time.

At **Canhas**, about 10km past Ribeira Brava, roadside Stations of the Cross lead to an ugly hooped concrete monument to St Teresa, the patron saint of lacemakers. Some 10km farther on you come to **Loreto**. Dona Joana de Eça, one of Zarco's daughters-in-law, commissioned the building of the village chapel here. The south portal is a beautifully preserved example of Manueline style. Inside, the ceiling combines Mudéjar geometry with Manueline stalactites and twirls. Bright blue and white paint and (for once) careful gilding heighten the effect. The church is worth every minute of the extra travel time it takes to see it – but bear in mind that, like most Madeiran churches, it is usually kept closed. If your visit coincides with afternoon Mass (*around 5pm*), you can usually have a look inside before or after the service. You'll probably find it quicker to take the coast road to Calheta, then double back to Loreto.

Calheta to Ponta do Pargo

Ten kilometres past Loreto you come to the turn-off to **Calheta**, a coastal village with another remarkable church. Begun in 1430, though much altered since, the church of **Espírito Santo** has a perfectly preserved Mudéjar ceiling and an enormous tiered ebony sacrarium, encrusted with silver carving, that was a gift from Dom Manuel I. There is a small lido at one end of the long beach and the remains of an *aguardente* distillery (built 1909) on the beachfront.

At **Lombo dos Reis**, about 3km farther along the main road near Estreito da Calheta, is the **Capela dos Reis Magos**. The chapel has a wooden retable of the *Adoration of the Magi*, carved with extraordinary vitality – and with wry attention to detail – in Antwerp in the 16th century. The writer Ann Bridge, casting her eyes over the relief in the 1960s, couldn't help noticing 'the saucy soldier with the fat behind and his cap at a rakish angle [who] is as much a portrait today as when his...creator modelled him'.

From **Estreito da Calheta** a road winds down the cliff-face to the seashore and the village of **Jardim do Mar**. Perched on rocks above the Atlantic, 'Garden-on-Sea' is appropriately named. Vines and banana trees come down to the edge of the village. Bougainvillaea, passion flowers and geraniums, orange, paw-paw and avocado trees all seem ready to burst out of the walled gardens. The houses are small and simple and reached by cobbled stairways that climb up and down the rocks. On the eastern side of the village is the **Quinta da Piedade**, home to the Couto Cardoso family who originally settled here in the 15th century. The village church was built this century, funded by subscriptions from the villagers and money sent home by emigrants.

Sports and Activities

Swimming

Calheta: A wall of boulders encloses a large pool near the Calheta Beach hotel. Alongside is a small patch of sand with palm-umbrellas and a bar.

Shopping

There's a **supermarket** in Calheta, opposite the Calheta Beach hotel.

Where to Stay

The only accommodation we could procure was the upper floor over a venda *– three rooms small and dirty; but as there was a bright sun, we had the floors washed, and some whitewash, which happily was at hand in the* venda, *gave the walls a clean look.*

19th-century British traveller in Calheta

Prazeres

Jardim Atlântico, Prazeres, 9370-605 Calheta, **t** 291 820 220, **f** 291 820 221, *www.jardimatlantico.com*, *refugioatlantico@mail.telepac.pt* (*expensive–moderate; €65–94*). Quiet, isolated, clifftop resort hotel. Rooms have either a kitchen or kitchenette, and you can stock up on supplies at the hotel supermarket. Bungalows 5001–5004 are slightly more pricey, but are perched at the edge of the cliff with nothing between them and the Atlantic. The yoga room, sauna and medicinal baths are full of healthy middle-aged Germans.

Calheta

Calheta Beach, 9370 Calheta, **t** 291 820 300, **f** 291 820 301, *www.galoresort.com*, *calhetabeach@galoresort.com* (*expensive; from €102*). Large, rather impersonal, resort-style hotel that offers thalassotherapy (sea-cures), mud packs and other treatments for well-being.

A long tunnel burrows underneath a tall, contorted landscape of red tufa rocks to bring you to **Paúl do Mar**. Until the late 1960s Paúl do Mar could only be reached by boat, and it still exudes an eerie atmosphere of complete isolation. The silent looks you get from the groups of men standing at street corners put you uneasily in mind of stories of solitary travellers who have wandered into remote hillbilly villages, never to be heard of again. A concrete causeway runs the entire length of the beach and a tall concrete wall all but hides the sea from view, adding to the feeling of claustrophobia by making it appear that the town is below sea-level. At the end of the causeway is a small bay with a row of garish green fishing boats perched high above the waterline. At the foot of the launch ramp, below a towering dark cliff, women and children gut the day's catch. Gore piles up on the stones and blood trickles down to the sea.

After Paúl do Mar the countryside gets a little softer, with banks of grass and flowers, pine forests and copses of oak. About 8km farther along the main road you come to **Ponta do Pargo**, the westernmost tip of the island. Here the vegetation thins out to brown grass, wheat and thistles. It is a lonely spot where little seems to have changed in centuries. You might even see a traditional oxcart, complete with solid wooden wheels. High on a rocky, windswept promontory is a lighthouse; you can stand beside it on the cliffs looking out over the churning Atlantic and thinking your own free thoughts.

From Ponta do Pargo the road heads north, through eucalyptus and bracken, to Porto Moniz (*see* p.181). Just before Porto Moniz you can turn east and head back to Funchal across the open plains of **Paúl da Serra** (*see* p.182).

Jardim do Mar

Hotel Jardim do Mar, Sítio da Piedade, Jardim do Mar, 9370-402 Calheta, **t** 291 823 616, **f** 291 823 617 (*moderate–inexpensive; €35–45*). At last, somewhere to stay in what is probably the prettiest village on the island. An unobtrusively designed hotel, well-run and with some good sea views to add to the charm.

Cecilia's, Jardim do Mar, 9370-402 Calheta, **t/f** 291 822 642, *pontajardim@hotmail.com* (*inexpensive; €35*). Rooms attached to a private house, overlooking the sea. Space is a little cramped, but the owner is friendly and there is a communal kitchen for the use of residents.

Paúl do Mar

Casal São João, Sítio do Maçapez, Fajã da Ovelha, 9370 Calheta, **t** 291 872 660, **f** 291 741 040 (*moderate; from €40*). Rooms in a pretty cliff-side cottage, with a garden overlooking the sea, near Paúl do Mar.

Eating Out

Calheta

Marisqueria do Camarão, t 291 824 379 (*moderate; €22*). Delicious crab pâté served in the shell, lobsters that come with a wooden mallet for crushing out the juiciest bits and crowds of Madeirense out for a treat make this a real find in the area. On the coast road just east of Calheta.

Jardim do Mar

Tar Mar, Jardim do Mar, **t** 291 823 207 (*inexpensive; €17*). Pleasant, family-run restaurant on the path that leads down to the sea, good for an easygoing lunch.

Fajã da Ovelha/Paúl do Mar

Churrascaria O Precipício, t 291 872 425 (*moderate; €21*). Cheery family-run grill room on the cliff overlooking Paúl do Mar. They dry their own fish and sometimes come up with tasty special dishes.

Walks

These are suggestions for walks you can follow, not a detailed guide to the routes. It essential to go properly equipped and to take a good map with you (*see* pp.57–9).

The western coast doesn't have many *levada* walks, but there are two that are fairly easygoing and pass attractive parts of the coast and countryside.

Levada do Norte: Estreito de Câmara de Lobos–Garachico–Quinta Grande–Campanário

Easy, but danger of vertigo. 4hrs. Short tunnel.

The Levada do Norte ducks in and out of valleys along the coast, alternating inland views with grand vistas over the Atlantic. For much of its length it runs close to National Road 101, so you can break off the walk along the way. You join the *levada* just above the village of Estreito de Câmara de Lobos (at Calvário, bus 96 to 'Levada do Norte' stop) and walk in the direction the water flows. The walk is pretty straightforward – just keep following the *levada* through Garachico, Quinta Grande and on into the Campanário valley. Here buses 4, 107 and 139 all travel along road 101.

Levada Calheta–Ponta do Pargo: Raposeira–Ponta do Pargo

Easy. 2hrs.

You join the *levada* below the church in the village of Raposeira (8km past Estreito da Calheta, bus 107) and simply follow it west to Ponta do Pargo. Near Ponta do Pargo the *levada* joins another. Here you should keep left. If you want to see the lighthouse you will have to leave the *levada* at the village and follow the (signposted) track to the point. This *levada* also travels near road 101, so you can leave it at various points along the way and hop aboard bus 107. You could even begin the walk a little earlier, at Prazeres (add another hour).

Porto Santo and the Desertas

13

Porto Santo

Highlights

1 The healing volcanic sands of the long south beach

2 Fantastically patterned rocks, etched by the elements, at Fonte da Areia

3 Viewing misty Madeira from Pico das Flores

4 Christopher Columbus's house in the town of Vila Baleira

This can't be Madeira – there's too much sand.

Viscount Carrington, after the US Air Force had delivered him to the NATO base on Porto Santo by mistake

Porto Santo is Madeira's desert island annexe. It has 8km of unspoiled golden beach, a house once lived in by Christopher Columbus, and almost nothing else. But there is such an abundance of nothing as to make it austerely beautiful. Fifty kilometres to the south, the Desertas are wild, wind-buffeted rocks inhabited mainly by seabirds, rabbits and goats. They are now a nature reserve and are hard to visit, but hundreds of Madeirense head to Porto Santo in the summer for the novel experience of sunbathing on sand. The beach can easily accommodate them, and the climate is warm enough to keep northern Europeans happy all year round.

Windier and flatter than Madeira (the highest point is a mere 507m above the sea), Porto Santo lies 74km northeast of Funchal and is the only other populated island in the archipelago. Twelve kilometres long and 7km wide, with just three major hotels and a handful of restaurants, it is as 'undiscovered' as any European resort could be. To really appreciate the island you need to spend some time here, rather than come on a quick (and expensive) day trip from Funchal. To talk of slipping into Porto Santo's rhythm would be misleading. It doesn't appear to have one. Rather, you become part of a gentle stasis that becomes very difficult to leave.

Most of Porto Santo's 5,000 or so inhabitants live in Vila Baleira, the tiny port. Here tourists – mainly wealthy Funchalese – and fishing provide the most visible source of income. Porto Santo has hardly any local water and a low rainfall. Today most of the island is arid, though the grapes – which ripen spread out on the hot sand rather than propped on trellises – produce an especially flavoursome madeira wine.

Porto Santo

History

The first people to set foot on Porto Santo were probably sailors washed south in a storm while exploring the Barbary Coast. Word got back to Henry the Navigator, and the fleet he sent to colonize Madeira included a boat bound for Porto Santo.

The boat's commander, **Bartolomeu Perestrelo**, a noble of Genoese origin and a noted seaman and navigator, became the first captain of Porto Santo. He planted vines and sugar-cane and was quick to tap the indigenous Dragon Trees for 'Dragon's Blood', a red resin used for paints, dyes and medicines, and lucrative on the international market (*see* p.156). Unfortunately, he also introduced rabbits to the island. In a few years they had multiplied prodigiously and had nibbled everything bare, and Porto Santo has never really recovered. Disheartened, Perestrelo left for Lisbon, but Prince Henry persuaded him to return by granting his family the captaincy of Porto Santo in perpetuity – the island was a strategic springboard for the voyages of discovery into the Atlantic, and could not be allowed to fall into enemy hands. The Perestrelos ruled for five generations (even though one of them, Garcia Perestrelo, was beheaded for murdering his wife).

Always in the shade of its fertile neighbour, Porto Santo managed over the years to make a modest income from sugar, grain and wine. Between the 15th and 17th centuries, pirates on their way to rich pickings in Madeira would drop in for a warm-

Getting There

By Air

TAP, the Portuguese airline, offer around 12 flights a day (depending on the season) between Funchal and Porto Santo. Flying time is 25 minutes and tickets (available from travel agents in Funchal) cost around €100 return.

No buses serve Porto Santo Airport, but you can get a **taxi** down to the centre of Vila Baleira for €3.

HeliAtlantis, the helicopter company, can get you to the island in just ten minutes, for €670 (up to five people; *see* p.76).

By Boat

The most popular way of getting to Porto Santo is by the **ferry** which usually leaves Funchal around 8am and returns at about 6pm, though departure times may change on Fridays to accommodate weekends. There's a daily service, except Tuesdays. The journey takes 2hrs 40mins. To catch the best views on the way, follow the old cruise liner rule of Port Outward, Starboard Home.

Tickets cost around €42 for a return, but there are reductions if you stay longer than a day. You can buy tickets in advance and check on departure times at most travel agencies; current rates and **sailing schedules** are also available on *www.portosantoline.pt*.

The boat leaves from the quay next to the Loo Rock. Tickets are also sold from a kiosk on the quay just before boarding. Except at the height of the season, you should have no trouble getting a place.

Getting Around

All the hotels and most of the good restaurants are in Vila Baleira or along the five miles of beach that stretch west of the village. The terrain around Vila Baleira is completely flat, so walking is easy and enjoyable. Hiring a car is generally a waste of money, unless you want to venture into the interior – even then it is cheaper to hire a taxi for a couple of hours and enjoy the added benefit of the driver's knowledge.

The main **transport hub** for the island is beside the petrol station at the eastern end of Avenida Dr Manuel Gregório Pestana Júnior (!) (a section of the coast road). Here you'll find buses and a taxi rank, as well as a car-hire kiosk and postings of bus timetables and taxi rates.

By Car

Car hire: Rodavante (Porto Santo Airport), **t** 291 982 925. Cars from around €35 per day.

Taxis: t 291 982 334. Fare from the harbour into Vila Baleira, €4; from harbour to Hotel Porto Santo, €7; tour of island (½-day), €30. There is a 20 per cent surcharge on all prices over weekends and on public holidays.

Off-road: Angie Travel, Rua Levada do Canha 2, **t** 291 982 780, **f** 291 982 403. A three-hour, off-road tour of the island by Land Rover costs €19 per person.

By Bus

A bus waits for the ferry and will chug you the kilometre or so from the harbour to the centre of Vila Baleira for €1.

up raid on Porto Santo, and lookouts on the island formed part of an important early warning system (*see* p.158). Since then the island has sunk into sun-baked obscurity. Apart from **Christopher Columbus** (who lived here for a while after marrying Bartolomeu Perestrelo's daughter; *see* p.206), the isle's only other notable resident was **Fernando Nunes**. An early settler and one of Prince Henry's most gallant knights, Fernando the Brave climbed up into the hills one hot day in 1533, and came down ringing a bell and proclaiming that he was Jesus Christ, come to save the people of Porto Santo from the clutches of Beelzebub. He healed a few paralytics to prove his point, and soon had a fervent following. Fernando the Brave became Fernando the Prophet. The detached and somewhat bemused inhabitants of Madeira nicknamed the people of Porto Santo *profetas*, and the name has stuck. Nowadays *profetas* retort by calling their flash neighbours *americanos*.

Apart from that, just five buses jog along the coast and across the island, with one running on average every hour (timetables posted at the Moinho car rental kiosk near the taxi rank on Avenida Dr Manuel Gregório Pestana Júnior). You can tour the whole island by bus for €7 a ticket.

By Boat

Farwest Sailing Trips, **t** (mobile) 963 103 762 or **t** 914 843 985. Custom-made yacht trips around the island.

By Cart

Six-seater **horse-carts** with canopies and curtains are a sedate way of travelling up the coast. There are always one or two waiting for the ferry, or you can pick one up on the promenade. They cost €15 for 15mins, €40 for an hour.

Walking

The tourist office publishes a map of three different walks around the island – though the going can be tough, and the rewards not as great as on Madeira.

Tourist Information

The **tourist information office**, **t** 291 982 361, is across from the post office on the Rua Dr Vieira de Castro. There's a **bank** almost next door and another on the road out to the port. Both have *multibanco* machines, and these are the only means of getting money after hours, apart from facilities offered by hotels.

The **emergency clinic**, **t** 291 980 060, is also on the port road. There's a **pharmacy** just off the village square.

The **police** are on **t** 291 982 423.

Note: Tap water in Porto Santo is desalinated seawater and not really suitable for drinking. You can buy bottled water all over town, and larger hotels place a bottle in your room.

Festivals

St Francis Xavier: 28 Aug.

Shopping

There is a small **supermarket** at Rua J. G. Zarco 26 if you are self-catering or want to make up a picnic. A little further down, near the pier, you'll find a small covered daily **market** where you can buy fresh fruit, vegetables and fish. Nearly everything here has to be imported, and prices are slightly higher than on Madeira. At one time the people of Porto Santo were known for making chunky little clay figurines and dolls out of palm leaves, but these have all but disappeared.

Sports and Activities

Porto Santo Sub, Clube Naval do Porto Santo, **t** (mobile) 916 033 997. Scuba-diving equipment hire and tuition.

Centro Hípico do Porto Santo, Sítio da Ponta (western part of the island), **t** (mobile) 967 671 689. Stables and riding school.

Vila Baleira and the Beach

Largo do Pelourinho

Tiny and dusty, the town of Vila Baleira was founded by Bartolomeu Perestrelo and remains Porto Santo's main settlement. The village gathers itself around the small, triangular Largo do Pelourinho, where tall date palms and a few straggling Dragon Trees and olive trees offer just a touch of shade. There is no traffic. From the depths of the enclosed veranda of the solitary café twenty or so pairs of eyes stare out across the square. Occasionally someone will shamble out into the street to sit on one of the park benches under the palms. Vila Baleira seems constantly to be holding its breath.

Where to Stay

Expensive

Hotel Porto Santo, Campo de Baixo, 9400-015 Porto Santo, **t** 291 980 140, **f** 291 980 149, *www.hotelportosanto.com, hotelpsanto@mail.telepac.pt* (*from* €100). Right on the sea, a kilometre outside Vila Baleira. The cream of the island's hotels has a private country club atmosphere – yet it is extremely relaxed and down-to-earth, with exceptionally friendly staff. Well-groomed green lawns roll down gently to the beach, where there is a bar (which also serves good lunches). The hotel offers plenty to do within its own grounds, with a large swimming pool, a gym, tennis and mini-golf for the use of residents. The rooms are comfortable, and all have private sun balconies. Rooms 201 and 202 look directly out to sea; the others face sideways up and down the coast (those on the western side of the building have the best view).

Moderate

Hotel Lúamar, Cabeça da Ponta, 9400 Porto Santo, **t** 291 984 121, **f** 291 983 100, *www.portosantoline.pt, luamar.suite.hotel@net.pt* (*from* €68). Smart beach-side hotel 4km from Vila Baleira. All the rooms have well-equipped kitchenettes for those who prefer to self-cater, or at least make a cup of tea, and many have balconies overlooking the sea (those with a so-called 'mountain view' look backwards on to the scrub). The hotel pool is right on the sands.

Torre Praia, Rua Goulart Medeiros, 9400 Porto Santo, **t** 291 980 450, **f** 291 982 487, *www.portosantoline.pt* (*from* €77). New resort hotel built around an old cement factory on Vila Baleira's busy stretch of beach. There's squash, a gym, sauna and jacuzzi for the active-spirited, a panorama bar and disco and a small pool, but little actual atmosphere.

Hotel Praia Dourada, Rua D. Estevão d'Alencastre, 9400 Porto Santo, **t** 291 982 315, **f** 291 982 484 (€48). Not on the 'Golden Beach' at all, but in the middle of the village. Large, functional, quiet and waiting for tour groups, but good value compared with some *pensions*.

Inexpensive

Central, Rua A. Magno Vasconcelos, 9400 Porto Santo, **t** 291 982 226, **f** 291 983 460 (*from* €35). Small, newly renovated hotel on a ridge overlooking Vila Baleira. The rooms are simple, with terracotta floors and bright furnishings. Ask for one of the front rooms on the third floor, which have a view across the ocean.

The tourist office, Rua Dr Vieira de Castro, **t** 291 982 361, has a list of **private rooms** and **holiday apartments** available for hire around the island.

Camping

There is a shadeless, dusty **campsite, t** 291 983 111, alongside the Torre Praia. Adults (over 25yrs) €1 per day, 3–25s 450¢ per day, tents 90¢–€2.25, caravans €1.50–3.

Madeirans will tell you that the *profetas* are bone-idle. But, sitting on the Largo do Pelourinho, you get the impression that there just isn't a lot to be done in this world, and that you've got a lifetime in which to do it. Porto Santo got its first telephone in 1947, and its first electric light in 1954. It seems barely to have noticed the 20th century, let alone the 21st.

At the top end of the Largo do Pelourinho, flags flap outside a solid little **town hall**, most of which dates back to the 16th century. Next door is the parish church of **Nossa Senhora da Piedade**. The first chapel on this site was built between 1420 and 1446, but it was burnt down by pirates in 1667. The church the villagers rebuilt is, by and large, the one you see today. A small Gothic chapel jutting out of the south side of the building is all that remains of earlier structures.

Eating Out

Moderate

Calheta, t 291 984 380 (*€22*). At the very end of the coast road. A popular daytime destination after a long beach walk. More upmarket than the other beach restaurants, it's busy and a popular place for sunset cocktails. Seabass risotto is a speciality and they do a tasty *caldeirada* and mix a mean margarita. As with other places along the strand, you are perfectly welcome to sit down for just a coffee, ice-cream or drink.

Restaurante/Bar Mar e Sol, t 291 982 269 (*€18–20*). Friendly, family-run restaurant on the beach (follow the sandy lane just beyond the Hotel Porto Santo). You can splash out on a lobster, or tuck into a *fragateira* – a scrumptious home-made fish stew with a potato, tomato and onion base, served in the cooking pot, replete with prawns, octopus, *lapas*, *espada*, and with just a dash of curry. Or you can sit quietly on the beach-terrace sipping a sundowner, watching the mountains tinge pink. The locally made house wine is good too – dry, with a pinkish tint and a slaty, volcanic taste.

Colombo, Campo de Cima, **t** 291 982 122 (*€18–20*). Pastas and pizzas on a ridge overlooking the sea.

Taverna Grill Mix, Sítio da Camacha, **t** 291 982 478 (*€18–20*). Tiny inland restaurant, which you enter through the family living-room. Mum does the cooking, and her hearty offspring (who may well be doing their homework or watching telly when you arrive) bear ample testimony to the quality of her cuisine. Dried hams and sausages hang from the beams. The house speciality is a magnificent *feijoada* (Brazilian bean and sausage stew), here made with more flavours of sausage than you thought possible, and dished from a big pot that reappears from the kitchen every time you look like finishing what is on your plate.

Inexpensive

Baiana, Largo do Pelourinho, **t** 291 984 649 (*€8–11*). The café on the square. All of Porto Santo stops here at one time or another, for a coffee, a drink or lunch on the veranda.

Mercearia, Rua João Santa 2, **t** 291 982 580. Cheerfully decorated café and snack bar, where you can get home-made cakes and good toasted sandwiches for around €4.

Tia Maria, t 291 982 400. Popular bar on the sand's edge, a little way beyond Hotel Porto Santo, with an indoor section as well as tables and palm-umbrellas on the beach.

Entertainment and Nightlife

The larger hotels will sometimes organize theme evenings or stage 'folkloric dancing' in the high season. The island's sole discotheque, next to the cemetery, attracts local lads on their mopeds and disgruntled youth over from Funchal with their parents. Young folk also hang out in the local internet café (one terminal!), **Mercearia** (*see* above).

Christopher Columbus Museum

Open Tues–Fri 9.30–5.30, Sat and Sun 10–1; adm free.

In the alley behind the church you'll find the house reputedly once occupied by Columbus, today a small museum. Downstairs you can see an ancient *matamorra*, a narrow stone-lined pit used as a domestic granary. Upstairs there are prints of the great explorer and his exploits (all guesswork – no contemporary portrait of Columbus exists, and we don't really know what he looked like). You can also see a diagram showing the routes he took, and copies of 15th- and 16th-century maps charting our gradual increase in knowledge of the Americas. Some of the rooms are decked out with reproduction period furniture, including a rather unfortunate model of Columbus at his desk.

Christopher Columbus and Madeira

There is little hard evidence – and dates are in a contradictory tangle – but the general belief is that Christopher Columbus spent some time in Porto Santo and Madeira before his voyage to the Americas and after marrying Filipa Moniz, the daughter of the second Bartolomeu Perestrelo. (Perestrelo had inherited the captaincy of Porto Santo from his father and married Guiomar Teixeira, daughter of Tristão Vaz, the first captain of Machico.) How the couple met, what brought Columbus to the islands in the first place and how long he stayed has local historians banging the table at each other.

Like Columbus, the Perestrelos were Genoese in origin, and it is possible that Columbus made contact with the family through the expat community in Funchal or on the mainland. One story goes that Columbus first met Filipa at Mass in Lisbon, another has it that this was in Machico (a more feasible possibility as she was related to the captain of Machico on her mother's side, and spent a lot of time there). Others say that Filipa had been retired to a nunnery for some previous indiscretion, and that the low-born young Genoese merchant married her with an eye to the main chance – she was, after all, part of a well-to-do noble family. More romantic chroniclers argue that Columbus was in fact an illegitimate son of the daughter of the great Zarco himself, and that Filipa had been long promised to him; or that Filipa had inherited her seafaring family's collection of charts and log books, and that this is really what he was after.

We do know that Columbus was acting as an agent for a Genoese firm of sugar importers, and was based on Madeira around 1478. He got into a bit of a fix about unfulfilled contracts and is recorded as having appeared before a tribunal. What might have induced him to settle on Porto Santo rather than in the busier ports of Funchal or Machico is less clear. Maybe his in-laws gave him a house there, though there is also a theory that he wanted to corner the market in Dragon's Blood, and Porto Santo at the time was still a major source of the resin.

Some time after 1479, Filipa and Columbus were married. A year or two later she had their son, and died soon afterwards. Here the legends really start. They have Columbus fraternizing with visiting sailors to pick up tips about their voyages of discovery, scouring the beach at Porto Santo for vegetation washed across from distant lands and studying maps and currents to work out where it had come from. One story goes that he nursed a pilot and four seamen washed up after a wreck, and that the pilot whispered the secret of the existence of another continent on his deathbed. What we do know is that in 1480 Columbus put his plan for a voyage across the Atlantic to the king of Portugal, but was laughed out of court. It wasn't until 1485 that he managed to persuade Isabella of Spain to sponsor the expedition.

The Beach

From Largo do Pelourinho, the Rua Infante D. Henrique leads through an avenue of palms, past a small **municipal garden** and public **drinking fountain** to the beach. Drinking fountains – most dating back to the 19th century – are dotted about the island, offering trickles of tangy water, high in calcium and supposedly good for kidney ailments. Islanders arrive with plastic flagons to stock up, and the water is also bottled and sold on Madeira. To the east of a stumpy pier is a modest new **market**, its roof designed to resemble a wave.

West of the village stretches a seemingly endless golden beach. The soft sands are said to have healing properties. According to one local guide book, 'paralytics, persons with rickets, decalcified or rheumatic people, persons with varicose veins' and 'atrophied sufferers' especially benefit. From time to time you'll come across someone buried up to the neck. After a day or two on the beach your aches and pains really do seem to go away. Maybe the sand is radioactive; possibly there is 'a certain mysticism, integral union with God, and He has breathed great virtue into it'. Perhaps it is just the sense of total detachment you have here. Apart from the odd bar or restaurant, the 8km stretch of beach is completely undeveloped. There are no ice-cream vendors or deckchair hire firms, no seaside funfairs, just miles of sand and surf. At night the only sound you hear is the waves. The occasional electric light looks quite insignificant beside the cascades of stars and flashes of phosphorescence from the waves.

The West of the Island

A short way west of Vila Baleira a road branches up from the coast to **Campo de Cima**, a suburb of villas on a ridge overlooking the sea. The road continues west along the ridge, past ruins of the windmills that once ground the corn that grew here, then peters out into a dirt track. Following the track through a dry Wild West landscape (complete with the horses from the nearby riding school), you come to **Pico das Flores**, a viewpoint on a cliff 184m above the sea. To the southeast the Desertas stand out stark against the horizon. To the southwest Madeira simmers in its mauve mist. Porto Santo's long beach stretches out below.

Another fork of the track leads from the Pico das Flores turn-off to **Morenos**, a shady picnic spot beside jagged volcanic cliffs. There are tables, umbrellas made from palm leaves, and a small thicket of conifers, olives and Dragon Trees, all planted by the local government as part of a reforestation plan. A third branch of the road leads back down to the coast, and the restaurant Calheta (*see* p.205). Nearby, as part of the grotesque pink Vila Baleira hotel, is a **thalassotherapy centre**, **t** 291 980 800, which offers a variety of health treatments and special cures for anything from aching joints to poor cocktail-party technique, using water treatments and the magical properties of Porto Santo sand.

The North and East

Porto Santo's inland plain is largely taken up by the **airport**, built in the 1950s and extended in the 1970s to accommodate the package-holiday jets which never really came. Beside the airport, just north of Vila Baleira, is **Pico do Castelo** (437m), a steep, nipple-shaped mountain that was the refuge of townsfolk during pirate raids. Today tough little trees are trying to obey government orders and cover the slopes. After a gruelling climb you get a view over the whole island, including nearby **Pico do Facho** (517m), Porto Santo's highest point and the peak on which bonfires were lit to warn the Madeirense of pirate raids (*see* p.158).

Beyond Pico do Castelo the road winds through some bleak countryside which, like the rest of the island, breaks briefly into green after the spring rains. For most of the rest of the year, though, Porto Santo earns its brave tourist-brochure euphemism of 'The Tawny Isle'. Through the nondescript hamlet of **Camacha** you come to **Fonte da Areia** on the north coast. Here the cliffs are so soft that they seem little more than compressed sand. Water and wind have etched fantastical patterns into them, like incomprehensible graffiti. A little way down the cliff, the Fonte itself is an oasis of palms and flowers. There's a **drinking fountain** (built in 1843), as well as a thatched shelter over what were once communal laundry troughs. Beside the fountain there is a snack bar with a bright and friendly owner who has put tables, shaded by palm leaf umbrellas, along the cliff top. A narrow path leads through wild flowers and sugar cane to a pebbly beach with rock pools way below.

From Camacha a tarred road will take you in a circle around the **eastern part of the island**, and back to Vila Baleira. Empty, dry and eerily silent, the terrain is a patchwork of fawn, beige and lionskin-gold. You descend sharply into valleys and twist back up hillsides past the ruins of old stone farmhouses and abandoned corn-threshing circles. A few birds twitter invisibly, and here and there a brown cow nuzzles about in the grit for something to eat, but otherwise this part of the island is uninhabited, severe and compelling.

The Desertas

About 30km southeast of Madeira lie the three Deserta islands: the flat **Ilhéu Chão**, **Deserta Grande** (the largest) and **Bugio**. Just north of Ilhéu Chão, a spine of rock sticks up 50m into the air. Many years ago, so the story goes, a passing sea captain let off a salvo of fire at the rock because in the mist it looked like a ship under sail, and it had not responded to signals.

Deserta Grande, 14km long and just 1.6km wide, is the only island of the three that was ever inhabited. Descendants of Zarco settled here in 1420. In 1564 the settlers fended off a pirate attack by raining boulders on their invaders from the clifftops, staining the rock-face with blood for decades to come. The islanders made a modest

Getting There

To disembark on the **Desertas** you need a special permit, and these are very difficult to come by. You could try harassing the tourist office, but are likely to be told that the trip is 'impossible'. Your best bet is to try to get in on occasional privately arranged group visits. Keep an eye on the '*Tráfego Marítimo*' pages in *Diário de Notícias*.

Other travel agencies organize **cruises** around the Desertas, sometimes with 'swimming stops' – but this usually means that you anchor out at sea and do not get to explore the islands themselves.

living from their cattle and by selling *orchilha*, a lichen once used in dye. Four centuries after the first settlers arrived, the village still comprised little more than eight houses and a chapel. Then in 1802 a waterspout blew in off the ocean, destroyed the grazing land and flattened the village. Since then Deserta Grande has been left to the rabbits, wild goats, seals and sea birds.

Over the years the islands have belonged to various Madeiran notables, some of whom styled themselves 'Lords of the Desertas'. The most recent private owners were the Hinton and Cossart families, prominent British Madeirense who relished the huntin' and fishin' prospects. Prince Albert of Monaco and Admiral Fairfax were among guests who bagged a few wild goats and reeled in tunny and barracuda. In 1971 the Portuguese National Trust took over the islands, and they have turned them into a bird and marine life sanctuary.

You need a permit to go there, and visits are discouraged (*see* 'Getting There', opposite). Today, as you clamber over the reddish rock you may see rare seabirds, or a giant Deserta carrot (*Monizia edulis*), which grows 1.5m high and is peculiar to the Desertas and Selvagens. If you are very lucky you might glimpse a few monk seals, though *Lycosa ingens*, a enormous black spider whose bite is said to be fatal, would be a less felicitous encounter.

The Selvagens

The Selvagens are the last group of islands that fall under the administration of the Madeiran government, though at 280km south of Funchal they are much closer to the Canary Islands than Madeira. Like the Desertas, the Selvagens were also in private hands until the Portuguese National Trust took them over in 1971. Today they are a designated nature reserve and a complete no-go area to the casual visitor. Rocky, remote and even drier than the Desertas, they support wildlife made up mainly of sea birds, including rare grebes, puffins and petrels.

The Selvagens have attracted their fair share of treasure stories. Until quite recently they were a secret meeting point for diamond-smugglers from Angola. At least three Mexican buccaneers are said to have hidden booty here. And this is where Captain Kidd, the Scottish pirate, is said to have stashed his hoard before being captured and hanged in 1701. This story is perhaps more than rumour – or at least the powers that be in Britain would seem to think so. In the 19th century there were at least four expeditions, with government backing, to attempt to find the treasure, and, had Sir Ernest Shackleton not died during his expedition to the South Pole in 1922, he would have stopped on the way home for another search. Unfortunately, whatever information the authorities had about the treasure was lost with Shackleton – though there have been treasure-hunting expeditions to the Selvagens ever since.

Chronology

1418 Zarco and fellow mariners are blown off course and washed up on Porto Santo.

1419 Zarco and Perestrelo return to colonize Porto Santo.

1420 Zarco and Vaz land on Madeira. The first settlers start a fire which burns for seven years.

1425 Dom João officially makes Madeira a full province of Portugal.

1566 The French pirate Bertrand de Montluc raids Funchal with 1,000 men.

1580 Philip II of Spain lays claim to the Portuguese crown.

1640 End of Spanish rule in Portugal.

1665 King Charles issues his ordinance forbidding exports to English colonies, but excludes Madeira from the ban, giving the island an effective monopoly over wine exports to the New World.

1768 Captain Cook visits the island.

1801–1802 First British Occupation.

1803 Great flood in Funchal.

1807 French troops march on Lisbon.

1807–1814 Second British Occupation.

1808 General Beresford, commander of the occupying force, leaves Madeira with half the garrison.

1814 French finally defeated on mainland.

1815 The ship carrying Napoleon to exile calls in at Funchal.

1821 Dom João returns to Lisbon from exile in Brazil and accepts the restricted powers offered by a new Constitution.

1826 Dom Miguel declares himself absolute monarch.

1828 A new Miguelite governor arrives in Madeira together with 1,000 troops. Some Liberals escape to Britain; others are arrested and imprisoned.

1834 Dom Miguel defeated and exiled to Austria.

1838 The British Factory wound up during a dip in the wine trade.

1851 *Oidium tuckeri*, a mildew disease, strikes Madeiran vines. Wine production drops.

1856 Cholera epidemic. Over 7,000 people die in a few weeks.

1872 *Phylloxera vastatrix*, a vine louse, all but destroys the wine industry.

1910 Portugal proclaimed a republic.

1914 All German property on Madeira confiscated.

1916 Germany declares war on Portugal. Funchal shelled by German U-boats.

1917 Funchal suffers a second light shelling.

1926 Military coup on mainland. Dr António de Oliveira Salazar becomes minister of finance.

1931 General strike on Madeira after monopoly is granted to handful of mill owners. A coup establishes a short-lived military dictatorship on the island.

1932 Salazar becomes Prime Minister and virtual dictator.

1939–1945 Portugal remains neutral in the Second World War.

1968 Salazar leaves office after a stroke.

1974 Salazar's successor, Dr Marcello Caetano, is overthrown after a bloodless coup, and the modern state of Portugal established.

1976 A new constitution gives Madeira special status within Portugal as an Autonomous Political Region.

Language

Travellers in the 19th century were given such useful linguistic tips as the Portuguese for 'I wish you would do me the favour of recommending a guide who can conduct me to the finest views, and to where I can get fern roots. I also require two or three hammock men and a hammock'. When speaking to the lowly hammock men themselves, you didn't have to wax quite so eloquent: 'Do not swing the hammock', 'Hold your tongue, do not make so much noise', and 'I will not give any money for drink until the end of the journey' sufficed.

Today you will find that most people in shops, and nearly all waiters and hotel staff on Madeira speak reasonable English. Many of the younger workers in the service industries are the children of emigrants, returned from South Africa, Jersey or the USA, and have English as a first language. You will be hard put to it to find a menu that is not translated into English, even in more remote spots. But it is always useful to know some words and phrases – for market shopping, in case you get lost on walks, or simply to be friendly or polite.

See pp.68–69 for food and drink vocabulary.

Pronunciation

Portuguese is a Romance language, so a basic knowledge of Spanish, Italian or French will help you to make your way through the written word. Pronunciation is another matter entirely. The Madeirense munch vowels and slush 's' sounds in a way that will make you think you are hearing Russian or Polish, rather than a southern European language. Attempting to reproduce the same effect yourself proves fiendishly difficult.

An acute (´) or circumflex accent (^) or a tilde (~) denote a stressed syllable. If there is no written accent, then stress the final syllable, unless the word ends in 'e', 'a' or 'o', in which case you stress the penultimate syllable. Other syllables tend to be swallowed.

Portuguese is a nasal language – 'm' after a vowel at the end of a word is silent, but means the vowel is nasalized, as in the '*bom*' of *bom dia*, which is closer to the French *bon* than to 'bomb'. The common 'ão' sound (as in *não* – 'no') is pronounced 'ow'. Give it a nasal twang and a touch of the Eliza Doolittle and you're almost there.

'S' is pronounced 'sh' when it comes before a consonant or at the end of a word; 'ç' is pronounced 's', but seldom with crystal clarity. 'X' and 'ch' also come out as 'sh'. 'J' is said like the 's' in 'pleasure', so is 'g' – unless it comes before 'e' or 'i', in which case it is hard, as in 'go'. 'C' is soft before 'e' and 'i', but hard before 'a' and 'o'.

'Lh' and 'nh' are pronounced 'ly' and 'ny' respectively, as in 'mi**lli**on' and 'ca**ny**on'.

Glossary of Useful Terms

achada plateau
bordados embroidery
caixa booth/cashier
câmara town hall
capela chapel
casa de prazer garden teahouse
chão small, flat place
fortaleza fort
freguesia parish
igreja church
igreja matriz parish church
ilha island
jardim garden
levada irrigation channel
lombo/lombada ridge
miradouro viewpoint
morgado landowner
paragem bus stop
pico peak

quinta large house, usually with walled garden
São/Santo/Santa Saint
Sé cathedral
venda general store, sometimes with bar
vila village

Some Useful Phrases

General

Do you speak English/German/French/Spanish? *Fala inglês/alemão/francês/espanhol?*
yes/no *sim/não*
I don't understand *Não compreendo*
What do you call this? *Como se chama isto?*
How much is it? *Quanto custa?*
please *por favor*
thank you *obrigado* (said by man); *obrigada* (by woman)
excuse me *com licença*
I'm sorry *desculpe*

Greetings

good morning *bom dia*
good afternoon/evening *boa tarde*
good evening/night *boa noite*
goodbye/see you *adeus/até logo*
How are you? *Como esta?*
Very well, thank you *Muito bem, obrigado/a*
And you? *E você?*
Fine *Bem*

Asking Questions

Can I have...? *Pode dar-me...?*
I'd like... *Queria...*
Is it...? *É...?*
Is there/Are there...? *Há...?*
Where is...? *Onde está...?*
Where are...? *Onde estão...?*
Is this right for... (direction)? *Vou bem para...?*
Can you direct me to...? *Pode indicar-me o caminho para...?*
Do you sell...? *Vendem...?*
Have you anything for...(at chemist)? *O que tem para...?*
When? *Quando?*
What? *O quê?*
How? *Como?*
Why? *Porquê?*

Some Adjectives

cheap/expensive *barato/caro*
ugly/beautiful *feio/belo*
bad/good *mau/bom*
slow/quick *lento/rápido*
hot/cold *quente/frio*
empty/full *vazio/cheio*

Size

big *grande*
bigger *maior*
small *pequeno*
smaller *mais pequeno*
long *comprido*
short *curto*

Accommodation

a single room *um quarto simples*
a double room *um quarto de casal*
with private bathroom *com banho*

Money

the receipt *o recibo*
the change *o troco*
Can you change...? *Pode trocar...?*
Do you take...? *Aceitam...?*
a bank *um banco*
money *dinheiro*
notes *notas*
coins *moedas*

Post Office

What is the postage... on this letter? *Quanto é a franquia... nesta carta?*
postcard *bilhete postal*
parcel *volume*
by air mail *por via aérea*
stamps *selos*

Time

What time is it? *Que horas são?*
When do you open/shut? *Quando abrem/fecham?*
yesterday *ontem*
today *hoje*
tomorrow *amanhã*

this afternoon *logo à tarde*
this evening *logo à noite*
now *agora*
later *mais tarde*

Numbers

one *um*
two *dois*
three *três*
four *quatro*
five *cinco*
six *seis*
seven *sete*
eight *oito*
nine *nove*
ten *dez*
eleven *onze*
twelve *doze*
thirteen *treze*
fourteen *catorze*
fifteen *quinze*
sixteen *dezasseis*
seventeen *dezassete*
eighteen *dezoito*
nineteen *dezanove*
twenty *vinte*
twenty-one *vinte e um*
thirty *trinta*
forty *quarenta*
fifty *cinquenta*
sixty *sessenta*
seventy *setenta*
eighty *oitenta*
ninety *noventa*
one hundred *cem*
one thousand *mil*

Days of the Week

Sunday *domingo*
Monday *segunda-feira*
Tuesday *terça-feira*
Wednesday *quarta-feira*
Thursday *quinta-feira*
Friday *sexta-feira*
Saturday *sábado*

Further Reading

Specialist Books

Flora

Da Costa, António and Franquinho, Luis de O, *Madeira, Plants and Flowers* (Francisco Ribeiro). Well illustrated ready-reference guide to the island's flora.

Grabham, Michael, *The Garden Interests of Madeira, Plants seen in Madeira, Madeira's Flowering Plants and Ferns* (HK Lewis/Will Clowes & Sons). The Grand Old Man of Madeira's books are still among the most interesting treatises on the island's plant life, but are difficult to come by.

Lowe, Richard, *A Manual of Flora of Madeira & Adjacent Islands of Porto Santo & Desertas* (John van Voorst, 1857). When he wasn't stirring up trouble (*see* pp.129–30) the Rev. Richard Lowe was researching the island's flora and fauna. Over a century later his book on Madeira's plants is one of the best there is, but sadly this is also one in the Rare Books Department.

Press, JP and **Short, MJ**, *Flora of Madeira* (HMSO, Natural History Museum). Scholarly work for the real enthusiast, with hardly any illustrations at all.

Vieira, Rui, *Flowers of Madeira* (Francisco Ribeiro). Not as comprehensive, nor as lavishly illustrated as Da Costa and Franquinho, but with more informative texts.

Walks

Underwood, John and Pat, *Landscapes of Madeira* (Sunflower). The Underwoods have been pottering about the island for years, and their book is the 'Walkers' Bible'.

Wine

Cossart, Noël, *Madeira, the Island Vineyard* (Christie's Wine Publications). Informative insider's view on Madeiran wines. The late Noël Cossart was a member of one of the island's most venerable wine-making families, and peppers his instructive book with personal reminiscences about island life. Currently out of print, but a new edition is on the cards.

Background and History

Liddell, Alex, *Madeira* (Faber and Faber). Thorough, informative and up-to-date book on Madeira.

Gregory, Desmond, *The Beneficent Usurpers* (Associated University Presses). An exhaustively researched account of the British in Madeira.

Kaplan, Marion, *The Portuguese* (Penguin). Not directly about the Madeirense, but an interesting investigation of their cultural heritage nonetheless.

Nash, Roy, *Scandal in Madeira* (The Book Guild). The full story of the Lowe affair. Witty and well-written.

Weaver, HJ, *Reid's Hotel, Jewel of the Atlantic* (Souvenir Press). Illustrated history of Reid's, published to commemorate the hotel's centenary. Available from the hotel.

Travellers' Accounts

Over the centuries many visitors to Madeira have felt moved to write about their experiences on the island. Most of these books are out of print, but can probably be found in a good library.

Bridge, Anne and Lowndes, Susan, *The Selective Traveller in Portugal* (Evans Brothers, 1949). Interesting chapter on Madeira.

Bryans, Robin, *Madeira, Pearl of the Atlantic* (Robert Hale, 1959). A pearl of a book. Amusing and sensitively written.

Coleridge, HN, *Six Months in the West Indies in 1825* (John Murray, 1826). Nephew to the Romantic poet, Coleridge was a traveller and explorer. His chapter on Madeira is effusive, but a good read.

De França, Isabella, *Journal of a Visit to Madeira and Portugal* (Junta Geral Distrito Autónomo do Funchal). You will struggle to find a copy, even on Madeira itself, but it is worth the effort. Isabella de França's journal is written with perception and delicious wit and stands supreme among contemporary accounts of island life.

Sitwell, Sacheverell, *Portugal and Madeira* (BT Batsford, 1954). The island viewed from the comfort of Reid's.

Taylor, Ellen, *Madeira, Its Scenery and How to See It* (Edward Stanford, 1882). Provides the best laughs of all the 19th-century guides. There is an intriguing appendix of letters home.

In Portuguese

Clode, Luiza Helena and Adragão, José Victor, *Madeira* (Novos Guias de Portugal). Beautiful photographs and a full text. Especially good on art and island culture.

Islenha. An illustrated journal available from good bookshops all over the island. Articles on everything from parish church architecture to rare birds. Some editions have English synopses or translations.

Pestana, Cesar, *A Maideira Cultura e Paisagem* (Região Autónoma da Madeira). An overview of island culture and literature.

Index

Main page references are in **bold**. Page references to maps are in *italics*.

Madeira & Porto Santo touring atlas

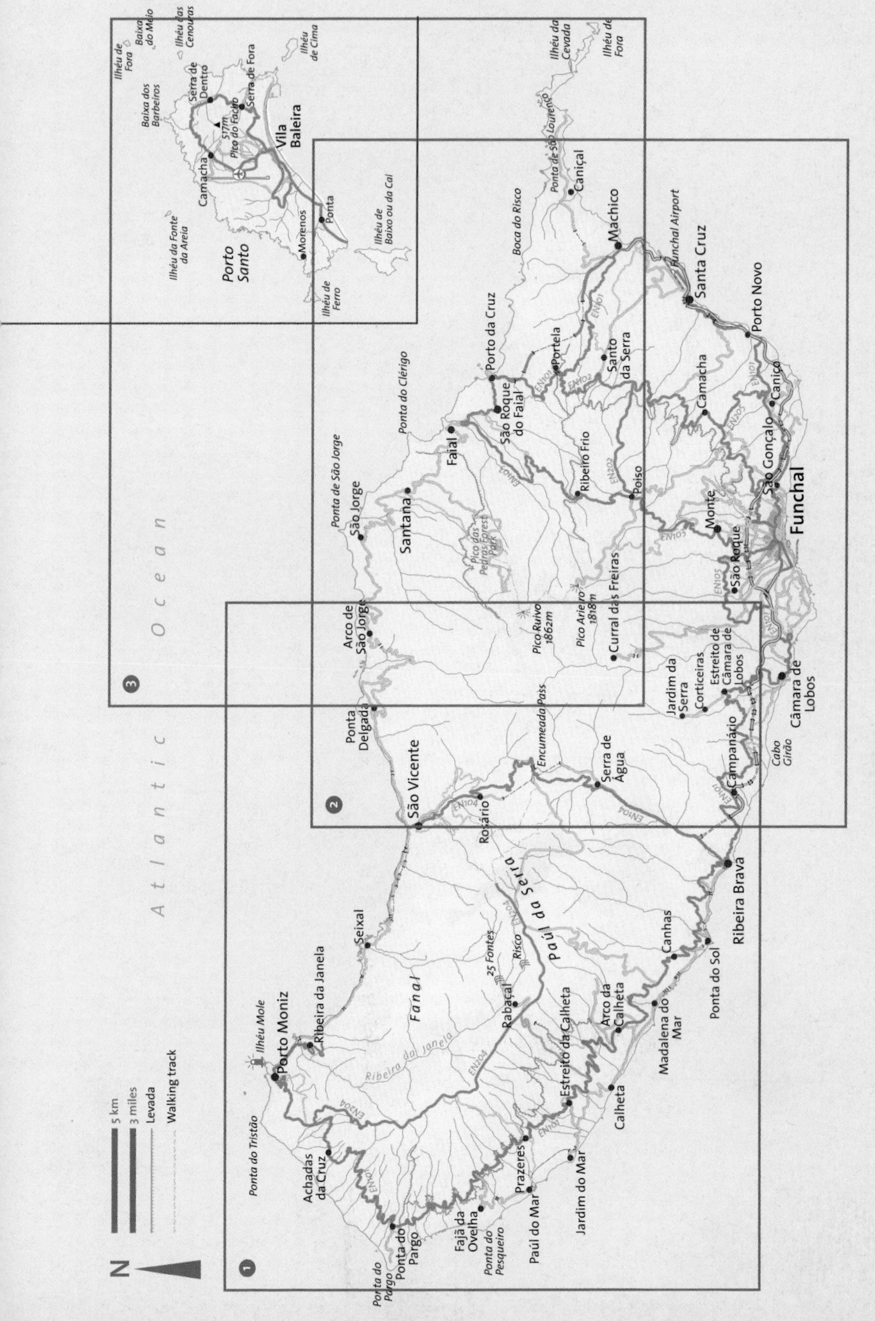

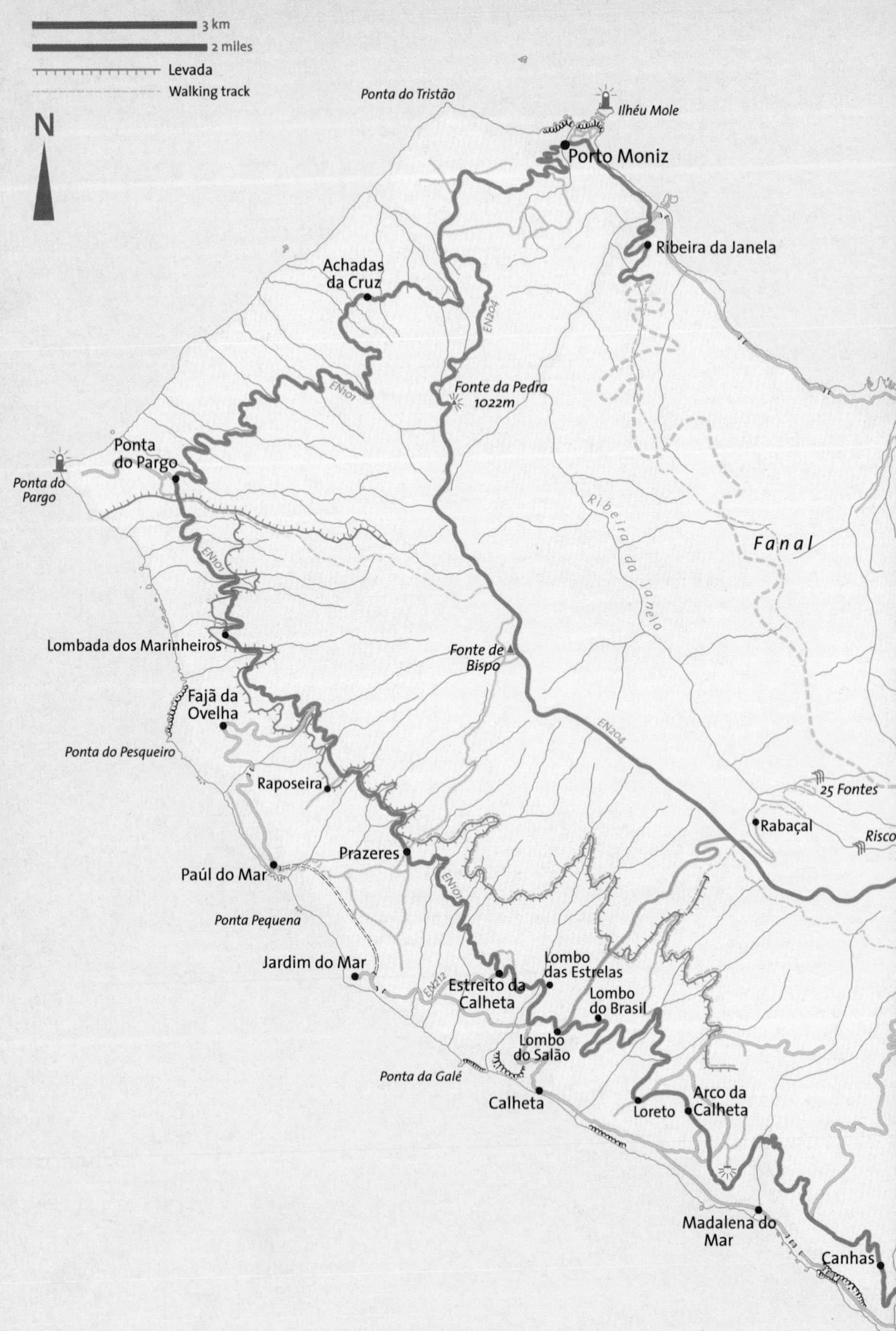

3 km
2 miles
Levada
Walking track
N
Ponta do Tristão
Ilhéu Mole
Porto Moniz
Ribeira da Janela
Achadas
da Cruz
EN204
EN101
Fonte da Pedra
1022m
Ponta
do Pargo
Ponta do
Pargo
Ribeira da Janela
Fanal
Lombada dos Marinheiros
Fonte de
Bispo
Fajã da
Ovelha
Ponta do Pesqueiro
Raposeira
25 Fontes
Rabaçal
Risco
Prazeres
Paúl do Mar
Ponta Pequena
Jardim do Mar
EN212
Estreito da
Calheta
Lombo
das Estrelas
Lombo
do Brasil
Lombo
do Salão
Ponta da Galé
Calheta
Loreto
Arco da
Calheta
Madalena do
Mar
Canhas
Ponta do S

1

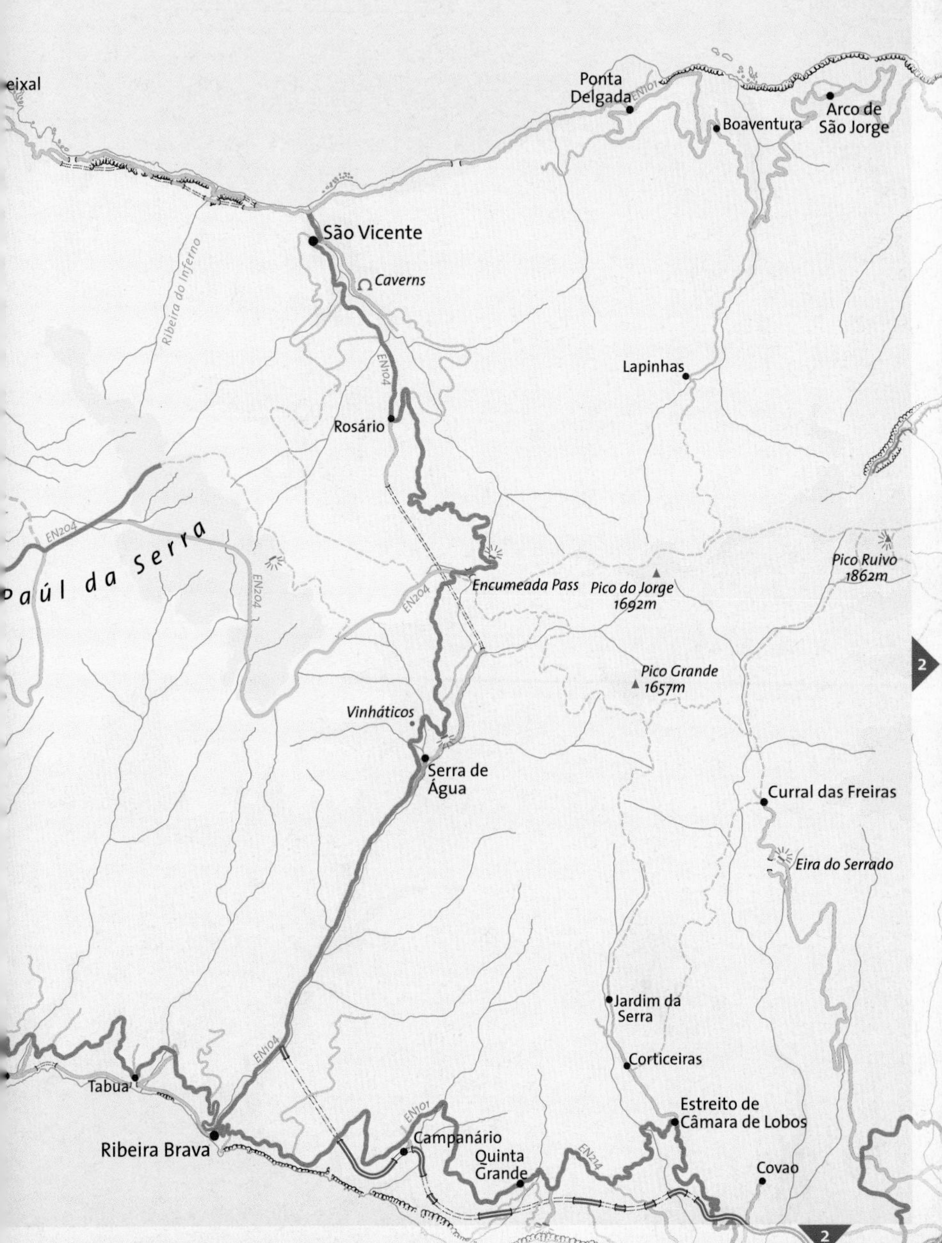

Atlantic Ocean
eixal
Ponta Delgada
EN101
Boaventura
Arco de São Jorge
São Vicente
Caverns
Ribeira do Inferno
EN104
Lapinhas
Rosário
EN204
Paúl da Serra
Encumeada Pass
Pico do Jorge 1692m
Pico Ruivo 1862m
Pico Grande 1657m
Vinháticos
Serra de Água
Curral das Freiras
Eira do Serrado
Jardim da Serra
Corticeiras
Tabua
Estreito de Câmara de Lobos
Ribeira Brava
Campanário
Quinta Grande
EN214
Covao

2

2

Ponta de São Jorge
Ponta de Santana
São Jorge
Ponta Delgada
EN101
Arco de São Jorge
Boaventura
Santana
São Vicente
Caverns
EN104
Lapinhas
Queimadas 900m
Pico das Pedras Forest Park
Rosário
Caldeirão Verde
Caldeirão do Inferno
Pico Ruivo 1862m
Encumeada Pass
Pico do Jorge 1692m
EN204
Pico des Torres 1851m
Balcões
Botanic
Pico Grande 1657m
Pico do Juncal 1800m
Ribei Frio
Vinháticos
Pico Arieiro 1818m
Trout Hatchery
Serra de Água
Curral das Freiras
Poiso
Eira do Serrado
Pico Alto 1129
EN103
EN201
Jardim da Serra
Terreiro da Luta
Corticeiras
Curral dos Romeiros
Estreito de Câmara de Lobos
Monte
EN105
Campanário
Quinta Grande
EN214
São Roque
Botanical Gardens
Levada dos Tornos
Covao
Pico dos Barcelos 355m
Quinta do Poco
EN102
Cabo Girão
Pico da Torre 205m
São Martinho
EN215
São Gonçalo
Câmara de Lobos
Funchal
Praia Formosa
Ponta da Cruz
Lido
Porto Santo
1

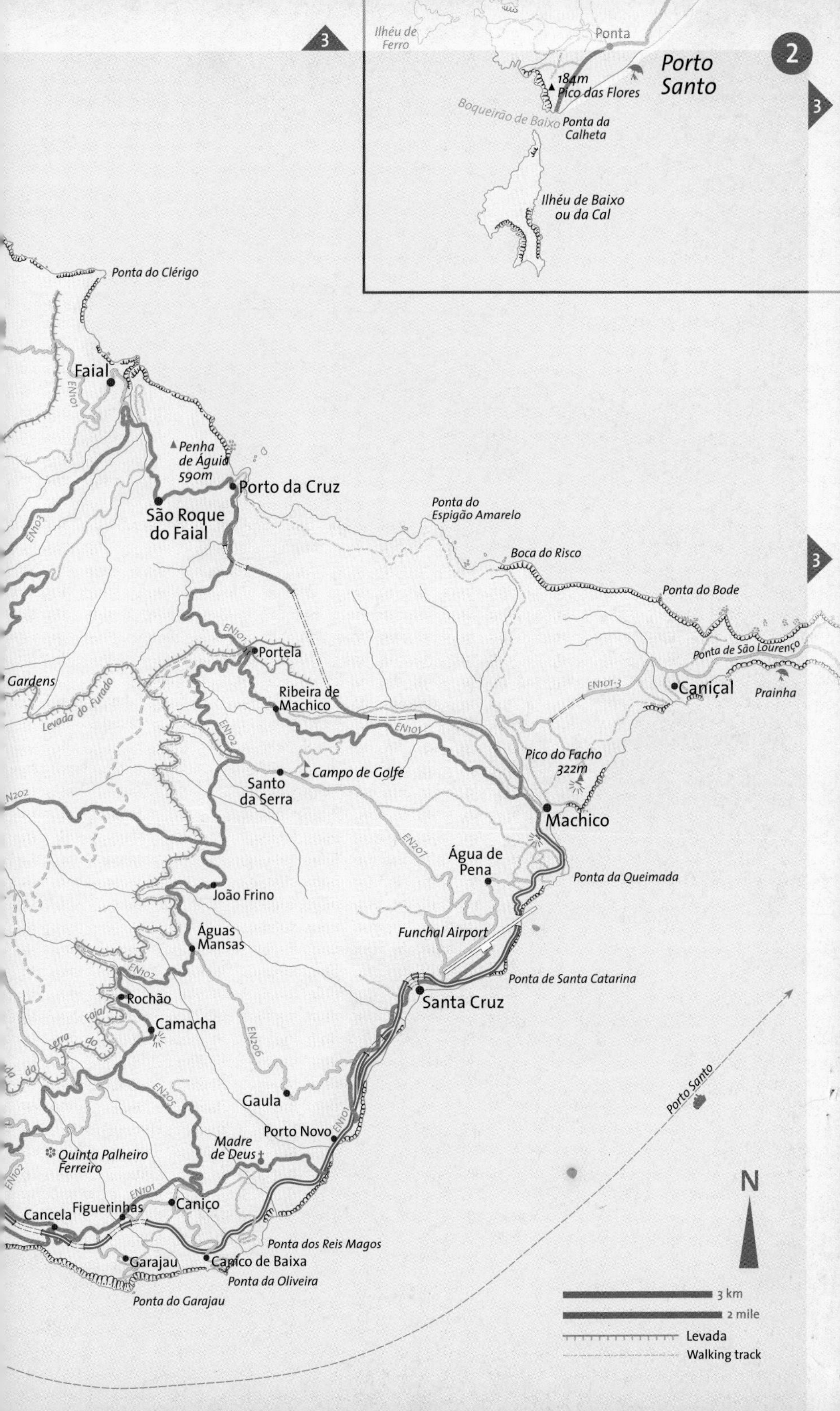

3
2
Porto Santo
3
3
Ilhéu de Ferro
Ponta
184m
Pico das Flores
Boqueirão de Baixo
Ponta da Calheta
Ilhéu de Baixo ou da Cal
Ponta do Clérigo
Faial
EN101
Penha de Águia 590m
Porto da Cruz
São Roque do Faial
EN103
Ponta do Espigão Amarelo
Boca do Risco
Ponta do Bode
Ponta de São Lourenço
Caniçal
Prainha
EN101-3
Portela
Gardens
Levada do Furado
Ribeira de Machico
EN101
EN102
Santo da Serra
Campo de Golfe
Pico do Facho 322m
Machico
EN202
EN207
Água de Pena
Ponta da Queimada
João Frino
Águas Mansas
Funchal Airport
EN102
Ponta de Santa Catarina
Santa Cruz
Rochão
Camacha
EN206
Gaula
EN205
Porto Novo
Madre de Deus
Quinta Palheiro Ferreiro
Porto Santo
EN101
Caniço
Figuerinhas
Cancela
Garajau
Caniço de Baixa
Ponta dos Reis Magos
Ponta da Oliveira
Ponta do Garajau
N
3 km
2 mile
Levada
Walking track

3 km
2 mile
Levada
Walking track

N

Atlantic Ocean

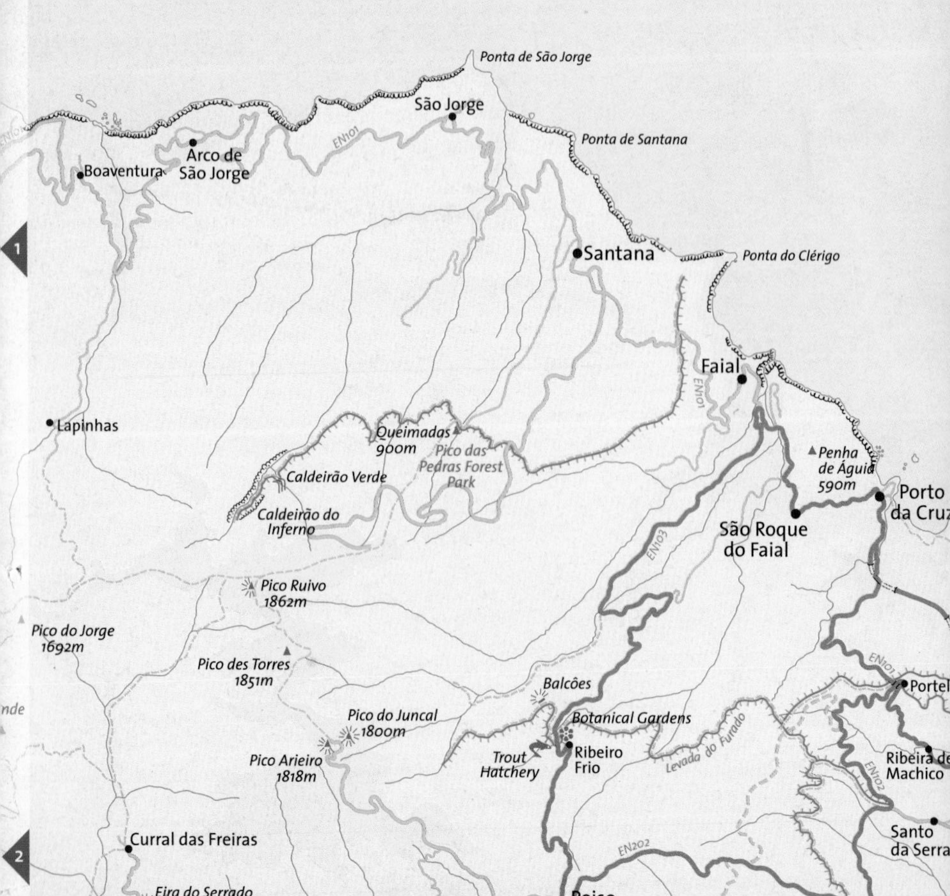

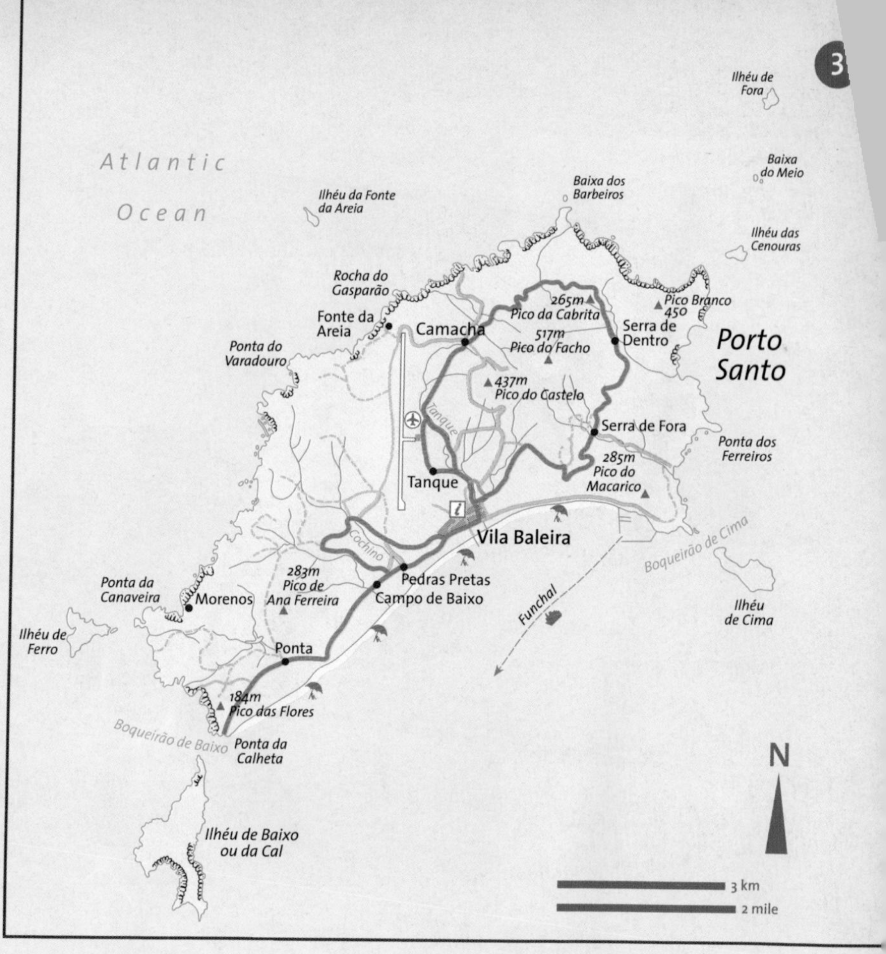
3
Atlantic
Ocean
Ilhéu de Fora
Baixa do Meio
Baixa dos Barbeiros
Ilhéu da Fonte da Areia
Ilhéu das Cenouras
Rocha do Gasparão
Fonte da Areia
Camacha
265m
Pico da Cabrita
Pico Branco 450
Serra de Dentro
517m
Pico do Facho
Porto Santo
Ponta do Varadouro
437m
Pico do Castelo
Tanque
Serra de Fora
Ponta dos Ferreiros
285m
Pico do Macarico
Tanque
Vila Baleira
Cochino
Boqueirão de Cima
283m
Pico de Ana Ferreira
Pedras Pretas
Campo de Baixo
Ponta da Canaveira
Morenos
Ilhéu de Cima
Funchal
Ilhéu de Ferro
Ponta
184m
Pico das Flores
Boqueirão de Baixo
Ponta da Calheta
N
Ilhéu de Baixo ou da Cal
3 km
2 mile

Ponta do Espigão Amarelo
Boca do Risco
Ponta do Bode
Ponta do Castela
Ponta de São Lourenço
Baia de Abra
EN101-3
Caniçal
Prainha
Nossa Senhora da Piedade
Ilhéu da Cevada
EN101
Pico do Facho
322m
mpo de Golfe
Ilhéu de Fora
Machico
EN207
2
Ponta da Queimada

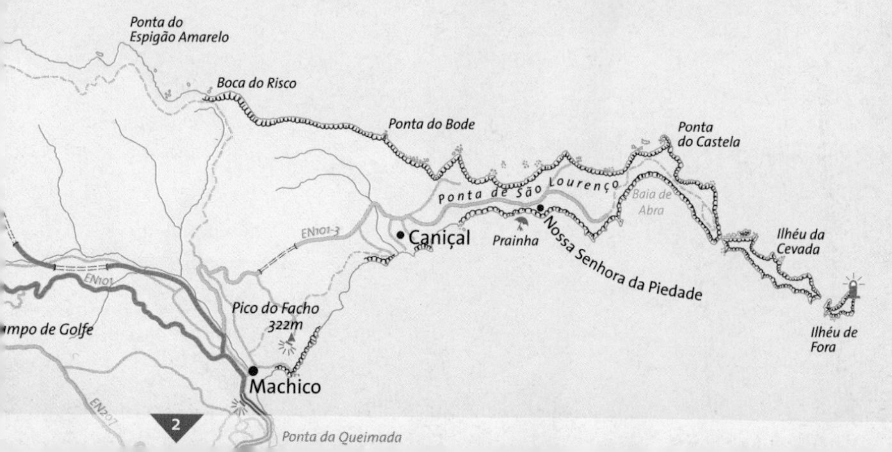

CORSICA
Dana Facaros & Michael Pauls
CADOGANguides

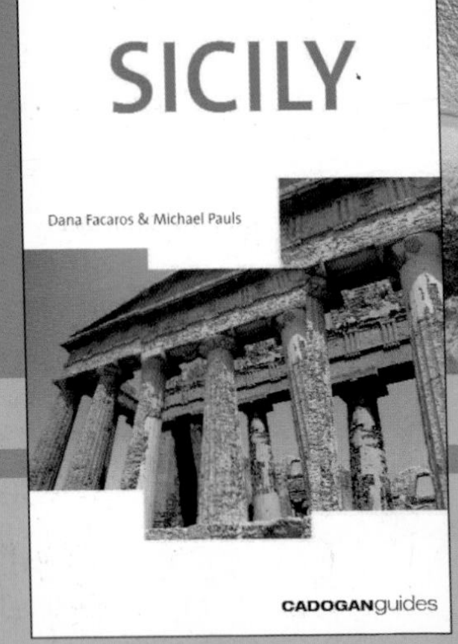
SICILY
Dana Facaros & Michael Pauls
CADOGANguides

CRETE
Dana Facaros & Michael Pauls
CADOGANguides

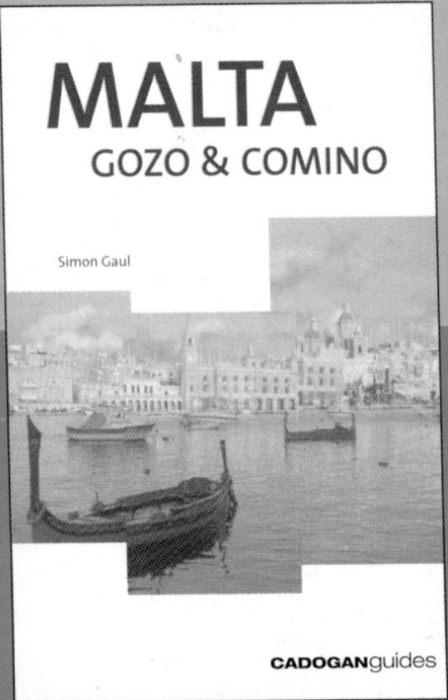
MALTA
GOZO & COMINO
Simon Gaul
CADOGANguides